ASPEN

PUBLISHERS

Medical Records Review
Third Edition

by Kristyn S. Appleby and Joanne Tarver

2004 Cumulative Supplement

The **2004 Cumulative Supplement** to Medical Records Review 3rd edition continues to build upon both the medical and the legal information contained in the 3rd edition. It is the authors' intent that the information contained in the 2004 Supplement will enhance the book's utility as an important resource for the legal professional.

Highlights of the **2004 Cumulative Supplement** include:

- New section on Health Insurance Portability & Accountability Act's (HIPPA) Privacy Rule (**§ 4.15A**);
- New Table on States Recognizing Psychologist-Client Privilege (**Table 4–2**);
- Revised and updated Table on States Recognizing Physician-Patient Privilege (**Table 4–1**);
- Revised and updated section on determining which medical records to obtain (**§ 6.1**);
- New section on the initial client interview (**§ 6.1A**);
- Updated and revised sections on National Committee for Quality Assurance and Foundation for Accountability (FACCT) (**§§ 8.18 and 8.20**);
- Revised Appendix O on State Statutes Regarding Use of Genetic Tests/ Information;
- Updated Appendix N on Internet Resources; and
- Updated Bibliography and Index.

9/03

For questions concerning this shipment, billing, or other customer service matters, call our Customer Service Department at 1-800-234-1660.

For toll-free ordering, please call 1-800-638-8437.

A WoltersKluwer Company

MEDICAL RECORDS REVIEW

Third Edition

2004 Cumulative Supplement

KRISTYN S. APPLEBY

JOANNE TARVER

1185 Avenue of the Americas, New York, NY 10036
www.aspenpublishers.com

This publication is designed to provide accurate and authoritative information in regard to the subject matter covered. It is sold with the understanding that the publisher is not engaged in rendering legal, accounting, or other professional services. If legal advice or other expert assistance is required, the services of a competent professional person should be sought.

—From a *Declaration of Principles* jointly adopted
by a Committee of the American Bar Association
and a Committee of Publishers and Associations

© 2004, 2003 Aspen Publishers, Inc.
A Wolters Kluwer Company
www.aspenpublishers.com

Printed in the United States of America

1 2 3 4 5 6 7 8 9 0

Library of Congress Cataloging-in-Publication Data

Appleby, Kristyn S.
   Medical records review / Kristyn S. Appleby, Joanne Tarver. — 3rd ed.
     p. cm
   Includes bibliographical references and index.
   ISBN 0-7355-0337-0 (cloth)
   ISBN 0-7355-4221-X (supplement)
   1. Medical records—Law and legislation—United States.
I. Tarver, Joanne. II. Title.
KF3827.R4A96 1999
344.73'041—dc21
                                                    98-49309
                                                      CIP

About Aspen Publishers

Aspen Publishers, headquartered in New York City, is a leading information provider for attorneys, business professionals, and law students. Written by pre-eminent authorities, our products consist of analytical and practical information covering both U.S. and international topics. We publish in the full range of formats, including updated manuals, books, periodicals, CDs, and online products.

Our proprietary content is complemented by 2,500 legal databases, containing over 11 million documents, available through our Loislaw division. Aspen Publishers also offers a wide range of topical legal and business databases linked to Loislaw's primary material. Our mission is to provide accurate, timely, and authoritative content in easily accessible formats, supported by unmatched customer care.

To order any Aspen Publishers title, go to *ww.aspenpublishers.com* or call 1-800-638-8437.

To reinstate your manual update service, call 1-800-638-8437.

For more information on Loislaw products, go to *www.loislaw.com* or call 1-800-364-2512.

For Customer Care issues, e-mail *CustomerCare@aspenpublishers.com;* call 1-800-234-1600; or fax 1-800-901-9075.

Aspen Publishers
A Wolters Kluwer Company

SUBSCRIPTION NOTICE

This Aspen Publishers product is updated on a periodic basis with supplements to reflect important changes in the subject matter. If you purchased this product directly from Aspen Publishers, we have already recorded your subscription for the update service.

If, however, you purchased this product from a bookstore and wish to receive future updates and revised or related volumes billed separately with a 30-day examination review, please contact our Customer Service Department at 1-800-234-1660, or send your name, company name (if applicable), address, and the title of the product to:

ASPEN PUBLISHERS
7201 McKinney Circle
Frederick, MD 21704

CONTENTS

Sections listed below have been updated in the supplement.

CONTENTS

PREFACE

The 2004 Supplement to Medical Records Review 3rd edition continues to build upon both the medical and the legal information contained in the 3rd edition. It is the authors' intent that the information contained in the 2004 Supplement will enhance the book's utility as an important resource for the legal professional.

Highlights of the 2004 Supplement include:

- New section on Health Insurance Portability & Accountability Act's (HIPPA) Privacy Rule (**§4.15A**);
- New Table on States Recognizing Psychologist-Client Privilege (**Table 4–2**);
- Revised and updated Table on States Recognizing Physician-Patient Privilege (**Table 4–1**);
- Revised and updated section on determining which medical records to obtain (**§ 6.1**);
- New section on the initial client interview (**§ 6.1A**);
- Updated and revised sections on National Committee for Quality Assurance and Foundation for Accountability (FACCT) (**§§ 8.18 and 8.20**);
- Revised Appendix O on State Statutes Regarding Use of Genetic Tests/Information;
- Updated Appendix N on Internet Resources; and
- Updated Bibliography and Index.

MEDICAL RECORDS REVIEW

2004 Cumulative Supplement

CHAPTER 1

BODY STRUCTURE AND FUNCTION

§ 1.6   Body Structures

Page 7, add to subsection **Cells:**

Cells have a finite life. Cell regeneration occurs on a periodic basis, with the length of time depending on the type of cell. New cells are formed by a process known as *mitosis*. During this process, the parent cell divides into two daughter cells. Although some characteristics of the two new cells may differ (e.g., weight), they carry the same genetic instructions that govern their activities and reproduction. These instructions are known as the *genetic code* of the cell.

The genetic code of the cell, carried in DNA (deoxyribonucleic acid), is contained in structures called *chromosomes.* Humans have 46 chromosomes, grouped into 23 pairs. One half of each pair originates from the father, the other from the mother. These chromosomes have approximately 80,000 genes (hereditary units). Genes carry both species and individual-specific information that is transmitted from generation to generation. The DNA structure itself is a coiled structure of double-stranded DNA molecules (double-helix structure). The strands are linked by hydrogen bonds that are relatively weak. During cell division, the DNA separates at the weak point in the hydrogen bond, a process of immense complexity; sometimes mistakes are made in copying genetic information before cell division. Genes can be lost or can mutate. Mutations may be favorable, unfavorable, or neutral. Unfavorable mutations can result in cell abnormalities that lead to structural and functional problems for the cell that cause heredity diseases such as sickle-cell anemia, hemophilia, cystic fibrosis, and several neurologic diseases. See § **3.50** for a discussion of treatment options available for genetic disorders.

BODY STRUCTURE AND FUNCTION

Page 53, add new § 1.29A at end of page:

§ 1.29A —The Inflammatory Response

When tissue injury occurs, the body responds immediately via a mechanism known as the *inflammatory response*. The inflammatory response is immediate and non-specific, that is, it is triggered by any condition causing tissue injury. Conditions that trigger the immune response include:

- infection
- immune reactions, such as allergic reactions
- thermal injuries, such as frostbite or burns
- chemical injuries from agents such as corrosive chemicals
- tissue death resulting from insufficient blood supply
- traumatic injuries

During this process, the body sends cells and chemical substances to the site of injury to wall off the area, destroy toxins, clean the area of cell debris, and repair damaged tissue. There are main phases of the inflammatory response:

1. Vascular phase—characterized by an immediate and transitory constriction of blood vessels followed by a lengthier period of vascular dilation and increased vessel permeability. Dilation occurs as a result of the body's release of the chemical histamine, which results in redness and warmth of the affected area. The increase in vessel permeability causes fluid normally in the vascular system to leak into the surrounding tissues, causing edema.

2. Cellular phase—occurs within the first hour of the event. This process involves the migration of neutrophils or polymorphonuclear leukocytes (referred to in the lab results as PMNs or polys) from the blood vessels into the tissues at the site of injury. Luekocytes comprise approximately 60% of white blood cells and are the first cells to be mobilized in the event of tissue damage. This movement occurs with aid of histamine. Once in the tissues, the leukocytes engulf and destroy harmful organisms through phagocytosis. The end result of this process is pus formation.

2

3. Tissue healing phase—begins approximately one day after the event and continues until the tissue is healed. If all compromised tissue cannot be removed, chronic infection results.

In its most severe form, inflammatory response can be systemic. This is a life-threatening condition that can result from massive tissue damage that can occur from sepsis (systemic infection) or severe burns.

The Process of Infection

As stated previously, the immune system plays a critical role in protecting the body against infection and infectious diseases. Infection has been noted as a cause of serious illness and death from the earliest documentation of medical diseases and their treatment. For hundreds of years, the cause of infection was not known. In the 17th century, microscope-maker Anton van Leeuwenoek reported the existence of microorganisms (germs). However, the significance of his observations was not recognized for nearly 200 years, when three critical discoveries were made:

1. Louis Pasteur discovered the relationship between microorganisms and disease, i.e., that microorganisms caused infection.
2. Dr. Ignaz Semmelwiess pioneered the use of antiseptics in obstetrics and dramatically reduced the incidence of death from infection following childbirth.
3. Joseph Lister demonstrated the efficacy of using antiseptic agents to kill microorganisms on the skin and surgical instruments before surgery.

Additionally, in the early part of the 20th century, improvements in environmental sanitation and development of vaccines dramatically reduced morbidity and mortality from infectious disease. The development of antibiotics, hailed as miracle drugs, enabled effective treatment of infections never before possible. As history has shown, however, that use of antibiotics has created other unique problems. Widespread antibiotic use has resulted in changes in bacteria structure and genetic makeup that allows them to survive in the presence of these drugs. Today, some bacteria are resistant to most antibiotics and cause severe illness and death in U. S. hospitals and health care institutions. Infectious diseases are the leading cause of death worldwide and as recently as 1992 ranked third as cause of death in the U.S.

Litigation involving infectious disease can be related to prompt diagnosis of infection or infectious disease, as well as the efficacy of its treatment including choice, dosage, and frequency of antibiotic/anti-infective therapy. In litigation involving trauma and prolonged hospitalization, development of infection in the course of treatment can add another component to damages if it has sequellae that impact recovery. Many types of litigation involving HIV infection are possible, including wrongful termination, issues involving workplace compliance with the Americans with Disabilities laws, and discrimination. It is helpful to have a basic understanding of how infection occurs and effects that may occur as a result of the infection. This knowledge will help you determine pertinent information that should be included in your medical record summary.

Infectious Disease Terminology

1. Agent—pathogen, organism, microorganism (such as bacteria or virus) that can cause infection. These terms are often used synonymously in describing the process of infection.

2. Carrier—a person or animal who harbors an infectious agent without any symptoms of disease.

3. Colonization—establishment of organisms in or on the body. In a colonized state, organisms do not cause infection, but co-exist within the body without causing disease. This state may continue indefinitely unless the body's defenses become compromised.

4. Iatrogenic—term commonly used to refer to an undesirable outcome that develops as a result of a medical treatment or intervention, e.g., an infection acquired in the hospital.

5. Incubation period—the time interval between initial contact with an infectious agent and the first appearance of symptoms associated with infection.

6. Infection—invasion of normally sterile body tissue by organisms that produce tissue injury. Infection may progress from mild inflammatory response to severe systemic infection that can cause death.

7. Infectious disease—caused by a variety of pathogens. Infectious disease has the potential for transmission to others by a variety of means.

8.   Infectivity—the ability of a pathogen to invade and replicate in the host.

9.   MRSA (methicillin-resistant staph aureus)—a strain of staphylococcus aureus that is resistant (not killed) by the antibiotic, methicillin. Methicillin is typically effective in killing this organism even when it is resistant to other antibiotics.

10. Normal flora—organisms normally present on body surfaces such as the mouth, skin, gastrointestinal tract, etc. These organisms do not normally cause disease in healthy individuals.

11. Nosocomial infection—an infection that develops in a hospital or health care institution that was not present or incubating at admission. Nosocomial infections can occur for many reasons, including use of invasive devices, weakened immune system, use of antibiotics, and chemotherapy or other treatments that weaken the body's immune system.

12. Pathogenicity—the ability of an organism to consistently produce disease. For example, the rabies virus always produces disease when introduced into the body, however, the tuberculosis bacteria often does not.

13. Virulence—the potency of the pathogen in producing severe disease as measured by case-fatality rates.

14. VRE (vancomycin-resistant enterococcus)—a strain of enterococcus that is resistant (not killed) by the antibiotic, vancomycin. Vancomycin is typically effective in killing this organism even when it is resistant to other antibiotics.

Development and Transmission of Infection

Development of an infectious disease begins with *exposure* to the causative agent. Following exposure, three outcomes are possible:

1.   Colonization—the pathogen can only contaminate body surfaces and not cause disease. A pathogen that colonizes an individual can be transmitted and cause active disease in a new host.

2.   Symptomatic active disease—body experiences destructive effects of the pathogen or its toxic products. The effects of the pathogen cause symptoms within the body.

3. Asymptomatic active disease—body experiences disease that is sub-clinical or without symptoms. Active disease that is asymptomatic can still be transmitted and cause disease in a new host.

If active disease develops, exposure is followed by an *incubation period* in which the pathogen begins to invade the body tissues. Whether colonization or active disease exists, infection can be transmitted to a new host after exposure.

Six elements must be present for infection to be transmitted: a pathogen or agent, a reservoir, a portal of exit, a mode of transmission, a portal of entry, and a susceptible host. This transmission process is commonly referred to as the chain of infection.

Pathogen or agent.   Virus, bacteria, fungus, or other agent capable of causing disease. Pathogens exist in the world around us and most of the time cause no harm to the human body. However, when the balance of pathogen/host symbiosis is upset, infection may result. There are numerous classifications of pathogens that are discussed in more detail in sections below.

Reservoir.   A place where the agent can live and multiply. Reservoirs can be living organisms such as people, animals, or plants, or inanimate substances such as soil, food, or water. A reservoir must provide essentials for the survival of an organism, including growth and multiplication.

Portal of exit.   A route by which the pathogen can escape the reservoir. This is usually the site of growth for the organism and can correspond to the portal of entry in the new host. For example, if an organism lives in the gastrointestinal tract a common portal of exit is the feces and portal of entry is the mouth of the new host. Common portals of exit from the body include respiratory secretions such as sputum, urine, feces, drainage from open wounds, tears, semen, and vaginal secretions.

Mode of transmission.   Method by which agent or pathogen travels from a reservoir to a new host. Transmission occurs by direct or indirect routes. Direct transmission occurs when there is immediate transfer from one person to another, as occurs in sexually transmitted diseases. Indirect transmission requires a vehicle for transmission such as soil, water, or food. Successful indirect transmission requires that the organism be able to survive until it reaches its new portal of entry.

Portal of entry.   Route by which pathogen gains entrance to a new host. Entry to a new host can be accomplished by:

- inhalation—through the respiratory tract by inhalation of infected particles, e.g. tuberculosis
- mucous membrane contact—through break in mucous membrane integrity, e.g. sexually transmitted diseases
- ingestion—through ingestion of contaminated food or water, e.g. food poisoning
- percutaneously—through non-intact skin, e.g. boils, abscesses
- transplacentally—from mother to baby through the placenta, e.g. measles

Susceptible host.   A new reservoir for the pathogen to grow and live. Normally, the body successfully defends against disease-causing pathogens through numerous anatomical structures and functions such as skin, mucous membranes, cough reflexes, etc. Many factors alter these defenses and influence the ability of a pathogen to cause disease in a new host. Among these influencing factors are age (the very young and the very old are more susceptible), heredity, general health, nutritional status, presence of concurrent disease (chronic or acute), and lifestyle choices such as drug use and sexual practices. Medical treatments can also increase host susceptibility to infection. Some risk factors related to medical treatment are prolonged hospitalization, splenectomy, medication that compromises the body's immune system (e.g. chemotherapy), invasive procedures such as catheters, intravenous lines, and respiratory intubation.

To interrupt the chain of infection transmission, only one of the essential "links" in the chain needs to be disrupted. The most efficient way to break the chain is determined by the type of pathogen, site of infection, and mode of transmission. The Centers for Disease Control and Prevention (CDC) has defined specific techniques known to be effective in preventing the transmission of infection. These are commonly known as Category-Specific Isolation Precautions and are used in hospitals and other health care institutions to control transmission. The choice of the type of isolation category to prevent transmission of an infectious disease should be driven by the causative agent of the disease, its virulence, and the mode of transmission. There are six categories of isolation precautions:

1. Strict Isolation—to prevent spread of highly contagious infections that can be transmitted by both air and contact, e.g. chickenpox and plague

2. Contact Isolation—to prevent spread of highly transmissible organisms that do not warrant Strict Isolation. All diseases in this category are spread by direct contact and include anyone with infection or colonization with multiply-resistant bacteria.

3. Respiratory Isolation—to prevent transmission of diseases primarily spread over short distances through the air by infected droplets, e.g. measles, whooping cough, meningitis.

4. Acid fast bacilli Isolation (Tuberculosis Isolation)—used to prevent spread of *active* pulmonary tuberculosis. Active tuberculosis is commonly defined as an individual with a positive acid fast bacilli (AFB) smear and/or a chest film that strongly suggests active disease.

5. Enteric Precautions—to prevent spread of diseases transmitted by direct or indirect contact with feces, e.g. hepatitis A, salmonella, shigella, specific types of E. coli.

6. Drainage/Secretion Precautions—to prevent spread of infection transmitted by direct or indirect contact with drainage from an infected body site, e.g. abscesses, surgical wound infections.

In addition to the above category-specific isolation precautions, the CDC has mandated the use of Universal Precautions when contact with blood or body fluids from any individual is anticipated. Universal Precautions are designed to prevent transmission of pathogens such as HIV and hepatitis B and C when infection may not be apparent. They require use of gloves, gowns, and protective eyewear when exposure to blood or body fluids is likely. Although the above isolation guidelines are used principally in hospitals and health care institutions, they are often modified for use in other settings such as the home to prevent transmission to family members or significant others.

In litigation involving infection or infectious disease, the definitive source for information on diagnosis of infectious disease and transmission prevention is the Centers for Disease Control and Prevention, specifically, the National Center for Infectious Diseases (NCID) branch. The stated mission of the NCID is to prevent illness, disability, and death caused by infectious diseases in the United States and around the world. The agency works in partnership with state and local public health agencies to control and prevent morbidity and mortality from infection and infectious disease.

Public health departments have authority to develop requirements for reporting diseases of importance to the health of the general public. This structure exists at many levels:

- County and local public health departments derive authority to require reporting from state health departments.
- State health departments derive authority to require reporting of specific infectious disease through state statutes.
- Nationally, over 50 diseases require reporting to health departments.
- Internationally, agreement has been reached on the following diseases requiring quarantine: plague, cholera, and yellow fever.

Although the CDC has no independent authority to require reporting of infectious diseases, the agency is responsible for collating and publishing health statistics based on infectious diseases required to be reported at the national level. This information is available in their publication, *Mortality and Morbidity Weekly Report.*

An additional excellent resource on infectious diseases is a publication of the American Public Health Association, *Control of Communicable Diseases Manual.* The scope and content of this publication includes (for all communicable diseases):

- identification of the disease
- infectious agent
- occurrence
- reservoir
- mode of transmission
- incubation period
- period of communicability
- susceptibility of the host

BODY STRUCTURE AND FUNCTION

In litigation involving infections acquired in health care facilities or as a result of medical intervention or treatment, facility policies and procedures relating to infection control should be requested. These represent internal standards of care and it is important to evaluate compliance with these standards in the context of the complaint.

Human Infectious Agents

The classification and nomenclature of microorganisms (microbiology) is very orderly. Nevertheless, it can be daunting to those unfamiliar with microbiology. In litigation involving infections or infectious diseases, microbiology or infectious disease reference texts are essential; however, a brief overview of microbiology is provided below.

There are several classifications of pathogenic organisms. The size, shape, and chemical composition of an organism, its growth requirements, its ability to survive under adverse conditions, and its ability to produce toxins determines its classification. Knowledge of pathogens' properties permits specific identification of an organism causing disease and allows rapid initiation of appropriate therapy, including appropriate isolation precautions to prevent transmission.

The most recognized classifications of organisms that account for the majority of infectious diseases are viruses, bacteria, fungi, and parasites. Lesser known are organisms classified as mycoplasma, rickettsiae, and chlamydia. Major characteristics of organism classifications and examples of some of the diseases they cause are discussed below.

Viruses. The smallest pathogens. Viruses are classified by their composition of a single or double strand of DNA (deoxyribonucleic acid) or RNA (ribonucleic acid) that contains their genetic information. They cause a wide variety of diseases in people. Antibiotics are not effective in the treatment of viral diseases; treatment strategies lie in prevention in the form of vaccines. However, some viral diseases, such as HIV, have no effective vaccines; for these diseases antiviral drugs are available. Common viral diseases are:

- DNA viruses, such as hepatitis B, herpes simplex, herpes zoster (chickenpox and shingles)

- RNA viruses, such as influenza, mumps, measles and German measles, HIV

Bacteria.   Most organisms are extracellular (live outside body cells) and are classified by their shape, their gram stain positivity or negativity, and their oxygen requirements.

1. Bacteria shape:
- round—cocci, diplococci, streptococci, staphylocci
- spiral shaped—spirochetes
- rod shaped—bacilli

2. Gram stain properties—bacteria are gram positive or gram negative. Gram staining is done with a dye that is applied to the bacteria. If the bacteria "take" the dye, they are designated as gram positive, if no staining is seen, the bacteria are gram negative. The shape of a bacteria is also determined during this process. For example, you may see gram stain laboratory results noted as "many Gm positive cocci present". Gram stain results are available from the laboratory within hours. This information gives direction to the physician as to the appropriate antibiotic treatment.

3. Oxygen dependence:
- aerobic—survive in the presence of oxygen
- anaerobic—survive without oxygen
- facultative—can live with or without oxygen

Examples of Bacterial Infections

Common Gm Negative Bacterial Infections & Causative Agents	*Common Gm Positive Bacteria Infections & Causative Agents*
Urinary tract infections (E. coli, Pseudomonas aeruginosa)	Urinary tract infections (Staphylococcus aureus)
Gonorrhea (Neisseria gonorrhea)	Gas gangrene (Clostridium perfringens)
Whooping cough (Bordetella pertussis)	Tetanus (Clostridium tetani)
Typhoid (Salmonella typhi)	Skin and wound infections (Staphylococci aureus)

Legionnaire's disease (Legionella pneumophilla)

Pneumonia (Haemophilus influenza, Pseudomonas aeruginosa)

Rheumatic fever (Group A beta-hemolytic streptococcus)

Pneumonia (Staphyloccus aureus, Streptococcus pneumonia or pneumococcus)

Fungi.   Mainly extracellular organisms (live outside body cells) that resemble plants because they grow as branching filaments. Common fungal diseases include vaginal or systemic candia (yeast) infections and coccidiomycosis. Systemic fungal infections, especially in individuals with compromised immune systems, can be extremely serious and are often fatal.

Mycoplasma.   Extracellular organisms (live outside body cells). Mycoplasma organisms cause few diseases in humans. The most common are atypical mycoplasma organisms that cause pneumonia and pelvic inflammatory disease (PID) in women.

Chlamydia.   Intracellular organisms (live inside body cells) that contain both DNA and RNA; like mycoplasma, these organisms can cause pneumonia and cervicitis/PID in women.

Rickettsiae.   Can multiply only within cells. Transmission to humans occurs through bites of ticks, fleas, mites, or lice. Human rickettsial diseases include Rocky Mountain Spotted Fever and typhus.

Protozoa.   Intracellular parasites (live inside body cells) that can move easily from place to place. Parasitic infections in humans include malaria, pneumonia, and toxoplasmosis.

Helminths.   Multi-cellular organisms shaped like worms. Offspring (larvae) are excreted in the urine or feces and transmitted to humans by ingestion or bites that cause breaks in the skin. Helminth infections include trichinosis, schistosomiasis, and enterbiasis.

Signs and Symptoms of Infection

The exact signs and symptoms of infection depend on the causative agent, location of infection, and stage of the disease. Manifestations result from direct effect of pathogen or its toxins, the body's inflammatory response, and resultant cell damage.

Organ Specific Effects of Infection

System	*Effects*
Generalized Effects	Fever, chills, aching muscles
Skin	Inflammation, rash, redness, tenderness
Gastrointestinal	Nausea, vomiting, weight loss, abdominal pain, loss of appetite, jaundice
Respiratory	Sore throat, cough with or without sputum production, foul sputum, lung congestion
Cardiovascular	Rapid heart beat, heart murmurs, alteration in blood pressure and clotting mechanisms
Genitourinary	Frequency/urgency of urination, blood in urine, cloudy or foul smelling urine, flank pain
Musculoskeletal	Muscle weakness, aches; joint redness, tenderness or swelling
Nervous	Confusion, headache, seizures, stiff neck

When infection becomes advanced, systemic effects occur. Systemic infection is known as sepsis and often compromises multiple body systems. In life-threatening sepsis, the following abnormalities in systemic functions are often present:

- blood culture positive for the causative infectious agent
- low blood pressure and cardiac output requiring drugs to support circulation
- low white blood cell (WBC) count—initially high in presence of infection, low WBCs indicate overwhelmed immune system
- abnormalities in blood clotting leading to disseminated intra-vascular coagulation
- impaired renal function or renal failure

Mortality resulting from overwhelming sepsis is extremely high.

BODY STRUCTURE AND FUNCTION

Diagnosis and Treatment of Infections

Diagnostic tests for infection include:

- Gram stain—results of gram positive or negative give important information quickly to health care professionals. Whereas cultures take a minimum or 24–48 hours to grow and identify a specific organism, gram stain results are available within hours.
- Smears—performed along with gram stain, smears determine the shape of the bacteria. A smear and gram stain result will read "many gram positive cocci present."
- Culture and sensitivity—specimen is transferred to a medium that supports bacterial growth (culture medium or agar) and incubated for 24–48 hours. At the end of this time, the bacteria can be identified, e.g., Staphyloccus aureus. This is the *culture* portion of the testing. The bacterial growth is then tested against a range of antibiotics to determine which inhibit or kill the growth of the organism and which do not. This is *sensitivity* testing.
- Hematologic tests:
  - ___ Differential white blood cell (WBC) count—quantifies each type of white blood cell in context of what is "normal". Results can be used to help determine type/causative agent of suspected infection, for example:
    - ___ neutropenia—low neutrophil count occurs in many viral infections, overwhelming bacterial infections, and in some rickettsial infections.
    - ___ neutrophilia—high neutrophil count occurs mainly in bacterial infections.
    - ___ eosinopenia—low eosinophil count. Eosinophils help regulate inflammation and protect against infections caused by helminths.
    - ___ eosinophilia—high eosinophil count occurs mainly in infections caused by helminths and some other parasites.
    - ___ lymphopenia—low lymphocyte count occurs in HIV and as a result of immunosuppressive drugs.
    - ___ lymphocytosis—occurs as a result of viral infections and chronic bacterial infections such as tuberculosis.

14

_____ Erythrocyte sedimentation rate (ESR)—nonspecific blood test that detects an inflammatory process, but cannot determine if caused by infection.

_____ C-reactive protein (CRP)—increased during inflammatory response

• Urinalysis—results extremely helpful in determining presence of urinary tract infection (UTI).

• Scans—simple CAT scans or scans that are dye enhanced such as Gallium or Indium-111 can help determine presence of abscesses in body tissues.

Treatment of infection or infectious disease is dependent on the causative agent and the symptoms the infection produces. Anti-infective medications are used as appropriate. Some of these can be toxic to specific body systems such as kidneys, liver, and hearing. Appropriate monitoring must be done if these agents are prescribed. Anti-infectives include antibiotics for bacterial infections, anti-virals for viral infections, and anti-fungals for fungal infections. For additional information on antibiotic therapy, refer to Table 3.3, pages 160–166. For additional information on anti-viral and anti-fungal agents, refer to insert to Table 3.3 in the supplement.

Page 63, add the following new sections at end of the page:

§ 1.39   —Sensory Organs

In addition to the body systems outlined in the previous material, the body also has sensory organs that allow us to interpret the external environment through sight, sound, smell, taste, and touch. Two of the main sensory organs are the eye and the ear.

§ 1.40   —The Eye: Structure and Function

The eye is the organ of sight. The purpose of the (two) eyes is to connect the human body to the environment. This is done in collaboration with the other sensory organs and the nervous system. The eyes do not actually see, but are the external portion of the visual pathway to the brain.

BODY STRUCTURE AND FUNCTION

Eye Structure

The eyes are composed of groups of structures that include the eyeballs, muscles, nerves, fat, and bones.

1. External eye structures (Ocular adnexa)—function to protect the eyeballs and provide optical clarity. They are composed of:
   - Ocular muscles—rotate eye in circular movements to allow vision at all angles.
   - Eyelids—elastic folds of skin that close to protect the eye and distribute film of tears over the eye surface to prevent drying of the eyeball.
   - Lacrimal apparatus—composed of lacrimal glands and ducts. The glands generate tears, and the ducts direct the flow of tears that are generated.

2. Internal eye—converts light rays and images into neural (nerve) messages that are sent to the brain.
   - Conjunctiva—transparent layer of mucous membrane that links eyelids and covers eyeballs.
   - Cornea—transparent structure that covers eye. The cornea is very delicate, has no blood supply of its own (it derives oxygen from the environment) and is very susceptible to injury. The cornea is convex in shape and acts on the lens to bend and direct rays of light to the retina.
   - Sclera—protective coating of the eye that is continuous with the cornea.
   - Uveal tract—composed of several structures:
     - ___ Iris—thin pigmented structure with a central opening, the pupil.
     - ___ Ciliary body—in direct continuity with the iris. It secretes the aqueous humor and supports the lens.
     - ___ Aqueous humor—clear fluid between the iris and the cornea that is secreted by the ciliary body. The aqueous humor circulates from the posterior chamber into the anterior chamber and is eventually filtered into the venous drainage system through Schlemm's canal, a vascular structure near the anterior edge of the sclera.

§ 1.40   THE EYE: STRUCTURE AND FUNCTION

_____ Choroid—posterior segment of the uveal tract between the retina and the sclera.

* Angle structures—angle that is formed where iris and cornea meet. These structures filter the aqueous humor and directs it into the venous drainage system.

* Lens—biconcave, avascular, transparent structure behind the iris. The sole purpose of the lens is to focus light on the retina. The elasticity of the lens allows changes that enable focus on near or far objects.

* Vitreous humor—clear jelly-like structure that occupies space of the vitreous chamber, the largest cavity of the eye. The vitreous humor helps maintain the shape of the eyeball.

* Retina—semi-transparent layer of nerve tissue that forms the innermost lining of the eye. The retina contains all the sensory receptors for light (photoreceptors). There are two types of photo-receptors, rods and cones. Rods function best in dim light and damage to them may result in night blindness. Cones are responsible for perception of fine details and color vision. The retina covers most of the eye's interior surface with the exception of two spots:

  _____ Macula—an area in the center of the retina that appears as a yellowish spot

  _____ Fovea—depressed area in the center of the macula. Only cones are present in the fovea; it is the point of finest vision.

* Optic nerve—transmits visual impulses from the retina to the brain. The head of this nerve is the optic disk. The optic disk contains no sensory receptors and represents a blind spot in the eye. Half of the visual field of each eye is projected to the other side of the brain, i.e. the right visual field is projected to the left occipital lobe of the brain and vice versa.

Refer to **Figure 1-15.**

Eye Function

The eye forms images that are analyzed by the retina. Receptors in the retina convert the images into neural (nerve) signals that are transmitted to visual centers in the brain. The two eyes collaborate to project at the

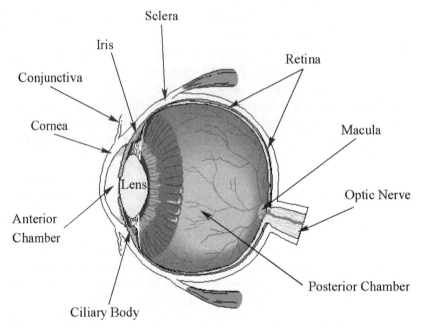

Figure 1–15. The eye.
© *Life*ART, Lippincott Williams & Wilkins 2002.

same point, fuse images, and transmit a single mental image to the brain. This process is referred to as binocular vision.

§ 1.41   —Diseases of the Eye

1. Astigmatism—rays of light are not bent equally in all directions by the cornea. In astigmatism, the cornea is not spherical.

2. Blepharitis—chronic, bilateral inflammation of the eyelid margins.

3. Cataract—thickness and density of lens increases, lens becomes yellow and opaque, affecting vision clarity. Treatment of cataracts is by surgical removal.

4. Chalazion—sterile inflammation of the eyelid gland. There is swelling without redness. If the chalazion is large enough to distort vision it may be surgically excised.

5. Conjunctivitis—inflammation of the conjunctiva secondary to bac-

terial or viral infection, allergy, or irritants, or as a result of systemic or other ocular disease.

6.   Corneal abrasion—scratch or defect in the outer layer (epithelium) of the cornea. Abrasions may be caused by foreign bodies or injury.

7.   Corneal dystrophies—group of conditions that affect the cornea. These conditions are relatively rare, usually hereditary and may progress to the need for corneal transplant.

8.   Diabetic retinopathy—microscopic damage to retinal vessels leads to their occlusion. The occluded vessels cannot supply the retina with blood, which results in death of the retinal tissue and blindness. This stimulates growth of new vessels to supply areas that do not have adequate blood supply. These new vessels are fragile and prone to bleeding into the retinal tissue. Laser therapy is directed to the new vessels to stop growth and thus prevent hemorrhage.

9.   Foreign bodies—usually as a result of trauma or injury. Effects from foreign bodies may range from minor to major depending on the type, size, and depth of foreign body penetration.

10.   Glaucoma—increase in pressure within the eye (intra-ocular pressure). There several types of glaucoma:
   • Primary open angle—insidious in onset and slow to progress. Symptoms appear late in the disease when vision is impaired by damage to the optic nerve.
   • Angle closure—attacks occur suddenly as a result of anterior angle blockage by the base of the iris. This type of glaucoma requires surgical intervention.
   • Low tension—resembles primary open angle glaucoma, however develops in the presence of normal intra-ocular pressures.
   • Secondary—occurs as a result of increased intra-ocular pressure secondary to trauma or as a postoperative complication.

Glaucoma treatment is dependent on the type of glaucoma and may be medical or surgical in nature.

11.   Hordeolum (style)—infection of the eyelid gland, characterized by localized redness and swelling. May resolve spontaneously or need to be surgically incised.

12.   Macular degeneration—degenerative process that affects the macula and surrounding tissues. The tissue degeneration results in central

vision defects. Macular degeneration may be classified as wet or dry. Wet degeneration can be treated with laser therapy to arrest associated bleeding.

13. Photophobia—an abnormal (painful) sensitivity to light. Photophobia is commonly associated with some eye diseases such as corneal abrasions, acute keratitis, and acute uveitis.

14. Refractive disorders—light rays are not focused appropriately on the retina. Refractive disorders are broken into three types:
    • Myopia or nearsightedness—light rays are focused in front of the retina. In many cases, this is caused by a longer than normal eyeball.
    • Hyperopia or farsightedness—light rays are focused in back of the retina. In many cases, this is caused by a shorter than normal eyeball.
    • Astigmatism—see 1., above.

15. Retinal detachment—tear in retina which allows seepage of vitreous fluid through it. This leads to accumulation of liquid between the retina and the retinal pigment epithelium. This process separates the retina from its blood supply and, if left untreated, can lead to blindness. Retinal detachments are surgically repaired. The goals of surgery are twofold: to place the retina back in contact with the choroid (scleral buckling) and to seal the accompanying holes and breaks (cryopexy or laser photocoagulation).

16. Retinitis pigmentosa—hereditary, degenerative disease of the retina eventually causing loss of vision.

17. Strabismus—abnormal deviation of one eye in relation to other. Strabismus may be convergent (cross-eyed) in which one eye is directed too far inward, or divergent, in which one eye is directed too far outward.

18. Uveitis—inflammation of uveal tract that can affect one or more of the following structures: iris, ciliary body, or choroid. Commonly arises from hypersensitivity reactions.

§ 1.42 —Evaluation of Eye Function

Eye function is evaluated as a routine part of the history and physical (see §§ 2.10–2.16). Commonly seen in history and physicals is the notation

§ 1.42 EVALUATION OF EYE FUNCTION

"eyes—PERRLA". This acronym stands for "*p*upils *e*qual, *r*ound, and *r*eactive to *l*ight and *a*ccommodation". Additional eye function tests are commonly used to assess eye function; some of the most common are:

1. Pupil response—both pupils should be equal and react to light, that is, constrict when light is shone into the pupil and dilate when it is removed. Normal pupil size is between 2 and 6 mm. Pupil response to light may be described as brisk or sluggish.

2. Pupil accommodation—ability to adjust focus from near to far. Determined by placing a finger 12–18 inches from the nose and slowly moving toward subject. The eye should follow the finger.

3. Corneal reflex—eye will blink when cornea is touched. This test assesses nerve function of the fifth cranial (trigeminal) nerve.

4. Blink reflex—normally the eye blinks 15–20 times per minute.

5. Ocular motility—evaluates alignment of eyes and movements independently and together. Motility can be impaired by strabismus; neurological conditions, e.g., cranial nerve paralysis; or weakness of the extra-ocular muscles. Three different types of motility tests can be done:
   - Hirschberg's test—determines presence or absence of strabismus.
   - Cover, uncover test—determines presence or absence of ocular muscle problems.
   - Six cardinal positions of gaze—determines ability of eye to look in six directions: right, left, up and right, up and left, down and right, down and left. Muscle weakness will prevent the eye from turning to a particular position.

6. Visual acuity—assesses macular function using the Snellen eye chart at a distance of 20 feet. Findings are measured relative to how far the average person can see at 20 feet. For example, a reading of 20/40 would indicate that individual can see at 20 feet what the average person can see at 40 feet.

7. Visual fields—assesses central fields of vision and peripheral vision. Defects can occur in glaucoma, retinal detachment, retinitis pigmentosa, and central nervous system disorders such as brain lesions or strokes.

8. Direct ophthalmoscopy—done using hand-held ophthalmoscope.

Provides a magnified image of the interior portion of the eyeball. The visibility of the eye structures can be enhanced using drops to dilate the pupil and a darkened room.

9. Indirect ophthalmoscopy—done using a head-mounted light that enables examiner to view a larger area of the retina.

10. Tonometry—measures intra-ocular pressure used to detect increase in pressures as seen in glaucoma.

11. Slit lamp evaluation—provides magnified view of external eye structures such as cornea, anterior chamber, iris. A yellow dye (Fluroscein) is applied from a paper strip and is used to detect defects in the cornea.

12. Refraction—used to quantify optical errors and determine correction needed with glasses or contact lenses. It distinguishes between refractive errors such as myopia, hyperopia, or astigmatism and abnormalities of the visual system itself.

§ 1.43 —The Ear: Structure and Function

The ear is the sensory organ for both hearing and balance. It is divided into three sections: the outer, middle, and inner ear. Sound is transmitted from the external ear through the middle ear (which amplifies the sound) to the inner ear. The inner ear then transforms the sound energy into neural (nervous system) elements that are carried to the brain. Balance organs in the inner ear send impulses to the brain that enables the body to maintain balance.

Ear Structure

The ear structure is divided into distinct sections:

- External ear has the following components:
    —Pinna/auricle—the most visible part of the ear. The pinna is composed mostly of cartilage and serves to protect the more delicate internal ear structures as well as to amplify sound. The concha is the deepest part of the pinna.
    —External auditory canal (ear canal)—extends from the concha to the tympanic membrane. Its funnel shape collects and directs sound waves to the eardrum.

§ 1.43 THE EAR: STRUCTURE AND FUNCTION

—Tympanic membrane—thin, translucent membrane that covers the end of the auditory canal and separates the canal from the middle ear. It conducts sound vibrations from the external ear to the ossicles (bones) in the middle ear.

- Middle ear—contains the three smallest bones in the body, the ossicles. Together the ossicles transmit sound vibrations mechanically. Individually, the ossicles are named are follows:

—Malleolus (hammer)—the outermost bone that is attached to the tympannic membrane.

—Incus (anvil)—middle bone of the three.

—Stapes (stirrup)—innermost bone which lies in contact with the oval window of the inner ear.

- The windows:

—Round window—opening into the middle ear through which sound vibrations exit the middle ear.

—Oval window—opens into the inner ear. Sound vibrations enter the inner ear through the oval window. The footplate of the stapes bone covers the oval window.

- Eustachian tube—narrow channel connecting the middle ear to the nasopharynx. Its function is to provide air passage from the nasopharynx to the middle ear to equalize pressure from both sides of the eardrum.

- Mastoid—section of the temporal bone of the skull composed of interconnected air-filled cavities and air cells that help middle ears adjust to changes in pressure. The mastoid also helps lighten the skull.

- Inner ear (labyrinth)—located deep within a section of the temporal bone, the inner ear contains the sensory organs for hearing and balance as well as the eighth cranial nerve. The inner ear is composed of two main structures: the bony labyrinth and the membranous labyrinth. The bony labyrinth surrounds and protects the membranous labyrinth. The space between the two structures contains *perilymph fluid*. Main structures of the membranous labyrinth are as follows:

—Utricle and saccule—position the head as it relates to the pull of gravity.

—Semicircular canals—sense rotational movements, such as movements or changes in position.

—Cochlea—a spiral shaped cavity within the inner ear in which a membraneous tube, the cochlear duct is suspended. The cochlear

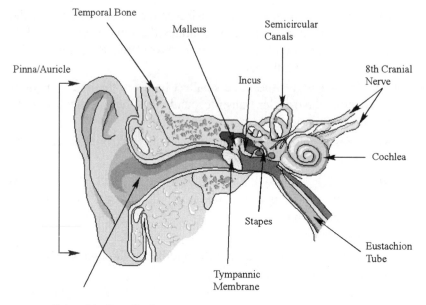

Figure 1–16. The ear.
© *Life*ART, Lippincott Williams & Wilkins 2002.

duct is filled with endolymph fluid that transmits impulses responsible for balance to the vestibular portion of the acoustic nerve.
• The organ of Corti—located at the end of the membraneous labyrinth, the organ of Corti is the end organ for hearing. It transforms mechanical sound into different frequencies.

Refer to **Figure 1-16.**

Ear Function

Sound vibrations pass through the external ear into the middle ear. From the stapes footplate, they pass through the oval window and move the perilymph. Vibrations of the perilymph are then transmitted through the vestibular membrane to the endolymph that fills the cochlear duct to the organ of Corti. The organ of Corti then transforms the mechanical sound into neural activity and separates sound into different frequencies. Electrochemical impulses then travel from the organ of Corti to the temporal cortex of the brain via the cochlear portion of the eighth cranial (acoustic) nerve. The impulses are decoded from sound to speech in the brain. Impulses responsible for balance are transmitted to the brain via the vestibular portion of the acoustic nerve.

§ 1.44   —Diseases of the Ear

Disorders and disease of the ear can affect external, middle, or inner ear. Some of the most common diseases/disorders affecting the ear are listed below.

1. Balance disorders—caused by dysfunction of vestibular system and balance reflexes located in the inner ear. Balance disorders may be extremely debilitating and also cause gait problems. They may originate in the central nervous system or the peripheral nervous system. Common disorders are:
    - viral neuronitis—characterized by sudden vertigo without hearing loss. As the name implies, this disorder is caused by viral infection; it is usually self-limiting.
    - viral labyrinthitis—affects both hearing and balance. Balance is usually recovered, however, hearing loss is usually permanent.
    - benign paroxysmal positional vertigo—characterized by short periods of vertigo precipitated by quick head movement or sudden changes in position.
    - Meniere's disease—characterized by presence of vertigo, hearing loss, and tinnitus. Recurring episodes of this disease frequently occur.

2. Eustachian tube disorders—usually some type of blockage resulting from middle ear infection, upper respiratory infection, enlarged adenoids in children, or barotrauma.

3. Hearing impairment—can range in severity from difficulty understanding specific words or sounds to total deafness. Many factors influence development of hearing impairment including heredity, trauma, age, noise exposure, infectious disease, arteriosclerosis, drugs potentially toxic to the eighth cranial nerve, and tumors. Hearing loss is categorized by its underlying pathophysiology:

- sensorineural hearing loss—results from disease or trauma to the structures or nerve pathways of the inner ear that lead to the brain stem. Sensorineural hearing loss is usually progressive and is not correctable.
- conductive hearing loss—interference in the conduction of sound impulses through the external auditory canal, the eardrum, or the middle ear. Most conductive hearing loss is correctable by either medical or surgical treatment.
- noise induced hearing loss—diminished hearing occurs in higher frequencies. Treatment is by avoiding noise and/or by wearing ear protection.
- central deafness—central nervous system cannot interpret normal auditory signals.

4. Infections—can affect both external and middle ear:
   - External ear infection (external otitis) is caused primarily by bacteria or fungi. The most common external ear infection is swimmer's ear that results from water retained in the external ear canal. Infections can also involve the cartilage of the external ear (see perichondritis below).
   - Middle ear infection (otitis media) is caused by various types of bacteria, depending on age of patient. Infection can be acute or chronic. Chronic infections commonly involve presence of drainage and perforation of the eardrum and, over time, can result in hearing loss. Less commonly, otitis media is seen in conjunction with upper respiratory infections and allergies.

5. Mastoiditis—infection of the mastoid bone. Acute mastoiditis has become rare since the discovery of antibiotics; however chronic mastoiditis can still occur with repeated middle ear infections.

6. Obstructions:
   - External ear—most common causes are impacted ear wax and foreign bodies. Both can cause decreased hearing, pain, and complaints of "blocked ear". Treatment consists of removal of the blockage through instillation of ear drops and/or ear irrigation.
   - Middle ear—see Eustachian tube disorders below.

7. Otosclerosis—involves excess bone formation around the stapes that prevents normal movement that results in conductive hearing loss.

8. Perichondritis—infection involving the cartilage of the external ear (the pinnal).

9. Presbycusis—hearing impairment resulting from degeneration of the organ of Corti that commonly occurs from age.

10. Tinnitus—commonly referred to ringing in the ears, but may include other noises as well. Tinnitus is not a disease per se, but a symptom. It is often a warning of hearing loss or other problems such as tumor.

11. Trauma:
    - External ear—may be blunt or sharp and should be treated promptly to prevent the development of inflammation in surrounding ear cartilage.
    - Middle ear—can result from a blast or blunt injury. These injuries can dislocate or fracture the ossicles and rupture the tympanic membrane.

12. Tumors or masses—can be malignant or benign.
    - External ear—most benign masses are usually cysts arising from the glands present in the external ear structure. Malignant tumors can occur in the external ear as well.
    - Middle ear—most common benign masses are infectious polyps. Malignant masses involving the middle ear can be primary or as a result of metastasis from a primary in another body location.

13. Tympanosclerosis—hardening of the tympanic membrane as a result of repeated bouts of infection. Tympanosclerosis results in conductive hearing loss secondary to hardening of the membrane around the inner ear ossicles.

14. Tympanic membrane perforation—can be caused by infection or fluid accumulation behind the membrane or from trauma.

§ 1.45   —Evaluation of Ear Function

Hearing testing is not commonly done as part of a routine history and physical. If through the history and physical process, the patient exhibits symptoms of hearing or balance pathophysiology, additional tests may be ordered. Such tests may assess auditory acuity or vestibular acuity. Auditory acuity tests include:

BODY STRUCTURE AND FUNCTION

1. Weber test—tuning fork is set into vibration; the rounded tip of the handle is then placed on the center of the nasal bone. The patient is asked whether the tone is heard in the center of the head, the right ear, or the left ear. Normally the sound is heard equally by both ears.
2. Rinne test—vibrating tuning fork is shifted between two positions against the mastoid bone. As the position of the fork is changed, the patient is asked which tone is louder. This test is useful to differentiate between conductive and sensorineural hearing loss.
3. Schwabach test—using the tuning fork, the hearing of the patient is compared to that of the examiner.

Vestibular acuity tests include:

1. Romberg test—assesses inner ear for balance. Patient stands with feet together, arms out in front and eyes open, then with eyes closed. Balance should be maintained with minimal amount of swaying. Also see § **2.15** for additional information.
2. Test for nystagmus (involuntary movements of the eye)—finger is placed directly in front of patient at eye level. The finger is moved slowly from the midline toward the right ear and left ear, but not more than 30 degrees. The eyes should follow without any jerking movements. Nystagmus is associated with vestibular nerve dysfunction.

CHAPTER 2

DIAGNOSTIC TESTING MODALITIES

§ 2.3 —Blood Tests

Page 73, add at end of section:

Adrenocorticotropic Hormone (ACTH):   Normal value ranges:

   AM: 15 to 100 pg/ml or 10 to 80 ng/L (SI units)
   PM: <50 pg/ml or <50 ng.L (SI units)

One of the anterior pituitary gland's primary functions is the secretion of the hormone cortisol. ACTH blood test measures levels of this hormone and is used to diagnosis Cushing's syndrome (overproduction of cortisol) or Addison's disease (underproduction of cortisol). In Cushing's syndrome, increased levels may indicate pituitary or nonpituitary tumor. In Addison's disease, decreased levels of cortisol may indicate primary adrenal gland failure.

Ammonia level: Normal value ranges:

   Adult: 15 to 110 µg/dl
   Child: 40 to 80 µg/dl
   Newborn: 90 to 150 µg/dl

Ammonia, produced when the body breaks down protein, is usually excreted by the liver. Serum ammonia level tests are usually performed to support the diagnosis of liver failure in diseases such as hepatitis or cirrhosis.

Antidiuretic Hormone (ADH):   Normal value ranges:

   1 to 5 pg/ml or <1.5ng?L (SI units)

ADH, also known as vasopressin, is formed by the hypothalamus and stored in the posterior pituitary gland. Its primary function is to regulate the amount of water reabsorbed by the kidney. This test is used to support the diagnosis of diabetes insipidus (ADH secretion is inadequate) or the syndrome of inappropriate ADH secretion (SIADH), caused by inappropriately high levels of ADH secretion.

Antistreptolysin O titer (ASO titer):   Normal value ranges:

Adult: ≤160 Todd units/ml
Newborn: similar to mother's value
Child (2 to 12 years):   ≤160 to 330 Todd units, depending on age.

An ASO titer is used to determine if a specific disease was caused by a prior streptococcus infection. Principal diseases associated with streptococcal infections are glomerulonephritis, rheumatic fever, bacterial endocarditis, and scarlet fever.

Breast cancer genetic screening (BRCA genetic testing):   Normal value ranges:

No genetic mutation in the BRCA 1 or 2 gene

Mutation in these genes indicate an increased susceptibility for developing breast cancer. BRCA 1 also indicates an increased susceptibility for developing ovarian cancer.

CA 27.29 and CA 15-3 tumor markers: Normal value ranges:

CA 27.29:   <38 U/ml
CA 15-3:   <22 U/ml

These two antigens are used to stage breast cancer and monitor its treatment. Their use as a screening tool is quite limited because of the high incidence of elevated markers in the general population; therefore, they are used most frequently to monitor treatment of metastatic disease.

CA 19-9 tumor marker: Normal value ranges:

<37 U/ml

This test is used primarily to evaluate a patient's response to treatment for pancreatic or hepatobiliary cancer and periodically as a post-treatment surveillance tool for tumor recurrence.

§ 2.3 BLOOD TESTS

CA 125 tumor marker: Normal value ranges:

0 to 35 U/ml

This marker is used to screen for ovarian cancer and to monitor its treatment. It is an extremely sensitive screening tool.

Cytomegalovirus (CMV).   Normal value ranges:

No virus isolated

This test is used to diagnose CMV infection. CMV is a virus, related to herpes simplex and varicella zoster viruses as well as to the Epstein-Barr virus. Infection is common and often goes undiagnosed. However, CMV does have serious implications during pregnancy, when infection may cause birth defects in the fetus.

Disseminated Intravascular Coagulation (DIC) screening.   Normal value ranges:

No evidence of DIC in a panel of tests that includes bleeding time, platelets, protime, PTT, and coagulation factors.

This test assesses the adequacy of the clotting mechanism. In DIC, the clotting mechanism is triggered inappropriately, causing small clots to form in small vessels. Clot formation may eventually lead to anoxic injury of body organs.

Epstein-Barr virus (EBV).   Normal value ranges:

Titers ≤10 nondiagnostic
Titers 1:10 to 1:60 indicate infection some time in past
Titers ≥1:320 may indicate active infection

EBV infection is highly prevalent in the U.S. population. The virus is the causative agent of infectious mononucleosis as well as other types of infections. After active infection, the virus becomes dormant in the body but can become reactivated at a later time.

Hepatitis virus studies: Hepatitis A.   Normal value ranges:

Blood negative for hepatitis A virus (HAV)
Positive HAV blood test with antibody immunoglobulin G (IgG) indicates past infection

DIAGNOSTIC TESTING MODALITIES

Positive HAV blood test with antibody immunoglobulin M (IgM) indicates active infection

Originally called infectious hepatitis, hepatitis has a short incubation period and is highly contagious. It is transmitted by the fecal oral route and has no carrier state.

Hepatitis virus studies: Hepatitis B.   Normal value ranges:

Blood negative for hepatitis B virus (HBV)
Positive blood test for hepatitis B surface antigen (HBsAg) indicates active infection or a carrier state
Positive blood test for hepatitis B surface antibody (HBsAb) indicates convalescent stage of infection and immunity to HBV

Hepatitis B, commonly known as *serum hepatitis,* has a longer incubation period than hepatitis A and is transmitted by exposure to blood (including blood transfusions) and other body fluids such as semen and breast milk. HBV infection can become a chronic infection.

Hepatitis virus studies: Hepatitis C.   Normal value ranges:

Blood negative for hepatitis C virus (HCV)

HCV infection, formerly called non-A, non-B hepatitis, like HBV infection is transmitted by blood and body fluids.

Herpes simplex virus (HSV) titers.   Normal value ranges:

No virus present in the blood.

The herpes simplex virus is classified as Type 1 or Type 2. HSV Type 1 is responsible for oral lesions such as cold sores. HSV Type 2 is transmitted sexually and can cause painful lesions on both male and female genitalia. Both types of HSV remain latent in the body and can be reactivated periodically to cause active infection.

Lipoproteins: High density lipids (HDLs) and low density lipids (LDLs).   Normal value ranges:

HDLs—male: >45 mg/dl or >0.75 mmol/L
      female: >55mg/dl or >0.91 mmol/L
LDLs—60 to 100 mg/dl or <3.37 mmol/L

§ 2.3   BLOOD TESTS

This test is used to assess risk of coronary heart disease. Lipoproteins are blood proteins that transport cholesterol, triglycerides, and other insoluble fats. HDLs carry cholesterol. Known as "good cholesterol," HDLs remove cholesterol from body tissues and transport it to the liver for excretion. LDLs, or "bad cholesterol," deposit cholesterol in body tissues such as arteries. Over time, these deposits may lead to cardiac disease.

Magnesium (Mg).   Normal value ranges:

> Adult: 1.2 to 2 mEq/L
> Child: 1.4 to 17 mEq/L

This test measures levels of magnesium in the blood. Mg is essential to normal organ functions, including those of neuromuscular tissue. Magnesium levels must be measured in patients with cardiac and renal disease.

Monospot.   Normal value ranges:

> Blood negative, titer $<1:28$

This test is used to diagnose infectious mononucleosis, a disease caused by the Epstein-Barr virus.

Partial thromboplastin time (PTT).   Normal value ranges:

> 60 to 70 seconds
> 1.5 to 2.5 times the control value (in seconds) for patients receiving anticoagulation therapy

PTTs assess the body's blood clotting mechanism. Sequential tests are commonly performed routinely when a patient is on anticoagulation therapy such as heparin. When an individual is at risk for developing blood clots, PTTs are kept elevated to prolong blood clotting time.

Prostate specific antigen (PSA).   Normal value ranges:

> <4 ng/ml

This test is used to detect prostate cancer. The higher the level, the greater the tumor burden.

33

Prothrombin time (Protime, PT or international normalized ratio (INR)). Normal value ranges:

11.0 to 12.5 seconds; 85% to 100%
1.5 to 2 times the control value; 20% to 30% in anticoagulation therapy

These tests are used to assess the adequacy of the body's clotting system. Factors such as liver disease, gallbladder disease, and the use of certain types of drugs can prolong clotting time. (Also see main text, page 72.)

Therapeutic drug monitoring. Normal (therapeutic) value ranges:

drug-specific

This test is performed periodically to assess therapeutic blood levels and detect toxic levels of a specific drug. Common drug classes for which therapeutic blood monitoring is done include certain antibiotics, anticonvulsants, cardiac medications, and antipsychotics. Lab results include therapeutic and toxic ranges along with the individual's result.

Triglycerides. Normal value ranges:

Adult male: 40 to 160 mg/dl or 0.45 to 1.81 mmol
Adult female: 35 to 135 mg/dl or 0.40 to 1.52 mmol/dl

Triglycerides, a form of fat present in the bloodstream, are produced in the liver, carried by low density lipids (LDLs) in the blood, and deposited in tissues. This test is commonly part of a lipid "profile" that includes measurement of cholesterol and lipoproteins.

§ 2.6 —Noninvasive Radiology Procedures

Page 77, add at end of section:

13. Videofluoroscopy—identifies swallowing mechanism problems. After barium or a meal containing barium is ingested, X-rays follow the progression of the food or liquid during the swallowing process. Impairment of the swallowing mechanism can be identified, possibly as a consequence of stroke or obstruction by tumor.

§ 2.7   —Invasive Radiology Procedures

Page 78, add at end of section:

12.   Hysterosalpingography—after injection of contrast dye through the cervix, the fallopian tubes and uterine cavity are visualized radiographically for patency of fallopian tubes and abnormalities of the uterine cavity.

13.   Percutaneous Transhepatic Cholangiography (PCT)—contrast dye is injected directly into a bile duct through the liver. Bile ducts both inside and outside the liver can be visualized and patency determined. The gallbladder may also be visualized and studied for obstruction due to tumor or gallstones.

14.   Electrophysiologic study (EPS) or cardiac mapping—multiple electrode catheters are placed through a peripheral vein into the right atrium and/or ventricle. Under close cardiac monitoring, the electrodes are used to pace the heart and potentially induce cardiac arrythmias. Abnormalities in the heart's conduction system can be identified and treated.

§ 2.8   —Computerized Radiology Technology

Page 80, add at end of subsection, ***Positron Emission Tomography (PET)*** *scan:*

PET scans are also used to assess cardiac function. Because both structure and function are studied, PET scanning can combine information about adequacy of myocardial blood perfusion and viability of myocardial cells. Two different radioisotopes (tracers) are injected intravenously. The first tracer travels through the bloodstream to the vessels supplying the myocardium with blood. A computer reconstructs images of the tracer's distribution in the vessels. Next, a glucose tracer is injected and localizes in the myocardium. The uptake level of the glucose tracer is determined by the metabolic activity of the myocardial cells, which gives a picture of cell viability. There is said to be a "match" when a perfusion study shows poor blood flow and the metabolic study shows low levels of glucose uptake, indicating nonviable myocardial cells. A "mismatch" occurs when a perfusion study shows poor blood flow and the metabolic study shows viable myocardial cells.

A less common use of PET scanning is in diagnosing cancers. Because cancer cells burn glucose at a higher rate than normal cells, PET scans can diagnose malignant tissue.

§ 2.9 —Additional Diagnostic Tests

Page 84, add to numbered list:

26. Cardiac nuclear scan—a radioisotope is injected intravenously and a radiation detector is placed over the heart. An image of the heart is then recorded and photographed to detect conditions such as myocardial ischemia, infarction, and dysfunction of the myocardial wall. It is most frequently used as part of cardiac stress testing. This test is also known as *heart scan, thallium scan,* or *MUGA scan.*

27. Electromyogram (EMG)—see § 2.15 of main text.

28. Electroneurogram (ENG)—also known as nerve conduction studies. See § 2.15 of main text.

29. Sleep studies—used to diagnose obstructive sleep apnea. Sleep apnea is defined as complete obstruction of the upper airway that results in no ventilation for at least 10 seconds. Apneic episodes may result in low oxygen levels in the blood, heart disturbances, muscle spasms, sleep interruption, and insomnia. During sleep studies, airflow adequacy through the nose and mouth are carefully monitored. Additional monitoring is provided through EKG, EMG, and pulse oximetry.

CHAPTER 3

THERAPEUTIC TREATMENT MODALITIES

Page 116, revise title to § 3.6, insert the following before the first paragraph:

§ 3.6   Federal Drug Administration (Revised Title)

The Federal Drug Administration (FDA) is *the* authoritative federal agency regulating many facets of the drug industry. The official FDA charge is to protect the American consumer by enforcing the Federal Food, Drug, and Cosmetic Act as well as several related public health laws. To help the agency make sound decisions based on scientific information in the review of regulated products, the FDA works with Advisory Committees comprised of individuals who are recognized as experts in their fields. Experts are from many different sectors in society and include medical professionals, scientists, researchers, industry leaders, and patient and consumer representatives. The agency fulfills its mission, in part, through publication of information on regulatory and reinforcement activities, such as:

- Drug recalls—list actions taken to remove problem drugs from market. The manufacturer can initiate these actions, or they can be initiated by FDA request, or by FDA orders under its statutory authority.
- Warning letters—issued by FDA to provide information on regulatory matters to companies under their jurisdiction.
- Enforcement reports—provides weekly reports of FDA regulatory activities.
- Import alerts—report problem commodities and shippers and provide guidance to FDA field investigators about import coverage.
- Import detentions—list products detained because of questionable compliance with FDA regulations.
- On-line sales of medical products—identify information on websites with potentially illegal on-line prescription drug sales.

- Debarment list—names firms or individuals barred from participating in drug industry because of conviction of crimes related to FDA regulations.
- Information on clinical investigators—list disqualified, restricted, or reinstated clinical investigators.
- Public Health Service administrative actions—list researchers with actions imposed against them by the Office of Research Integrity.
- Notices of initiation of disqualification proceedings—contain letters issued to clinical investigators when repeated violation of FDA regulations relating to clinical trials is suspected.
- Investigators reports—publish cases in FDA Consumer magazine that illustrate FDA administrative actions.
- Summaries of court actions—report cases involving seizure, criminal, and injunction proceedings.

When a problem arises with a product under its authority, the FDA can take a number of actions:

1. Initially work with manufacturer to correct a problem voluntarily.
2. If efforts fail, initiate legal actions, including product recalls, product seizure by federal marshals, or detention of imports at port of entry.
3. Request court injunctions against and/or prosecute those that deliberately violate the law. When warranted, criminal penalties, including prison sentences, are sought.

More in-depth information on FDA enforcement activities can be found in their web site http://www.fda.gov/oc/enforcement.htm.

In addition to the agency's enforcement activities, it also participates in the 1996 amendment to Freedom of Information Act that mandates publicly accessible electronic reading rooms that also provide agency response materials. The web address for Freedom of Information materials is http://www.fda.gov/foi/foiaz.htm.

To assist the FDA to meet its public health responsibilities, the agency promotes leveraging activities. These activities involve working with companies in the private sector to develop ideas and proposals that will enhance delivery of mission-related FDA functions, but do not require FDA funding. For example, a leveraging venture could involve contractor or third party development and operation of a system beneficial to FDA as well as to others in the private sector. The developer would then charge a fee for use of the system and the revenue generated would be used to maintain and improve the system. More in-depth information on leveraging activities can be found on their website, including an information guide that lists past and present activities and leveraging contacts at FDA. The website address is http://www.fda.gov/oc/leveraging/default.htm.

A final service of the FDA that bears mention is *MedWatch,* an internet-based resource for timely safety information on drugs and other medical products regulated by the FDA. *MedWatch* services both health professionals and consumers and covers medical products such as prescription and over the counter (OTC) drugs, biologicals, dietary supplements, and medical devices. *MedWatch* website address is http://www.fda.gov/medwatch/index.html

Page 117, add at end of § 3.6:

Researching Drug Information

An often-overlooked aspect of medical records review is investigation into the types and quantities of medications used by the plaintiff and any possible relationship to alleged symptoms or injuries. For example, a plaintiff involved in a motor vehicle accident is now claiming low back pain and sexual dysfunction. An examination of the plaintiff's medical records discloses a history of depression that predates the subject accident. Plaintiff's physician has prescribed Fluoxetine Hcl (Prozac), a selective serotonin reuptake inhibitor, as an antidepressant medication. A common side effect of this medication is sexual dysfunction. It is the responsibility of the consultant or expert to relate a condition to injury or medication; moreover, potentially valuable information has been discovered by examining this area of an individual's medical history.

When preparing to research drug information, make certain you have the correct pronunciation and spelling of the drug as there are many, similar-sounding members of a drug class (e.g., Cefazolin Cephalexin, and Cefotetan). Learn both the generic and brand names of the drug. A medication may have many brand names, but only one generic name. For example, within the histamine receptor antagonist category is the generic drug, ranitidine, and four different brand names (Zantac, Zantac EFFERdose, Zantac GELdose, Zantac 75).

Internet Drug Information Resources

- Biological Therapies in Psychiatry (http://www.btpnews.com)
  Psychopharmacology newsletter; good resource on new drugs and drug interactions.

- Internet Medical Health (http://www.mentalhealth.com)
  Covers the most used psychiatric medications with links to other drugs not included.

- The Medical Letter on Drugs and Therapeutics
  (http://www.medletter.com)
  Peer-reviewed publication with critical evaluations of new drugs.

- Pharmaceutical Research and Manufacturers of America
  (http://www.phrma.org)
  Information about issues of significance including drugs in development and facts and figures about drugs in current use.

- Pharmacists' Guide to the Internet (http://www.altimed.com)
  Canadian site that is well organized by disease and drug category; other drug information sites are rated; some information in French.

- PharmInfo Net: Pharmaceutical Information Network
  (http://www.pharminfo.com)
  Database of articles, list of frequently-asked questions (FAQs) about drugs with answers from drug manufacturers, archive of drug-related discussion threads, links to other sites.

- PharmWeb (http://www.mcc.ac.uk/pharmacy)
  Annotated listing of publications, electronic products, journals related to pharmacology, links to pharmacy-related sites, including pharmaceutical companies.

- Rx List—The Internet Drug List (http://www.rxlist.com)
  List of the top 200 most prescribed medications; also includes some foreign drugs.

- U.S. Food and Drug Administration (FDA) (http://www.fda.gov)
  The most important consumer protection agency in the federal government; includes information on new drug approvals, recalls and product alerts, drug evaluations, adverse drug reactions; research programs and approved products.

§ 3.7 Actions, Indications, and Side Effects

Page 166, insert at end of **Table 3–3:**

Table 3–3 (*continued*)

Drug	Action	Indications	Common Side Effects
		ANTI-VIRAL DRUGS	
Acyclovir sodium (Zovirax®)	interferes with DNA synthesis and inhibits viral multiplication	initial and recurrent herpes simplex virus infections, varicella in immunocompetent patients, acute herpes zoster infection in immunocompetent patients, herpes simplex encephalitis	malaise, headache, nausea, vomiting, transient elevation of creatinine and BUN levels. *Major, but uncommon side effects*: seizures, coma, acute renal failure, thrombocytopenia
Amantidine hydrochloride (Symmetrel®)	unknown; may prevent release of viral nucleic acid into host cell	prophylaxis or treatment of influenza A infection	dizziness, irritability, insomnia, nausea. *Major, but uncommon side effects*: heart failure
Famciclovir (Famvir®)	inhibits viral DNA synthesis	acute herpes zoster infections (shingles), recurrent mucocutaneous herpes simplex infections in HIV patients	headache, nausea

Table 3–3 (*continued*)

ANTI-VIRAL DRUGS

Drug	Action	Indications	Common Side Effects
Foscarnet sodium (Foscavir®)	interferes with viral DNA synthesis	cytomegalovirus (CMV) retinitis in AIDS patients; acyclovir resistant herpes simplex infections	headache, fatigue, malaise, dizziness, neuropathy, hypertension, abnormal EKG, flushing, nausea, vomiting, diarrhea, anorexia, abnormal renal function, anemia, granulocytopenia, blood electrolyte abnormalities, rash. *Major, but uncommon side effects:* seizures, pancreatitis, acute renal failure, blood cell disorders, bone marrow suppression, bronchospasm
Ganciclovir (Cytovene®)	inhibits viral DNA synthesis	CMV retinitis in AIDS patients, prevention of CMV disease in patients with advanced HIV infection, prevention of CMV disease in transplant recipients (normal renal function must be present)	nausea, vomiting, diarrhea, anorexia, increased creatinine levels, anemia, rash. *Major, but uncommon side effects:* seizures, coma, blood cell disorders
Oseltamivir phosphate (Tamiflu®)	interferes with viral replication	influenza infection in patients with symptoms for <2 days	no significant common side effects

Table 3–3 (*continued*)

Drug	Action	Indications	Common Side Effects
Ribavirin (Virazole®)	unknown, possibly by inhibiting RNA and DNA synthesis	respiratory syncyntial virus in hospitalized infants & children	no significant common side effects. *Major, but uncommon side effects:* cardiac arrest, slow heart rate, apnea
Rimantadine hydrochloride (Flumadine®)	unknown, possibly interferes with viral replication	prophylaxis of influenza A	no significant common side effects

HIV drugs are listed below; often more than one drug is used in treatment. Consult a comprehensive drug text for specific drug indications, side effects, and therapy regimens.

Abacavir sulfate (Ziagen®)

Amprenavir (Agenerase®)

Delavirdine mesylate (Rescriptor®)

Didanosine (Videx®)

Efavirenz (Sustiva®)

Indinavir sulfate (Crixivan®)

Lamivudine (Epivir®, Epivir-HBV®)

Lamivudine/zidovudine (Combivir®)

43

Table 3–3 (*continued*)

Drug	Action	Indications	Common Side Effects
	ANTI-VIRAL DRUGS		
Nelfinavir mesylate (Viracept®)			
Nevirapine (Viramune®)			
Ritonavir (Norvir®)			
Saquinavir (Fortovase®)			
Saquinavir mesylate (Invirase®)			
Stavudine (Zerit®)			
Zalcitabine (Hivid®)			
Zidovidine azidothymidine, AZT (Retrovir®)			
	ANTI-FUNGAL DRUGS		
Amphotericin B (Amphocin®, Amphotericin B for Injection®)	alters cell permeability to allow leakage of intracellular components and eventual fungal cell death	systemic fungal infections such as coccidiomycosis, histoplasmosis, disseminated candidiasis; for GI tract infections caused by candida albicans	headache, malaise, thrombophlebitis, anorexia, nausea, vomiting, abnormal renal function, anemia, weight loss. *Major, but uncommon side effects:* seizures, arrhythmias, GI bleeding, renal impairment, blood cell disorders, hepatitis, liver failure, bronchospasm

Table 3–3 (*continued*)

Drug	Action	Indications	Common Side Effects
Floconazole (Diflucan®)	inhibits fungal cell synthesis and weakens cell walls	oropharyngeal candidiasis, prevention of candidia infections in bone marrow transplant patients	nausea and vomiting. *Major, but uncommon side effects:* blood cell disorders, anaphylaxis
Grisefulvin (Fulvicin U/F, Fulvicin V, Grisactin 500®)	stops fungal cell activity	ringworm infections of skin, hair, or nails	rash, urticaria. *Major, but uncommon side effects:* GI bleeding, blood cell disorders, liver toxicity, hypersensitivity reactions
Ketoconazole (Nizoral®)	interferes with fungal cell wall synthesis and increases cell wall permeability	candida infections (local and systemic), coccidiomycosis, infections resistant to oral or topical grisefulvin	nausea, vomiting. *Major, but uncommon side effects:* blood cell disorders, fatal liver toxicity
Nystatin (Mycostatin®, Nilstat®, Nystat-Rx®)	unknown, probably alters cell wall permeability	intestinal, oral, and vaginal candida infections	no significant common side effects
Terbinafine hydrochloride (Lamsil®)	inhibits an enzyme critical in cell biosynthesis	nail infections caused by dermatophytes (tinea unguium)	headache. *Major, but uncommon side effects:* neutropenia, hypersensitivity reactions, anaphylaxis

Page 200, add new sections:

§ 3.45 —Pain (New)

In part because the term "pain" is difficult to define, numerous definitions of pain exist. McCaffrey, (1969) defines pain as "Whatever the patient says it is, existing whenever he says it does." The International Association of the Study of Pain describes pain as "an unpleasant sensory and emotional experience associated with actual or potential tissue damage, or described in terms of such damage."

All persons experience some type of pain in their lifetime. Pain is a normal physiologic response of the body, a subjective sensation caused by noxious stimuli that signal the body of actual or potential tissue damage. Pain can be perceived only by the person experiencing it. How pain is interpreted and responded to is unique to that individual and influenced by psychological and cultural factors—values, beliefs, religion, norms, and customs—that help determine the significance and meaning of pain for each person.

Chronic pain is one of the most costly health care problems in America. Billions of dollars are spent annually on medical expenses, lost income, lost productivity, compensation payments, and legal fees. Many personal injury and worker's compensation cases involve chronic pain as part of their damages. For the legal professional reviewing and summarizing medical records, extracting relevant information on the client's pain history and treatment can be challenging. Understanding some basic concepts about types of pain, assessment, and treatment is helpful to this process.

Theories and Beliefs Relating to Pain

Pain has always been considered a byproduct of injury or disease—that is, if the condition is treated, the pain will stop. Many theories and beliefs have supported this thinking. The specificity of pain theory developed in the 17th century was based on the concept of a fixed, one-to-one relationship between stimulus and sensation: a particular form of therapy administered by all physicians works for all patients and all pain. As recently as the 1980s, it was assumed that infants could not feel or remember pain.

46

§ 3.45 PAIN

In many cultures, high pain tolerance is valued. Individuals are encouraged not to verbalize their pain characteristics or manifest outward signs of discomfort, especially in the presence of chronic pain. Although society encourages stoicism in the presence of pain, it also widely subscribes to the acute pain model. The acute pain model holds that if someone has pain, some visible signs of discomfort will be present, behavioral or physiologic. Examples of these "appropriate" manifestations of pain could include grimacing, wincing, crying, or guarding the painful area. It is commonly believed that if an individual is laughing, resting comfortably, or conversing or joking with others that he/she cannot be in pain. Contrary to these popular and widespread beliefs, it is now known that over time both behavioral and physiologic adaptation to pain occurs, leading to periods of minimal or no visible signs of pain.

Another widely accepted belief is that all causes of pain are identifiable. If its cause is known, pain is more acceptable. Family and friends are more supportive of the individual and clinicians are almost always more attentive to achieving successful pain management if the cause is known. The term "psychogenic pain" is commonly used to refer to pain for which a physical cause cannot be found. Of interest to note is the fact that "Psychogenic Pain" as a diagnosis has been removed from the DSM-IV Manual (Diagnostic and Statistical Manual of Mental Disorders). When the cause is unknown or seems insufficient to account for severity of pain, the clinician may attribute it to anxiety or depression and minimize efforts to treat it. In reality, most pain is a combination of physical and psychological factors; cause and effect between pain and anxiety/depression is unclear as to which comes first.

Common Misconceptions about Pain

Society's beliefs around pain have helped develop many common misconceptions held by both the lay public as well as health professionals. These misconceptions may impede proper assessment of patients with pain by healthcare providers and impact the effectiveness of pain treatment. Some common misconceptions include:

- Health care providers are the authority on pain, the experts in treating it. In reality, the patient should always be considered the authority on his/her pain.

- There is a uniform pain threshold, that is, the intensity of the pain experienced from comparable stimuli will be the same from person to person. Not only do different intensities of pain result from comparable stimuli, but the threshold at which pain is perceived differs as well.

- Patients with low pain tolerance need to make more effort to cope with the pain. Pain tolerance is the duration or intensity of pain the patient is willing to tolerate. This will vary from person to person. Although an individual's coping skills may influence his/her pain tolerance, other factors affecting pain tolerance are past experience with pain, motivation to endure pain, and energy level.

- All real pain has an identifiable (physical) cause. Pain is a complex phenomenon with both physiologic and psychological components. As a relatively new science, many aspects of pain are still not fully understood.

- Persons in pain exhibit visible signs, either physical or behavioral. Because adaptation to pain occurs, lack of expression of pain does not necessarily mean that pain is not present.

- Pain is not perceived by the very young or the very old. Studies have demonstrated this not to be true. However, how pain is expressed may be altered in these patients.

- Individuals knowledgeable about opiod (narcotic) analgesia and who regularly request them are addicted. People who experience pain should be knowledgeable about their pain medications, including opiods, just as persons with diabetes should be knowledgeable about medication and diet that help control blood sugar.

- Opiods can easily cause addiction and, therefore, should be used sparingly and only for specific diagnoses, e.g. cancer. Numerous studies have demonstrated little risk of addiction associated with opiod administration for pain relief.

As a result of widely accepted theories and misconceptions, as well as of individual beliefs of health care providers, pain has often been undertreated in the United States. However, newer theories about pain perception and transmission that incorporate both the anatomy *and* physiology of pain transmission have advanced approaches to pain treatment. The Gate Control theory of pain (discussed in **§ 3.46**) is one of the foundations for these advances.

§ 3.46   —Physiology of Pain Perception (New)

As previously stated, pain is a complex phenomenon. To understand pain, it is helpful to understand the process of pain transmission, modulation, and perception. The basic process has the following components, also illustrated in **Figure 3–8:**

1. Noxious stimuli are perceived by a specific body part. Stimuli can be thermal, chemical, mechanical, or electrical.
2. Peripheral tissues are damaged by stimuli. Damage results in the secretion of chemical substances that stimulate free nerve endings call *nociceptors*. Located in various tissues throughout the body, nociceptors convert pain stimuli into electrical impulses. Nociceptors react to changes proximal to them and require relatively increased levels of stimulation to be activated.
3. Electrical impulses travel along afferent nerve fibers to the dorsal horn of the spinal cord, where chemicals called *neurotransmitters* are secreted. These substances either inhibit or excite transmission of pain impulses.
4. The dorsal horn acts as a clearinghouse for these impulses (see gate control theory of pain, below) and transmits pain information to higher centers in the thalamus and cerebral cortex.
5. The brain identifies the stimulus as pain, precisely identifies the site, and sends this information back down the spinal cord to the site of pain, telling affected muscles to contract and block pain and withdraw from stimulus. *It is important to note that noxious stimuli are not identified as pain until this stage of the transmission process.*
6. The brain also prods the body's autonomic nervous system into action to adjust body functions such as breathing, blood flow, and pulse.

Gate Control Theory of Pain

The gate control theory of pain as described by Melzack and Wall in the 1960s suggests that specialized neural tissue, located in the dorsal horn of the spinal cord, acts as a gating mechanism to either increase or decrease the transmission of pain signals to the brain. This is accomplished via excretion of specialized chemicals, such as serotonin, adrenaline, and endorphins, which are all peptides similar to opium. The gate control the-

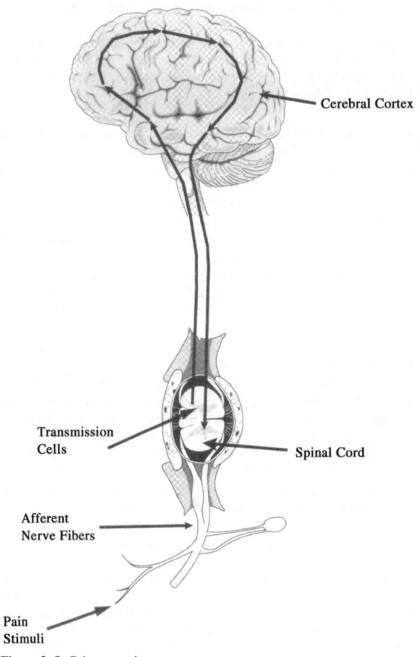

Figure 3–8. Pain perception process.

ory has been revised periodically since it was first described and now suggests that an inhibitory system in the brain stem may exist in addition to that previously described in the spinal cord. Evidence also exists that gates function differently in acute and chronic pain.

In acute pain, impulses are transmitted directly to the brain. For example, the entire pain perception process is complete in the time it takes for a hand to grasp a hot object and withdraw from it. However, in chronic pain, impulses appear to take a more circuitous route. Impulses received in the dorsal horn are not transmitted directly to the brain, but instead are transferred back and forth between interconnected nerves (the gates) that modulate the pain message as it travels up the spinal cord. Eventually, impulses are received in the cerebral cortex, which assesses the damage and sends back down the spinal cord messages that appropriately adjust body functions. This slower pathway is usually taken by duller, more persistent pain. Some evidence suggests that if pain persists long enough, the entire nervous system may reprogram itself to create a lower threshold of pain perception.

In an adult, both acute and chronic pain perception mechanisms are influenced heavily by past experience, culture, and psychological factors, which in turn determine "pain threshold." The pain threshold of an individual accounts, to a large extent, for variations in pain experience from person to person. The following types of thresholds have been described and can be assessed in the person with pain:

- Sensation threshold—lowest stimulus value that produces tingling or warmth.
- Pain perception threshold—lowest stimulus value that produces pain.
- Pain tolerance—lowest stimulus value at which person withdraws or asks to have stimulus withdrawn.
- Encouraged pain tolerance—same as pain tolerance, but person is encouraged to tolerate higher levels of stimulation.

Types of Pain

Many different classifications of pain exist and descriptions of pain vary widely. It is helpful both to know some of the most commonly used classifications of pain and to have a basic understanding of each category. This is critical to extracting relevant information for your summary. Pain can be described as follows.

THERAPEUTIC TREATMENT MODALITIES

- *Onset or time of occurrence.* It is important to determine when the pain began and what the client's situation was at this time. Since the onset, has there been a pattern to the pain—is it cyclical or does occurrence vary?
- *Duration.* Is the pain acute or chronic? Refer to the discussion below on the characteristics of acute and chronic pain.
- *Severity or intensity.* Individuals will use such terms as stabbing, dull, sharp, intermittent, excruciating, burning to describe their pain.
- *Location.* Is the pain internal or external? Is the pain always in the same location? In chronic pain, an exact location may be difficult for the individual to describe.
- *Causation.* Is the pain a result of stimulation of nerve pain receptors or nerve damage? See the discussion below for examples of these causes.

Pain is most commonly described in terms of its duration and location. Pain *duration* is classified as acute, chronic, and psychogenic. *Acute pain* is generally caused by tissue damage. It has a short duration, generally less than six months, an identifiable onset, and a limited/predictable duration. Acute pain diminishes gradually with appropriate interventions and the healing of damaged tissues. *Chronic pain* is of prolonged duration, generally persisting for longer than six months with no identifiable end. Some pain classifications include cancer pain as a separate classification and refer to chronic pain as chronic, nonmalignant pain. Based on certain characteristics, chronic pain can be further subcategorized as

- recurring acute pain—recurring episodes of pain that do not have a defined end (e.g., migraine headache pain);
- prolonged time-limited pain—pain that continues over a fairly lengthy period of time, but has a high probability of ending with appropriate treatment (e.g., burn pain);
- chronic benign pain—generally due to non-life-threatening causes, but refractory to common treatment modalities (e.g., arthritic pain).

As pain persists and becomes chronic, it no longer becomes a symptom of injury or disease, but a *pain syndrome*. Chronic pain is a medical problem in its own right that requires medical evaluation and treatment. The syndrome can affect social, family, and employment relationships and create a pattern of physical distress, emotional conflict, and long-term suffering. Major behavioral and affective changes can occur, such as:

- anxiety and/or depression;
- social withdrawal;
- appetite and weight changes—either increased or decreased;
- restricted physical activity leading to decreased work capacity, poor physical tone;
- preoccupation with physical symptoms;
- poor sleep patterns and chronic fatigue.

Pain is often labeled *psychogenic* when no physical cause can be found. It is a common belief that a person experiences psychogenic pain because he or she wants or needs it to avoid specific tasks, for economic gain, because of drug-related behavior, or to gain attention. This type of pain is also called pretended pain or malingering. There is evidence however, that chronic pain is the cause of psychogenic pain rather than the result of neurotic symptoms. The Minnesota Multiphasic Personality Inventory (MMPI) scores for individuals with "psychogenic" pain show increased scores in hysteria, depression, and hypochondria that improve when pain is relieved. Thus, even though it does exist, pretended pain should never be assumed.

Pain *location* classifications are as follows:

1. Cutaneous or superficial pain—usually well localized on the skin or body surface. The intensity of the pain usually correlates with the intensity of the stimulus. Treatment is relatively uncomplicated because the pain is localized.

2. Deep somatic pain—primarily affects muscles, bones, nerves, and blood vessels. Somatic pain is poorly localized because of poor innervation of affected organs. Pain is associated with autonomic central nervous systems symptoms, such as nausea, sweating, and blood pressure changes.

3. Visceral pain—affects large internal organs occupying body cavities and may be constant or intermittent in nature. Pain tends to be diffuse, but may become more localized over time.

4. Referred pain—occurs in an area of the body remote from the affected organ. For example, a heart attack exhibits no pain in the heart, but pain felt in the left arm, shoulder, or jaw pain.

5. Radiating pain—follows dermatome patterns from its site of origin.

The above are examples of *nociceptive pain,* that is pain caused by stimulation of pain receptors. Stimulation can be of chemical, mechanical, or thermal origin. Nociceptive pain should be differentiated from *neuropathic pain,* which is caused by damage to the nervous system when the flow of afferent nerve impulses is partially or completely interrupted. Neuropathic pain can be central or peripheral in origin. Examples include:

1. Muscular and bony origin—can affect ligaments, joints, fascia, tendon, and muscles. Pain may occur from rupture, sprains, ischemia, inflammation.

2. Vascular—precise mechanism not understood. This type of pain is believed to originate from pathology of vessels or surrounding tissues. Pain-producing chemicals also appear to play a role. The most common manifestation of vascular pain includes migraine headaches and headaches associated with arterial hypertension, brain tumors, and increased intracranial pressure.

3. Inflammation—caused by numerous agents and by bacterial or chemical stressors such as heat or cold. Symptoms include redness, swelling, heat, pain, inflammation secondary to swelling of tissues, and direct effect of released neuroregulators on afferent nerve endings. Chemical causes of inflammatory responses include secretion of histamine, bradykinen, prostoglandins, and leukoninens. These substances are acidotic and heighten sensitivity of pain fibers.

4. Central—due to central nervous system injury such as infarction or tumor. It is often severe and difficult to treat. Thalamic pain is one of the most common types of central pain. It occurs in one-half of the body after thalamic injury and is aggravated by specific stimuli.

5. Peripheral pathogenic pain—common cause is histologic changes in nerve structure, as occurs with post-herpetic neuralgic. This pain may be severe and unrelenting. Although its cause is not fully understood, scarring and degenerative changes in nerves and nervous tissue may play an important role in pain intensity. Common manifestations of peripheral pathogenic pain are:

- post-herpetic pain—occurs following infection of the dorsal nerve ganglia. Causative agent is herpes zoster or varicella zoster virus (chickenpox virus). Pain is caused by scarring and degenerative changes of the affected nerve roots.
- causalgia—result of peripheral nerve injuries. Peripheral nerves of extremities, such as brachial plexus, median, and sciatic nerves are most commonly involved. Nerve injury is usually a result of sprains, bruises, fractures, amputations.
- trigeminal neuralgia (tic douloureux)—occurs along the 5th or 9th cranial nerves. Pain results from a neuritis caused by degenerative changes that injure nerve roots. Trigeminal pain is often triggered by minimal stimuli such as cold air, temperature changes, clothing irritation against affected area.
- phantom pain—perceived in a nonexisting body part, such as after amputation of a limb. The mechanism of phantom pain perception is not well understood.
- headache—occurs in pain-sensitive structures in the head and may result from intracranial and extracranial causes. Although the brain itself is almost insensitive to pain, cerebral vasculature is all pain-sensitive, especially the middle meningeal artery. Causes of intracranial pain include infection, hemorrhage, changes in intracranial pressure. Migraine headaches are the best known example of this type of pain. Extracranial pain results from muscle tension, TMJ, ocular, sinus, dental, or malignant pain such as from cancer. Pain is caused by pressure on or displacement of nerves, interference with blood supply, or blockage within hollow organs.

§ 3.46A   —Differences in Types of Pain (New)

It is important to emphasize the differences in nocioceptive and neuropathic pain. Nocioceptive pain results from *normal processing* of sensory input by an intact nervous system. Neuropathic pain is distinctly different in that pain is sustained by *abnormal processing* of sensory input by the peripheral or central nervous system. It becomes critically important to thoroughly assess the underlying pathophysiology of the pain, as pain caused by different mechanisms responds to different treatment modalities. Chronic pain and cancer pain may reflect both types of pain (nocioceptive and neuropathic).

§ 3.46B —Harmful Effects of Unrelieved Pain (New)

To counter the belief held by some that individuals with low pain thresholds should learn to live with their pain, numerous potentially harmful effects from unrelieved pain have been observed. Unrelieved pain causes physiological stress responses in the body that affect many body systems. Pain also affects cognitive function, specifically, decreased ability to perform daily functions, and may precipitate mental confusion, especially in the elderly. Examples of some system-specific physiologic effects of pain are:

- Cardiovascular—increased heart rate, blood pressure, increased tendency of blood clotting (hypercoagulation). Hypercoagulation may lead to venous thrombosis or pulmonary embolism (blood clots).
- Respiratory—shallow breathing, decreased oxygenation of the lung alveoli, decreased lung capacity. Potential for these effects is increased if source of pain is from the thoracic or chest region. If pain is not adequately treated, complications such as pneumonia and atelectasis may develop.
- Endocrine and metabolic—excessive release of some hormones and decreased release of others. These imbalances have numerous effects on body metabolism. Unrelieved pain prolongs this situation and ultimately can delay recovery from trauma or surgery.
- Musculoskeletal—muscle spasms, impaired musculoskeletal function, fatigue. Especially significant in orthopedic injuries as these effects may interfere with the ability to participate in physical therapy, which may in turn affect return of mobility and functionality of injured area.
- Immune system—depression of the immune response that can cause susceptibility to infection; can predispose to post-operative infections such as pneumonia, wound infections, and sepsis.

In addition to physiological effects of unrelieved pain, behavioral effects are seen as well. Some studies have shown that poorly controlled acute pain can predispose to future chronic pain syndromes. Following surgery, cognitive function can become impaired, especially in the elderly. Finally, the impact on quality of life is significant, with effects noted that range from decreased physical activity to severe depression and suicidal ideation.

§ 3.47   —Assessment Tools (New)

Because pain is a subjective experience, pure objective tests for pain do not exist. As stated previously, an individual's pain response is influenced by cultural and societal factors, which must be taken into account during the evaluation process. It is impossible to predict how much pain a given stimulus can cause in an individual. Causes of pain can be obscure; pain psychological in origin can cause physiological responses. Because a physical cause for pain cannot always be found *does not mean that it is not real pain.*

Additionally, health-care provider myths and misconceptions about pain may influence assessment techniques. Personal beliefs about pain can cloud the pain assessment process. Irrespective of all barriers, the key to effective pain *treatment* is accurate *assessment.* As in any type of assessment, the provider must listen to the patient, establish physical findings, and form an objective conclusion. Shortcuts in this process may result in premature conclusions on the part of the provider and lead to less than adequate pain management.

Assessment of pain should include both subjective and objective findings; both types of data must be taken into consideration. Summarized information should contain the individual's description of pain as well as the examiner's observation of the person's behavior. It is not the role of a legal professional to interpret the meaning of the information in the medical record, but to summarize that information accurately and highlight discrepancies and conflicting information in the medical record. It is critical to include information on the client's baseline pain history prior to the current complaint.

As with any type of assessment technique, pain assessment should include both history and physical examination components:

1. History—should provide a chronology of events and include factors relevant to the location of pain, frequency, extension/radiation, surface versus deep, onset or pattern, duration, character, precipitating or aggravating factors, intensity, and symptoms. Key information includes the effects pain has had on the individual's ADLs and on his or her ability to perform job duties and responsibilities.

2. Physical examination—should focus on the objective signs of pain the patient exhibits, which can be divided into three categories:

- Sympathetic responses such as increased blood pressure, pulse, and respiration. Sympathetic responses often occur with pain of low to moderate intensity or superficial pain and are regulated by the autonomic nervous system (see § **1.22**).
- Parasympathetic responses, such as decreased blood pressure, vomiting, weakness, and pallor. These responses are often associated with pain of severe intensity or with deep pain. They are also regulated by the autonomic nervous system (see § **1.22**).
- Behavioral responses, which may include moaning, grimacing, crying, drawn facial expression, assuming a posture that minimizes pain, and others.

These responses are not diagnostic of pain, but may give clues as to its cause. The information obtained should then be evaluated within the context of cultural and psychological experiences of the individual.

Tools for Assessing Pain

More commonly, clinicians whose practice encompasses treatment of patients with pain (acute or chronic) will utilize some type of pain assessment tool. With the development of clinical practice guidelines, Patient Rights bills, and JCAHO pain standards (see § **3.48**), clinicians must now be able to demonstrate that they assess and manage their patients' pain actively. Several widely accepted tools have been developed to assist the clinician with pain assessment. For initial pain assessment, the Initial Pain Assessment tool and the Brief Pain Inventory Tool are commonly used. Both of these tools are included in the clinical guidelines for treatment of cancer pain published by the Agency for Health Care Policy and Research (AHPR). The clinician or the patient may complete either tool. The Initial Pain Assessment guides the systematic collection of pain history information. It is a 10-point tool that asks the patient to describe the following characteristics of his/her pain:

1. location
2. intensity
3. quality
4. onset, duration, variations, rhythms
5. manner of expressing pain

6. what relieves pain
7. what causes or increases pain
8. effects of pain
9. other comments
10. treatment plan.

The Brief Pain Inventory tool focuses on pain experience within the past 24 hours and includes a numeric rating scale along the following dimensions:

1. types of pain in the past 24 hours, other than "everyday" types of pain
2. identification of the worst area of pain
3. numerical rating of the worst pain in the past 24 hours
4. numerical rating of the least pain in the past 24 hours
5. numerical rating of the average pain in the past 24 hours
6. numerical rating of the pain presently
7. treatments or medications currently receiving for pain
8. maximum pain relief experience in the past 24 hours
9. numerical rating of how pain has affected (in the past 24 hours): general activity, mood, walking ability, normal work, relations with other people, sleep, enjoyment of life.

A third tool commonly used for initial pain assessment is the McGill-Melzack Pain questionnaire (see **Figure 3–9**). This tool is complex and time-consuming to use, but is gives the clinician in-depth information about the pain being experienced.

The McGill-Melzack test is designed to measure the patient's pain symptoms against five main components:

1. Pain Rating Index (PRI)—consists of words describing pain quality.
2. Number of Words Chosen (NWC)—a count of the number of words chosen from the 20 total responses in the group.
3. Present Pain Intensity (PPI)—selection of the word that most accurately describes pain intensity.

THERAPEUTIC TREATMENT MODALITIES

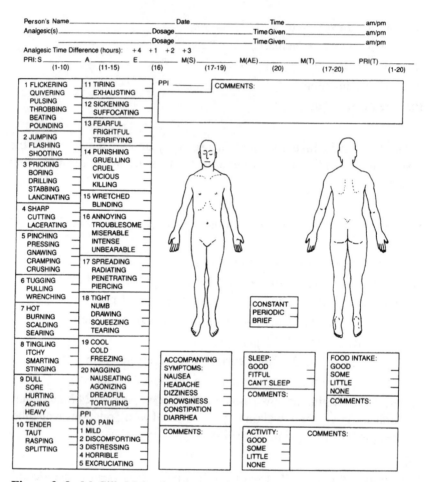

Figure 3–9. McGill–Melzack pain questionnaire.

4. Line Drawing of the Body—describes the location and frequency of the pain.

5. List of Symptoms—individual's description of symptoms experienced.

Responses are assigned scores used as a basis for pain treatment. Once treatment is initiated, this tool can be re-administered to assess the efficacy, or lack thereof, of the treatment.

Other pain assessment tools are designed for use in *daily* assessment of pain levels. Many such tools exist and are similar in that they all are used to help the individual describe pain severity. Some commonly used tools include:

- Visual analog scale with verbal anchors—individual is asked to rate pain on along a horizontal line with a scale of 0 (no pain) to 10 (worst pain).
- Numeric rating scale—verbally administered; individual is asked to rate pain on a scale of 0 to 5 or 0 to 10. This type of pain assessment is commonly used post-operatively and response levels are documented in the medical record.
- Word descriptor scale—individual is asked to rate pain intensity by using a verbal scale from no pain, slight, moderate, severe, or worst pain.
- Faces (Wong-Baker)—a variation of the above tools that describe pain in terms of facial expressions, ranging from a happy face (no pain) to a sad face with tears (worst pain). This tool is used widely to assess pain in children.

Assessment of Breakthrough Pain

Chronic pain that is more or less stable can have intermittent episodes of increased pain, known as breakthrough pain. Types of breakthrough pain can be classified as either *incident pain,* pain that occurs without warning as a result of an identifiable event, or *end of dose failure,* pain that returns at the end of a medication dosing period. As yet, no tool has been developed specifically for the assessment of breakthrough pain; however, 24-hour flow sheets can be helpful to individuals to track pain frequency, intensity, and duration. Typically, log sheets contain the following information: pain rating, activities, analgesics taken, and relief experienced.

Information gained from assessment tools requires ability of the individual to communicate information. These tools are not useful in patients with altered consciousness. Special considerations are critical to accurate pain assessment for children and the elderly. A child's cognitive and emotional development must be taken into consideration when assessing pain and planning treatment. Parents and child (if able) should participate in the treatment plan. Elderly patients are at risk for both over- and under-treatment of pain. It is common for the elderly to exhibit changes in drug distribution within the body, a factor that affects both drug absorption and excretion. Changes commonly occur in

- renal function
- central nervous system function
- sensitivity to opioids, antidepressants
- adverse interactions with drugs prescribed for existing chronic conditions
- cognitive impairment and dementia

§ 3.48 —Treatment/Management Modalities (New)

In this country, there is still evidence of continuing under-treatment of pain despite tremendous advancements in pain research, assessment tools, and management strategies. Although treatment of pain has become a clinical specialty, it still remains the responsibility of all clinicians to address pain management in the patient's treatment plan. As stated previously, a primary concept in effective pain management is that the individual is the authority on his/her pain. This concept does not require that clinicians totally agree with what a patient says, only that they accept what the patient says, convey acceptance to the patient, and take appropriate action. Clinicians can have doubts about the validity of the information relayed by the individual, but these cannot be allowed to interfere with the appropriate patient care. Therefore, observation and vital signs should not be used instead of self-report to assess pain levels.

To proactively address some of the issues related to the high incidence of under-treated pain, many professional organizations have issued guidelines and standards addressing effective pain management.

Recognition of the rights of people with pain has manifested itself in the growth of professional organizations that focus on pain, numerous patient rights statements, and guidelines that have been developed by professional organizations as well as by national and state agencies.

The Joint Commission of Accreditation of Healthcare Organizations (JCAHO) has had some standards relating to pain management since 1992. Over the years, these standards have expanded and as of 2000, JCAHO standards require that healthcare organizations develop and implement formal policies and procedures related to appropriate assessment and management of pain. Specific components of the standard that the organization is required to demonstrate are that:

- initial assessment and re-assessment of pain are performed and documented;
- provider education in pain assessment and management is given;
- patient and family education in pain management plan, including limitations and potential side effects of treatment, is given;
- communication of the importance of pain management to family has occurred, with considerations for cultural, personal, and spiritual beliefs.

Clinical practice guidelines for pain management have been developed by several organizations worldwide. Some of the more widely referenced clinical practice guidelines include:

Agency for Health Care Policy and Research (AHCPR)—guidelines for management of acute pain, cancer pain, and lower back problems. Guidelines are free of charge and may be ordered from AHCPR (see **§ 8.22**) or downloaded from their website http://www.ahcpr.gov/guide.

American Pain Society (APS)—guidelines for acute and cancer pain. For ordering information, visit their website, http://www.ampainsoc.org or contact:

American Pain Society
4700 W. Lake Avenue
Glenview, IL 600215–1485
Phone: (847) 375-4715

American Society of Anesthesiologists Task Force on Pain Management—guidelines for chronic pain management. Guidelines provide decision support to practitioners treating persons with chronic pain. They are intended to optimize pain control, minimize adverse outcomes, and minimize cost, enhance functional abilities and quality of life for individuals with chronic pain. Guidelines may be obtained by contacting

American Society of Anesthesiologists
270 North Northwest Highway
Park Ridge, IL 60068

THERAPEUTIC TREATMENT MODALITIES

Other strategies directed at improving pain management in a variety of settings are:

- Providing greater focus on patient/family and provider education, formally and informally. Provider education programs need to be incorporated into education curricula. The International Association for the Study of Pain (IASP) has published core curriculum for health care professionals.
- Incorporating pain assessment as a component of the vital sign record. This raises awareness of the health care professionals and prompts intervention.
- Greater utilization of expertise of professional organizations that focus on pain treatment as well as that of board certified specialists in pain treatment.

A fundamental goal of pain treatment is to identify and remove the cause of pain whenever possible. If this goal is not realistic, the treatment plan should focus on minimizing the adverse effects of pain on the individual's life. This approach is often necessary in treating chronic pain. The use of multiple treatment/management modalities may be necessary to achieve a successful level of pain control. The examiner should include the individual in the development of the plan and listen to what the individual feels will work and what will not. Promoting feelings of control over pain is an important component of successful treatment, as evidenced by studies demonstrating reduction of post-operative pain in patients who are taught coping techniques prior to surgery. Another key premise to consider in plan development suggests that attention be focused on pain and associated anxiety that usually results in more intense pain perception, whereas distraction from pain can diminish or relieve it. Distraction techniques can be an important component of the treatment plan. A comprehensive pain treatment plan may include noninvasive and/or invasive techniques.

Noninvasive Techniques for Pain Control

Noninvasive techniques are often used in combination with pharmacological pain management; they are seldom effective alone.

Commonly known as behavioral techniques, noninvasive modalities,

64

alone or in combination, can reduce pain in many individuals. To be successful, behavioral techniques require a great deal of participation from the individual. Some common techniques include the following:

1. Operant conditioning programs—diminishing frequency of pain-related behavior patterns. The overall goal of these techniques is to reduce pain behaviors by withdrawing positive reinforcement for undesired behaviors and increasing frequency of desired behaviors with positive reinforcement. Operant conditioning does not cure pain, but can reduce associated functional impairment.

2. Biofeedback—a variety of techniques that provide an individual with information about changes in body function of which he or she is usually unaware, such as blood pressure. Provides a vehicle for distraction and relaxation and a sense of control over one's body and, thus, over pain. It has some proven effectiveness in relieving pain associated with tension and stress, low back pain, headaches, and muscle spasms.

3. Hypnosis—induction of a trance state during which suggestions to alter the character of the pain may be introduced. In an altered conscious state, the individual becomes more receptive to these suggestions. The mechanism of pain control is not clear.

4. Acupressure—based on the principles of acupuncture. Pressure or other cutaneous stimulations are applied over acupuncture points.

5. Meditation—focuses attention away from the pain and can provide a sense of peace and relaxation to the individual. This technique is easily learned and can be practiced anywhere at any time by the individual.

6. Guided imagery—uses imagination to create images that focus attention away from the pain. This technique relieves pain through distraction, production of a relaxation response, and subsequent reduction in perceived pain.

7. Rhythmic breathing—combines both distraction and relaxation techniques. Rhythmic breathing combines rhythms such as music, a ticking clock, or a metronome with breathing rhythms and focuses attention on this process and away from the pain.

8. Relaxation or Progressive Relaxation Therapy (PRT)—emphasizes the relaxation of voluntary skeletal muscles. PRT reduces anxiety

associated with pain, encouraging the individual to first tighten, then relax various muscle groups in the body. The exercise proceeds from one area of the body to another.

9. Transcutaneous stimulation (TENS)—see § **3.38.**
10. Cold therapy—see § **3.39.**
11. Heat therapy—see § **3.40.**
12. Massage—involves superficial stimulation of the body by applying pressure to the skin in a patterned fashion using a variety of motions.
13. Multiple convergent therapy—combines multiple techniques to enhance effects of single therapy.

Invasive Interventions

Invasive interventions include nonsurgical procedures that involve the introduction of anesthetic or analgesic agents into the body and surgical procedures designed to interrupt pain pathways. For nonsurgical procedures, it is helpful to understand the difference between analgesia and anesthesia when summarizing this type of information. An *analgesic* is a pharmacologic substance that diminishes or eliminates pain without producing unconsciousness. An *anesthetic,* in addition to abolishing pain, causes loss of feeling or sensation within the body. There are various types of anesthesia. *General anesthesia* is accompanied by loss of consciousness and amnesia, whereas *local anesthesia* produces pain relief in a specific part of the body without loss of consciousness. Common types of invasive analgesia/anesthesia pain relief modalities are as follows:

1. Local anesthesia (nerve block anesthesia)—performed by injecting analgesics (generally divided into two classes) close to the nerves, thereby blocking conductivity and transmission of pain impulses. Several types of pharmacologic agents can be used. Nerve blocks are effective in relieving many different types of pain, related to varied conditions such as childbirth, herpes zoster, musculoskeletal problems, and some neuralgias.
2. Epidural infusions—deliver analgesia via catheter inserted into epidural space (see § **3.4**).
3. Intrathecal infusions—given into the subarachnoid space and do not cross the dura.

66

4. Patient controlled analgesia—refers to a method that allows the patient to control pain by using an intravenous drug delivery system (see § **3.4**).

5. Implantable infusion pump—intraspinal route for administering narcotics analgesics. Most commonly used for terminal cancer patients, who have not experienced adequate pain relief by other methods.

6. Neurosurgical interventions (surgical procedures)—include the following procedures:
   - neurectomy—severance of peripheral nerve fibers from the spinal cord, thus blocking the transmission of pain;
   - rhizotomy—resection of a posterior nerve root at the point just before it enters the spinal cord, used to control pain in the upper body;
   - sympathectomy—interruption of afferent visceral nerve fibers of the sympathetic nervous system;
   - cordotomy—accomplishes either bilateral or unilateral interruption of pain pathways, used to control pain in the lower body.

7. acupuncture—requires insertion of needles into specific points of the body, which produces mechanical stimulation to close the gate to pain stimuli.

Pharmacological Management

As stated previously, effective pain treatment is directly affected by the identification of its underlying cause(s). Once this has been determined, pharmacological intervention is likely to play a role in the treatment plan. For some providers, choice of drugs, dosage, and frequency is problematic, especially in the treatment of chronic pain. The problems may arise from several sources, such as personal beliefs and prejudices about pain treatment or lack of in-depth knowledge about current pain management techniques and treatment options. These problems may result in undertreatment of the pain.

A belief held widely by many clinicians is that the treatment of chronic pain with opiod drugs will cause addiction. While these drugs do have the potential to cause physical dependence, evidence exists that addiction as a result of taking opiods for relief of pain is extremely rare. Additionally, some physicians fear regulatory repercussions from perceived overprescription of opiods. To ease concerns, some state medical boards have issued guidelines and policies that clarify the appropriate role of opiods in pain treatment. Although guidelines have no legal status, they are an official statement by medical boards (which license physicians) and thus have been somewhat effective in addressing MD's fears of being disciplined. Professional organizations have also included statements on the appropriate role of opiods in pain management. In 1997, American Academy of Pain Medicine and the American Pain Society published a consensus statement on the use of opiods as an essential part of treatment of chronic pain.

Appropriate pain management is likely to become an escalating area of litigation. In the case of *Bergman v. Chin* (No. 20732, Cal. Super. Ct. Alameda Cty.), the children of a decedent brought suit against their father's physician for inadequate treatment of his pain. The California case involved an 85-year-old male with metastatic cancer. Days before his death, his daughter alleges that she heard her father moaning in pain frequently over a two day period, apparently obtaining little relief from pain medication that had been prescribed. His daughter called his physician and requested that her father's medication be changed to morphine; the physician refused the request. Finally, the daughter found a physician who did prescribe the morphine and she stated that her father finally obtained relief. He died two days later.

In California, survivors cannot seek damages for pain and suffering once an individual is deceased, so the case was tried under an elder abuse law in which reckless negligence must be proven. The jury found in favor of the plaintiffs and awarded $1.5M to the family, though California law caps pain and suffering damages at $250,000. In the judge's final ruling, the judgment was reduced to the $250,000 cap for pain and suffering, but attorneys' fees were also awarded, pushing the total judgment close to $1 million.

Other case law for pain and suffering exists. In a 1989 Georgia case, *State v. McAfee,* the court found in favor of the litigant that pain management was an integral part of medical care. Mr. McAfee was a quadriplegic who was respirator dependent. He sought court approval for discontinuing his respirator (right to refuse medical treatment). In addition, he sought sedation and pain management during this process. The court found in favor of Mr. McAfee, recognizing that in addition to his right to refuse treatment, he also had the right to be pain free.

The 1990 North Carolina case of *Estate of Henry James v. Hillhaven,* the nursing home was found liable for failure to treat pain appropriately.

§ 3.48   TREATMENT/MANAGEMENT MODALITIES

The complaint alleged that the dying days of Mr. James, who had meta-static cancer, were made intolerable because of inadequate pain relief. In this case, a nurse unilaterally decided that Mr. James had become addicted to the morphine that had been prescribed by the physician. She decided to implement her own pain management plan consisting of a mild tranquil-izer and placebos. After death, the family of Mr. James sued the nursing home proving to the jury that the "alternate treatment" failed to meet standard of care. The jury awarded $15 million, and the case was subse-quently settled out of court.

If pain management is an issue in litigation, research applicable state laws or guidelines on pain management, any guidelines developed by state medical boards, and examples of pain management guidelines. Although pain management litigation is relatively new, multiple pain treatment guidelines do exist that can guide the professional in prescribing analgesic medications for pain relief. It is valuable for the legal professional to have a basic understanding of pain management options, so that all pertinent information is included in the medical record summary.

Analgesics

Analgesics by definition are drugs with pain relieving properties. Com-monly analgesics are classified into three main categories: non-opiods, opiods, and adjuvant analgesics. Within each of these classifications, drugs are further classified into subgroups based on their mechanism of action for pain relief and how they are used in clinical practice (their effectiveness in relieving specific types of pain).

Non-opiods, include acetaminophen and non-steriodal anti-inflam-matory drugs, commonly referred to as NSAIDs. Acetaminophen, e.g. Tylenol®, has fewer side effects than do the NSAIDs, e.g. no effect on GI or platelet function. It can, however, cause liver toxicity and should be used with caution in patients consuming large amounts of alcohol. Acetaminophens have little anti-inflammatory effects. In contrast, NSAIDs were originally prescribed mainly for their anti-inflammatory properties for conditions such as arthritis. They are now recognized for their effectiveness in a wide variety of painful conditions. Some examples of NSAID's are:

- Ibuprofen (Motrin®, Advil®)

THERAPEUTIC TREATMENT MODALITIES

- Naproxen (Naprosyn®)
- Ketorolac (Toradol®)

Non-opiods drugs may be used to treat both nocioceptive and neuropathic pain, especially pain arising in muscles and joints. In higher doses, NSAIDS may effective for severe pain. Non-opiods can also be used to enhance the effectiveness of opiod drugs.

Opiod drugs have two subcategories: morphine-like drugs known as full agonists a second group known as agonist-antagonist drugs. Drugs within these two subcategories are used very differently in pain management. Examples of full agonist drugs are:

- Hydrocodone (Vicodin®)
- Morphine
- Methadone
- Codeine
- Hydromorphine (Dilaudid®)

Examples of opiod agonist-antagonist drugs are

- Butorphanol (Stadol®)
- Pentazocaine (Talwin®)

Full agonist opiods are effective in treating moderate to severe pain, both acute and chronic. They are the mainstay therapy for acute and cancer pain and are also effective treatment for breakthrough pain. Agonist-antagonists play a more limited role, effective only for certain types of acute pain. Opiods do have numerous side effects, the most common of which are nausea and vomiting, dizziness, confusion, constipation, urinary retention, and respiratory depression. They can cause physical dependence.

Adjuvant analgesics are comprised of several different drug classes, each of which is effective in treatment of different types of pain. Only selected drugs within a class may be effective as adjuvant analgesics. Classes and uses are:

- Antidepressants—some chronic pain, especially neuropathic pain.
- Anticonvulsants—some types of chronic neuropathic pain.

- Corticosteriods—some types of cancer-related pain, such as metastatic bone pain.
- Psychostimulants—a variety of painful conditions.

Examples specific drugs by class:

Antidepressants

- Amitriptyline (Elavil®)
- Desipramine (Norpramin®)

Anticonvulsants

- Carbamazepine (Tegretol®)
- Phenytoin (Dilantin®)
- Clonazepan (Klonopin®)

Corticosteriods

- Dexamethasone (Decadron®)

Psychostimulants

- Dextroamphetamine (Dexidrine®)
- Methylphenidate (Ritalin®)

Side effects caused by adjuvant analgesics differ by drug class. More detailed information on side effects cause by these drugs can be found in § 3.7.

Key principles of effective pharmacological analgesic therapy require individualizing the drug regimen and optimizing administration, that is dosage, frequency, and route. While the choice of a drug(s) depends on the type of pain being treated, other factors such as age, co-existing medical conditions, incompatibility with other medications being taken, and side effects experienced are also considered. Different combinations of analgesics may be, and in many cases, should be tried. Trials of several different regimens may be necessary before optimal results are obtained.

The World Health Organization (WHO) has developed a three-step approach for the treatment of chronic cancer pain. Originally developed in the 1980's, this model focuses on selecting analgesics or combinations of analgesic groups, based on the severity of the pain. The model has gained wide acceptance in the clinical community and is generally recognized as effective in managing chronic cancer pain. WHO recommendations include the following:

- Mild pain—non-opiod and possibly an adjuvant analgesic.
- Mild to moderate pain, or pain not relieved by non-opiod—addition of opiod to non-opiod and adjuvant.
- Moderate to severe pain—same combinations as recommended for mild to moderate pain, choice of opiod may be different.

When summarizing drug information related to pain, be sure to research medications with which you are not familiar. Understand a drug's actions, major side affects, adverse reactions, and interactions with other medications. Many excellent drug reference books are available for this purpose.

§ 3.49 —Sources of Pain Treatment/Management Information (New)

As more and more Americans live longer and develop chronic diseases, chronic pain is experienced by a greater percentage of the population, which has in turn led to a wealth of information on self-management of chronic pain, encompassing a wide range of options. Traditional treatment/management modalities have expanded as well. As with virtually all topics of individual concern, the Internet has contributed immensely to both quantity and quality of available information on pain management, including the following:

- *Alternative nonprescription pain-relieving agents.* In the past several years, there has been an explosion of these medications in the health care market, many of which are marketed as nutritional supplements and are therefore not regulated by the FDA. Implied benefits of a drug are published on the label; many excellent books on alternative drug therapy are available. One of the most popular alternative analgesic medications on the market is *glucosamine.* This drug is used to relieve the pain of osteoarthritis by impeding the breakdown of cartilage and assisting in the regeneration of new cartilage.

- *Self-help books.* Covering varied methods of chronic pain management, these books include many different approaches, including dietary and exercise regimens, exacerbation prevention, and techniques for handling psychological issues associated with chronic pain. Websites such as Amazon.com offer many titles from which to choose.
- *Holistic approaches.* These methods include herbal remedies, chiropractic treatment, acupuncture, tai chi, and others. Again, websites are a great source of available titles.

For more traditional management of chronic pain, multidisciplinary pain centers offer very comprehensive services. These centers use various treatment modalities to decrease the intensity of pain, minimize the use of potent analgesics, and maximize functionality in the presence of pain. Linkages between pain, emotions, and techniques that enable self-management of pain are also emphasized. Health care disciplines involved in these centers may include physicians from the subspecialties of anesthesiology, neurology, orthopedics, psychiatry, physiatry, and rheumatology. Ancillary disciplines—physical therapy, occupational therapy, social service, nutritional services, nursing and/or case management, osteopathic manipulation, and vocational counseling—may also be involved.

Additional miscellaneous information on pain management can be found from the following:

- American Pain Society—offers regular updates on various topics related to pain research and treatment (www.ampainsoc.org).
- American Society of Anesthesiologists Task Force on Pain Management, Chronic Pain Section (Clinical Practice Guidelines for Chronic Pain Management)—has developed Clinical Practice Guidelines for chronic pain management. Guidelines, which provide decision support to practitioners treating chronic pain, are intended to optimize pain control, minimize adverse outcomes and costs, enhance functional abilities and psychological well-being, and enhance the quality of life for individuals with chronic pain. Guidelines may be obtained by addressing reprint requests to:

American Society of Anesthesiologists
250 North Northwest Highway
Park Ridge, IL 60068
e-mail: mail@ASAhq.org

- Agency for Health Care Policy and Research (AHCPR)—Clinical Practice Guidelines for Acute Pain (see § **8.22**).

§ 3.50   Genetic Diseases (New)

Although genetic aspects of certain diseases have been recognized for many years, only recently has development of new technology allowed identification of the specific genes containing the disorder. To date, 2,000 to 5,000 genes have been identified that either cause or predispose humans to various diseases.

Biotechnologists now apply technological advances to the prevention and treatment of genetic diseases through a process known as *genetic engineering,* which became possible with the discovery of two substances: restriction enzymes and DNA ligase. *Restriction enzymes* are proteins that can cut DNA at predictable sites; *DNA ligase* is a genetic glue that can bind unrelated DNA fragments. Manipulation of these two substances can mix together or recombine genes.

Genes can also be removed from human DNA and joined to bacterial DNA. The bacteria begin producing proteins present in the human DNA, creating new generations of proteins or other substances. Examples of products produced by this technology are human insulin, human growth hormone, tPa, and interferon.

Gene Therapy

Because scientists have now identified the exact location of gene defects and successfully developed genetic engineering processes, certain genetic disorders can be treated by *gene therapy*. Using biological compounds such as hormones, proteins and other substances that already exist in the body, disease-specific "healthy" DNA fragments are injected into damaged cells. These fragments replace the cell's damaged DNA so that the cell can begin to function normally. To develop and produce gene therapy substances, biotechnology companies have expanded research at a rapid rate in an effort to secure competitive niches in this market.

§ 3.50   GENETIC DISEASES

The Human Genome Project

The Human Genome Project, a federally funded project that began in 1990, is an international effort charged with identifying the estimated 80,000 to 100,000 genes in human DNA and determining the sequences of DNA chemical bases. Additional project goals include storing information in databases, developing tools for data analysis, and addressing ethical, legal, and social issues (ELSI) that may arise from project findings. The project's charge is to have a working draft completed by the year 2003. The efforts of their first decade of work are impressive, leading to identification of approximately 500 biological targets for drugs. For more detailed information, the Human Genome Project has an excellent website at www.ornl.gov.hgmis. Some of the website's topics include:

- general information, including discussion on ethical, legal, and social issues;
- resources, including an excellent glossary;
- research;
- publications;
- medical applications.

As the availability of genetic information increases, complex issues will arise regarding its use. Some of these issues, as cited in the Human Genome Project Information, include:

- fairness in use of genetic information by insurers, employers, and others;
- privacy and confidentiality of genetic information—who owns this information?
- psychological impact and stigmatization due to genetic differences;
- genetic testing—for a specific condition due to family history and population screening;
- reproductive issues—use of genetic information in decision-making and reproductive rights;
- clinical issues—including education of healthcare providers, individuals with genetic disorders, and the general public;

- commercialization of products—property rights and accessibility of data.

Legislation

Some legislation to prevent genetic discrimination has already been passed and much more is pending. Common issues being addressed in legislation include provisions for:

- preventing insurers from denying, canceling, or changing premiums, terms, or conditions of coverage based on genetic information;
- prohibiting insurance companies from requesting or requiring genetic tests;
- requiring written informed consent of the individual when insurer desires third-party disclosure of genetic information;
- explaining risks and benefits of genetic screening tests (testing per se is not harmful; what is done with the information can be).

In April 2003, scientists announced the formal completion of the Human Genome Project. This major milestone marked the end of the initial chapter in the genetics work and signaled the beginning of the second, and perhaps more difficult phase, that of tracing the functions of all three billion DNA letters. This work will continue for many decades and drive advances in application for biotechnology as these functions become known. As this work progresses, the implications (many still unknown) for individuals, families, and society will continue to unfold. The potential exists to use information gained from genetic research to discriminate against individuals or groups of individuals. At the time of this writing (May 2003), no comprehensive anti-discrimination laws pertaining to genetic discrimination have been passed at the federal or state level. The following sections summarize existing laws pertaining to genetic discrimination.

Federal Laws

No federal legislation has been passed relating to genetic discrimination in individual insurance coverage or genetic discrimination in the workplace. In February 2000, President Clinton signed an executive order prohibiting every federal agency from using genetic information in hiring or promotion. No other legislation is currently pending.

State Laws

States have been more prolific in enacting anti-discrimination laws. However, at best they are a patchwork, and none of them are comprehensive. Some only prohibit discrimination against individuals with genetic disorders, while some regulate the use of genetic testing in employment decisions and the disclosure of genetic test results. The majority of laws generally prohibit employers from requiring genetic testing as a condition of employment. Nine states have sponsored genetics reports and published study findings. Cites for these state reports can be found on the Human Genome website @ www.ornl.gov/TechResources/Human_Genome/elsi/legislat.html. Also refer to Appendix O for a comprehensive state-by-state survey of statutes related to genetic information and its uses. This information can also be found on-line on the National Conference of State Legislatures website. See the National Institute of Health National Human Genome Research Institute (NIH NHGRI) chart of all genetics workplace discrimination that has been enacted at the state level (current as of April 2002 at date of publication). Web site address is www.nhgri.nih.gov/.

Existing Federal Anti-Discrimination Laws—How They Apply to Genetics

1. Americans with Disabilities Act of 1990 (ADA). This law, enforced by Equal Employment Opportunity Commissions (EEOC), doesn't explicitly address genetic information, but provides some protections against disability-related genetic discrimination in the workplace. In March 1995, the EEOC issued an interpretation of ADA related to genetic discrimination. However, this interpretation is

    • limited in scope and effect,
    • policy guidance only, and does not have same legal binding effect as statute, and
    • has not been tested in courts.

    There are two main points of the interpretation:

    • Entities that discriminate on basis of genetics are regarding indi-

77

viduals as having impairments. Such individuals are covered by ADA.

- Unaffected carriers, individuals with late onset genetic disorders who may be identified through genetic testing or family history as being at risk to develop disease are not covered.

2. Health Insurance Portability and Accountability Act of 1996 (HIPAA). This law applies only to employer-based and commercially issued group health insurance and is the only federal law that addresses the issue of genetic discrimination. There are no similar laws protecting individuals seeking to purchase insurance. Genetic discrimination is only one small part of the HIPAA scope. See § **4.3** for a more detailed discussion of HIPAA.

3. HIPAA National Standards to Protect Patients' Personal Medical Records, December 2002. This regulation was mandated when Congress failed to pass comprehensive privacy legislation, as required by HIPPA, by 1999. It seeks to protect medical records and personal health information maintained by health-care providers, health plans, health insurers, and health-care clearinghouses. The regulation does not contain language specific to genetics, but rather has sweeping regulations governing all health information. Scope of Standard:

- Limits non-consensual use and release of private health information.
- Gives patients new rights to access their medical records and to know who else has accessed them.
- Restricts most disclosure of health information to the minimum needed for the intended purpose.
- Establishes new criminal and civil sanctions for improper use of disclosure.
- Establishes new requirements for access to records by researchers and others.

HIPAA final recommendations can be found on the U.S. Department of Health and Human Services (DHHS) web site: http://www.hhs.gov/ocr/hipaa.

4. Title VII of Civil Rights Act of 1964. An argument could be made that genetic discrimination based on racially or ethnically linked genetic disorders constitutes unlawful race or ethnic discrimination. This argument would only apply if the discrimination was based on a genetic

trait that is substantially related to a particular race or ethnic group. Such relationships have been established for only a few diseases.

The Ethical, Legal and Social Implications Research Program (ELSI)

As part of the Human Genome Project, the Ethical, Legal and Social Implications (ELSI) Research Program was established. The program is organized around four areas:

- Privacy and fairness and use of genetic information
- Clinical integration of new genetic technologies
- Issues surrounding genetics research
- Public and professions education

The program takes the approach of identifying issues of human genetics at the same time the basic science is being studied. ELSI is very aware of the gaps in existing laws and, with other groups, has made recommendations for needed legislation. Their recommendations are based on the premise that information from the Human Genome Project should be used to improve health and not discriminate against workers or their families. Among ELSI's recommendations are:

- Employers should not require genetic testing as a condition of employment, or use genetic information to deprive individuals of employment opportunities.
- Employers can monitor employees for effects of a specific substance found in the workplace that may cause genetic damage. Informed consent of the employee should be required and information gained from monitoring should be kept in medical files, not in personnel files.
- Laws should apply to public and private sector employees.

ELSI and its partners have also developed recommendations on legislation needed to prevent genetic discrimination by insurance companies. The recommendations are that insurance providers should be prohibited from:

- using genetic information or a request for genetic services to deny or limit coverage, and

- establishing differential rates based on genetic information or a request for genetic services.

Proponents of comprehensive genetic non-discrimination legislation cite many reasons for legislation now rather that later. Among the arguments are:

- Employers fear the potential for increased costs associated with genetic disease/information.
- Economic incentive to discriminate is likely to increase as genetic research advances.
- Genetic information could be used in cases where workers are healthy and unlikely to develop disease or where genetic conditions have no effect on the ability to perform work.
- Insurers can still use genetic information in individual markets to make decisions about coverage, enrollment, and premiums.
- Individuals are not protected from disclosure of genetic information to insurers, employers (who buy health care coverage), and medical information bureaus (see **§ 4.16** for additional information on the medical information bureau) without their consent.
- Insurers can still require individuals to take genetic tests.
- HIPAA protection is not currently extended to individuals.

Practice Note: Because of this rapidly evolving field, any case involving genetic discrimination must be meticulously researched. Be aware of available resources and utilize them to obtain information pertinent to your case. You should, at a minimum, have a basic understanding of what the Human Genome Project is and its numerous societal implications. The field of genetics is complex and findings from the Human Genome Project will have many impacts, many unknown at this time, for years to come.

When reviewing a client's medical records, note any genetic testing or treatment for genetic diseases. Evaluate the pertinence of the information in regard to the issues of the case and include that information in your summary if appropriate.

See **Appendix O** for a comprehensive state-by-state survey of statutes related to genetic testing and its uses.

CHAPTER 4

CONFIDENTIALITY OF MEDICAL RECORDS

§ 4.2 —State Statutes

*Page 203, replace **Table 4–1** with the following:*

Table 4–1
States Recognizing Physician-Patient Privilege

State	Statute
Alaska	Rules of Evid. R. 504; Stat. § 9.25.400
Arizona	Rev. Stat. Ann. § 12-2235
Arkansas	Rules of Evid. R. 503
California	Evid Code § 993
Colorado	Stat. Ann. § 13-90-107(d)
Connecticut	Gen. Stat. 52-146(o)
Delaware	Uniform Rules of Evid. R. 503
District of Columbia	Code Ann. § 6-2001
Idaho	Code § 9-203(4)
Illinois	735 Comp. Stat. 5/8-802
Indiana	Code § 34-46-3-1
Iowa	Code § 622.10
Kansas	Stat. Ann § 60-427
Louisiana	Code of Evid. Art. 510(A), Rev. Stat. Ann. § 13:3734(A)(1)
Maine	R. Rev. R. 503
Michigan	Comp. Laws § 600.2157
Minnesota	Stat. Ann. § 595.02(1)(d)
Mississippi	Code. Ann. § 13-1-21
Missouri	Rev. Stat. § 491.060
Montana	Code Ann. § 26-1-805
Nebraska	Rev. Stat. § 25-504
Nevada	Rev. Stat. § 49.225
New Hampshire	Rev. Stat. § 329:26
New Jersey	Stat. §§ 2A:84A-22.1 and 22.2
New Mexico	Rules of Evid. 11-504
New York	Civ. Prac. L & R § 4504
North Carolina	Gen. Stat. § 8-53

Table 4–1 *(continued)*

State	Statute
North Dakota	Rules of Evid R. 503
Ohio	Rev. Code § 2317.02(B)(1)
Oklahoma	Stat. tit. 12, § 2503
Oregon	Rev. Stat. § 40.235
Pennsylvania	42 Pa. Cons. Stat. Ann. § 5929
Rhode Island	Gen. L. § 5-37.3-4
South Dakota	Codified Laws §§ 19-13-6, 19-13-7
Texas	Rev. Civ. Stat. Ann. art. 4495b, § 5.08
Utah	Code Ann. § 78-24-8(4)
Vermont	12 Vt. Stat. Ann. § 1612, 18 Stat. Ann. § 7101(13)
Virginia	Code Ann. § 8.01-399
Washington	Rev. Code Ann. § 5.60.060
Wisconsin	Stat. Ann. § 905.04
Wyoming	Stat. Ann. § 1-12-101

Unlike the physician-patient privilege, which is not recognized in multiple states, 49 states plus the District of Columbia statutorily recognize some form of a psychologist-client privilege. Clearly, the governing bodies in this country recognize the continued need for protection of the confidentiality of psychiatric/psychological communications.

Table 4–2
States Recognizing Psychologist-Client Privilege

State	Statute
Alabama	Code §§ 34-26-2, 34-8A-21
Alaska	Stat. §§ 08.29.200, 08.63.200, 08.86.200
Arizona	Rev. Stat. § 32-3085
Arkansas	Rules of Evid. R. 503; Code. Ann. § 17-97-105
California	Evid. Code § 1010 et seq.
Connecticut	Gen. Stat. §§ 52-146(d)–52-146(j)
District of Columbia	Code. Ann. § 7-1201.01
Colorado	Stat. Ann. § 13-90-107(g)
Delaware	Uniform Rules of Evid. R. 503
Florida	Stat. Ann. §§ 90.503, 456.059
Georgia	Code Ann. § 24-9-21
Hawaii	Rev. Stat. § 626; Rules of Evid. R. 504.1
Idaho	Code § 54-2314
Illinois	735 Ill. Comp. Stat. 5/8-802

Table 4–2 *(continued)*

State	Statute
Indiana	Code. Ann. 25-33-1-17
Iowa	Code § 622.10
Kansas	Stat. Ann. §§ 65-5601–65-5603, 74-5323, 74-5372
Kentucky	Rules of Evid. R. 507
Louisiana	Code of Evid. Art. 510(a), Stat. Ann. § 13:3734(A)(1)
Maine	R. Rev. R. 503
Maryland	Code Ann., Cts & Jud. Pro. § 9-109
Massachusetts	Gen. Laws ch. 233, § 20B
Michigan	Comp. Laws §§ 330.1750, 333.18237
Minnesota	Stat. § 595.02 subd. 1
Mississippi	Rules of Evid. R. 503, Code Ann. § 73-31-29
Missouri	Rev. Stat. §§ 337.055, 491.060
Montana	Code Ann. § 26-1-807
Nebraska	Rev. Stat. § 27-504 (Rule 504)
Nevada	Rev. Stat. § 49.209
New Hampshire	Rev. Stat. § 330-A:32
New Jersey	Stat. Ann. § 45:14B-28
New Mexico	Rules of Evid. 11-504
New York	C.P.L.R. 4507
North Carolina	Gen. Stat. § 8-53.3
North Dakota	Rules of Evid. R. 503
Ohio	Rev. Code § 4732.19
Oklahoma	Stat. tit. § 2503
Oregon	Rev. Stat. § 40.230
Pennsylvania	42 Pa. Cons. Stat. Ann. § 5944
Rhode Island	Gen. Laws § 5-37.3-6
South Carolina	Code § 44-22-90
South Dakota	Codified Laws §§ 19-13-7, 36-27A-38
Tennessee	Code Ann. § 24-1-207
Texas	Health & Safety Code §§ 611.002 and 611.003
Utah	Rules of Evid. R. 506, Code Ann. § 58-60-113
Vermont	Stat. Ann. § 7101(13)
Virginia	Code Ann. § 8.01-399
Washington	Rev. Code Ann. § 18.83.110
Wisconsin	Stat. Ann. § 905.04
Wyoming	Stat. Ann. § 33-27-123

Page 204, replace § 4.3 with the following:

§ 4.3 —Federal Legislation

Federal legislation has been developed to protect the privacy of certain types of information: educational records (1974), bank records (1978), cable television services (1984), electronic communications (1986), employee polygraphs (1988), video rentals (1988), and telemarketing (1988). Until 2000, there was no rule or regulation at the federal level which protected the confidentiality of medical information.

The Privacy Act of 1974

The Privacy Act of 1974 generally protects individuals against disclosure of information held by federal agencies in any "system of records." Hospitals operated by the federal government, such as the Veterans Administration and Indian Health Services, are subject to the Privacy Act, as are a small number of private health care and research facilities that maintain medical records under federal contracts. See § **4.25** for a discussion of the federal statutes and regulations controlling release of patient records at federally funded drug and alcohol treatment facilities.

Under the Privacy Act, any disclosure of information or data collected must be "relevant and necessary" to the agency's mission. Release of personally identifiable data requires consent, unless the disclosure is "compatible" with the purposes for which the data was collected, or if disclosure serves a public policy need for which statutory authority exists. In 1988 the Computer Matching and Privacy Protection Act amended the original 1974 Act. This amendment required agencies to develop agreements to control information exchange.

Health Insurance Portability and Accountability Act

Recognizing the serious need for a national patient record privacy standard, the Health Insurance Portability and Accountability Act (HIPAA) was signed into law on August 21, 1996. The first part of this legislation, the "portability" aspect, serves to protect the ability of people with current or pre-existing medical conditions to get or maintain health insurance if starting a new job. It also established medical savings accounts and tax deductions for long-term care insurance This portion of HIPAA has been fully implemented.

An August 21, 1999 deadline was established by HIPAA for Congress to pass comprehensive health privacy legislation. When Congress failed to meet this deadline, the Department of Health and Human Services drafted a proposed rule concerning the "accountability" aspect of HIPAA with regard to confidential medical information. The proposed rule was issued for public comment in October of 1999. During an extended comment period, HHS received more than 52,000 comments ranging from individual members of the public to entities such as the Health Privacy Project, the American Medical Association, the American Hospital Association, and the Health Insurance Association of America. As might be expected, there was a sharp division between health care providers, who felt that the rules would interfere with patient care and dramatically increase the cost of health care, and privacy advocates, who supported the proposed rule and asked that it be strengthened.

On December 20th, 2000, President Clinton announced the parameters of the final rule which extended the scope of protection to all individually identifiable health information in any form, electronic or non-electronic, held or transmitted by a covered entity. This included individually identifiable health information in paper records that had never been electronically stored or transmitted. The vast bulk of medical information is generated on paper and not transferred electronically, except perhaps by fax. Additionally, hospitals and clinics must keep medical records for periods ranging from a few years to more than 50 years. These records are all on paper or microform, and were untouched by the proposed rule, but covered by the final rule. This created a privacy system that covers virtually all health information held by hospitals, providers, health plans and health insurers and closed a gap in the proposed rule.

Practice Note: Public comments were submitted on the basis of the proposed rule that only addressed health information found in electronic records and any paper records that had at some point existed in electronic form. The final rule applies to all records in any form. A significant question has been raised as to whether the rule was properly promulgated, or whether it should be resubmitted for further comment. It is anticipated that several modifications will be made to the parameters of the rule before it goes into effect in 2003.

CONFIDENTIALITY OF MEDICAL RECORDS

The final privacy rule is available in the December 28, 2000 Federal Register online at www.access.gpo.gov/su_docs/fedreg/a001228c.html. The rule can be downloaded for free using Adobe Acrobat software or ordered from the Superintendent of Documents at (202) 512-1800.

Deadline for Compliance

The Final Privacy Rule became effective on April 14, 2001. Compliance by all covered entities was required by April 14, 2003. Small health plans are allowed an additional twelve months.

State Confidentiality Laws Not Preempted

State laws (such as those covering mental health, HIV infection, and AIDS information) which may be stronger than HIPAA continue to apply and will not be preempted by HIPAA. These confidentiality protections are cumulative; the federal rule sets a national "floor" of privacy standards that serve to protect all Americans, but in some states individuals enjoy additional protection. In circumstances where states have decided through law to require certain disclosures of health information for civic purposes, HIPAA will not preempt these mandates.

Protected Health Information (PHI)

HIPAA regulations apply to medical information that contains any of a number of patient identifiers, including the patient's name, Social Security number, telephone number, medical record number, or ZIP code. The regulations protect all identifiable health information held or disclosed by a covered entity in any form, whether communicated electronically, on paper, or orally.

Covered Entities

As required by HIPAA, the final rule covers all health care providers and health plans such as hospitals, medical practices (including solo practices), employers, rehabilitation centers, nursing homes, public health authorities, life insurance agencies, billing agencies and some vendors, service organizations, and universities. It also covers health care clearinghouses that generate and electronically transmit medical information such as billing, claims, enrollment, or eligibility verification.

Business Associate

An additional covered entity is the "business associate" which is defined as a person who, on behalf of a covered entity, performs or assists in the performance of functions or activities that involve the use or disclosure of individually identifiable health information (e.g. claims procession or administration, data analysis, processing or administration, utilization review, quality assurance, billing, benefit or practice management). A business associate is also that individual who provides legal, actuarial, accounting, consulting, administrative, accreditation or financial services to or for a covered entity (other than in the capacity of a member of the covered entity's workforce). Each business associate must enter into a written contract with the covered medical entity, which contract requires the business associate to maintain and to follow all of the provisions of HIPAA with regard to privacy of medical information. Further, the business associate itself must enter into contracts with other entities requiring these third parties to follow the provisions of HIPAA.

Practice Note: Conceivably, this would mean that defense counsel providing legal advice to a hospital is a "business associate" under HIPAA and must enter into a contract for services with the healthcare provider. Further, the defense counsel would be required to obtain appropriate contracts from all of the services it utilizes during the course of litigation—the subpoena services, expert witnesses, the document storage facility, other attorneys, services providing exhibits for trial, the company that destroys documents, etc. At this time, the business associate portion of the rule has elicited the most controversy.

Patient Inspection of Medical Records

Under the final privacy rule, patients have significant new rights to understand and control how their health information is used. An individual has the right to inspect and obtain a copy of their record, except for the following:

CONFIDENTIALITY OF MEDICAL RECORDS

- Psychotherapy notes
- Information compiled in anticipation or use in a civil, criminal, or administrative action or proceeding
- Health information protected pursuant to the Clinical Laboratory Improvements Amendments (CLIA) of 1988. (CLIA, 42 USC 263a is the federal law that defines the requirements for certification of clinical laboratories)
- Health information exempted from CLIA, e.g. information generated by facilities that perform forensic testing, research labs that do not report patient-specific results, and drug testing performed in a lab certified by the National Institute on Drug Abuse (DIDA).

Denial of Access to Medical Record

A covered entity may deny an individual access to his or her medical record when:

- The entity is a correctional institution (or healthcare provider acting under the direction of such an institution) and the inmate's request to obtain the information would jeopardize the individual, other inmates, or the safety of any officer, employee, or other person at the institution
- The individual agreed to a temporary denial of access when consenting to participate in research that has not yet been completed
- The records are subject to the Privacy Act of 1974 and the denial of access meets the requirements of that law
- The protected health information was obtained from someone other than a healthcare provider under a promise of confidentiality and access to that information would likely reveal the source of the information.

Under the following circumstances an entity may also deny an individual access:

- When a licensed healthcare provider has determined that the access is likely to endanger the life or physical safety of the requesting individual or another person
- The protected health information makes reference to another person who is not a healthcare provider, and a licensed healthcare professional

88

has determined that the access requested is likely to cause substantial harm to such other person

- The request is made by the individual's personal representative and a licensed healthcare professional has determined that access is likely to cause substantial harm to the individual or another person.

If the request for access is denied, the individual must be given the right to have the denial reviewed. Detailed requirements for denial review are outlined in § 45 CFR § 164.524.

Special Protection for Psychotherapy Notes

Psychotherapy notes (used only by a psychotherapist) are held to a higher standard of protection because they are not part of the medical record and never intended to be shared with anyone else. All other health information is considered to be sensitive and treated consistently under this rule.

Request for Amendment of Health Information

Under HIPAA, an individual has the right to request that a covered entity amend his or her health record if that individual feels that certain information is in error. Covered entities may require that a request to amend be in writing and that the individual provide a reason in support of the amendment. The covered entity may deny the request for amendment of the record if the health information that is the subject of the request:

- Was not created by the covered entity, unless the originator is no longer available to act on the request
- Is not part of the individual's health record
- Would not be accessible to the individual for the reasons stated above
- Is accurate and complete.

The covered entity must act on the individual's request for amendment no later than 60 days after receipt of the amendment. Provided the covered entity gives the individual a written statement of the reason for the delay, and the date by which the amendment will be processed, the covered entity may have a one-time extension of up to 30 days for an amendment request.

CONFIDENTIALITY OF MEDICAL RECORDS

Amendments to the Medical Record

If the request to amend the record is granted, the covered entity must:

- Insert the amendment or provide a link to the amendment at the site of the information
- Inform the individual that the amendment is accepted
- Obtain the individual's identification of and agreement to have the entity notify the relevant persons with whom the amendment needs to be shared
- Within a reasonable time frame, make reasonable efforts to provide the amendment to persons identified by the individual, and persons, including business associates, that the covered entity knows have the protected health information that is the subject of the amendment and that may have relied on or could foreseeably rely on the information to the detriment of the individual.

Denial of Amendments to the Record

If the covered entity denies the requested amendment, it must provide the individual with a timely, written denial in plain language that contains:

- The basis for the denial
- The individual's right to submit a written statement disagreeing with the denial and the procedure for filing such a statement
- How the individual's request for amendment and the denial be provided with any future disclosures of the protected health information
- A description of how the individual may complain to the covered entity with the name or title, and telephone number of the designated contact person who handles complaints.

Consent for the Use or Disclosure of Personal Health Information

Providers and health plans are required to give their patients a clear written explanation of how the entity can use, keep, and disclose their health information. Health care providers who see patients are required to obtain patient *consent* before sharing their information for treatment, payment, and health care operations purposes. Patient *authorization* to disclose information must be sought and granted for non-routine uses and most non-healthcare purposes, such as releasing information to financial institutions determining mortgages and other loans or selling mailing lists to interested parties such as life insurers.

Patients have the right to request restrictions on the uses and disclosures of their information. Providers and health plans generally cannot condition treatment on a patient's agreement to disclose health information for non-routine uses.

Limitations on Use and Release of Personal Health Information

With few exceptions, an individual's health information can be used for health purposes only. This means that patient information can be used or disclosed by a health plan, provider or clearinghouse only for purposes of health care treatment, payment, and operations. Health information cannot be used for purposes not related to health care—such as use by employers to make personnel decisions, or use by financial institutions—without *explicit authorization* from the individual.

Disclosures of information must be limited to the minimum necessary for the purpose of the disclosure. However, this provision does not apply to the transfer of medical records for purposes of treatment, since physicians, specialists, and other providers need access to the full record to provide the best quality care. The final rule gives providers full discretion in determining what personal health information to include when sending patients' medical records to other providers for treatment purposes.

Nonroutine disclosures with patient authorization must meet standards that ensure the authorization is truly informed and voluntary. The rule establishes the privacy safeguard standards that covered entities must meet, but it leaves detailed policies and procedures for meeting these standards to the discretion of each covered entity. In this way, implementation of the standards will be flexible, to account for the nature of each entity's business, and its size and resources.

Covered entities are required to develop policies and procedures to control and track the use of medical information, and maintain the privacy of that information by:

- Adopting written privacy procedures. These must include who has access to the protected information, how it will be used within the entity, and when the information would or would not be disclosed to others. They must also takes steps to ensure that their business associates protect the privacy of health information.

CONFIDENTIALITY OF MEDICAL RECORDS

- Training employees and designating a privacy officer. Covered entities must provide sufficient training so that their employees understand the new privacy protections procedures, and designate an individual to be responsible for ensuring the procedures are followed.
- Establishing grievance processes. Covered entities must provide a means for patients to make inquiries or complaints regarding the privacy of their records.

Accountability for Use and Release of Personal Health Information

Individuals have the right to complain to a covered provider or health plan, or to the Secretary of the DHS, concerning violations of the provisions of this rule or the policies and procedures of the covered entity. Penalties for covered entities that misuse personal health information are provided in HIPAA. Health plans, providers and clearinghouses that violate these standards would be subject to civil liability with civil penalties of $100 per incident, up to $25,000 per person, per year, per standard. Federal criminal penalties were also enacted for health plans, providers and clearinghouses that knowingly and improperly disclose information or obtain information under false pretenses. Penalties would be higher for actions designed to generate monetary gain. Criminal penalties up to $50,000 and one year in prison for obtaining or disclosing protected health information; up to $100,000 and up to five years in prison for obtaining protected health information under "false pretenses;" and up to $250,000 and 10 years in prison for obtaining or disclosing protected health information with the intent to sell, transfer or use it for commercial advantage, personal gain, or malicious harm.

Disclosures Without Authorization

HIPAA permits certain existing disclosures of health information without individual authorization for certain defined activities and for activities that allow the health care system to "operate more smoothly." All of these disclosures have been permitted under existing laws and regulations. Within certain guidelines found in the regulation, covered entities may disclose information for:

- Oversight of the healthcare system, including quality assurance activities
- Public health matters

- Research (generally limited to when a waiver of authorization is independently approved by a privacy board or Institutional Review Board)
- Judicial and administrative proceedings
- Limited law enforcement activities
- Emergency circumstances
- Identification of the body of a deceased person, or the cause of death
- Facility patient directories
- Activities related to national defense and security.

The rule permits, but does not require these types of disclosures. If there is no other law requiring that information be disclosed, physicians and hospitals will still have to make judgments about whether to disclose information, in light of their own policies and ethical principles.

Equivalent Treatment of Public and Private Sector Health Plans and Providers

The provisions of the final rule generally apply equally to private sector and public sector entities. For example, both private hospitals and government agency medical units must comply with the full range of requirements, such as providing notice, access rights, requiring consent before disclosure for routine uses, establishing contracts with business associates, among others.

Protecting Against Unauthorized Use of Medical Records for Employment Purposes

Companies that sponsor health plans will not be able to access the personal health information held by the plan for employment-related purposes, without specific written authorization from the individual.

Page 215, add after § 4.15:

§ 4.15A—HIPAA Privacy Rule

Following the 2001 passage of the Health Insurance Portability and Accountability ACT (HIPAA) Privacy Rule, the Secretary for Health and Human Services called for additional public comment. This was done to ensure that the rule would achieve its intended purpose and not inadvertently adversely affect the quality of, or create barriers to, patient care. In March 2002, HHS published the proposed modifications based on that public comment. This was followed by a second round of comment that resulted in additional modifications reflected in the final version of the Privacy Rule published in August 2002. Detailed information about the privacy rule is available on the HHS website: http://www.hhs.gov/ocr/hipaa. A summary of the some of the major components of the Privacy Rule that includes the modifications reflected in the August publication is provided below.

Summary of Privacy Rule

Incidental Uses and Disclosures.   General provisions permit incidental uses and disclosures of protected health information that occur as a result of permissible necessary disclosure as long as the entity has applied reasonable safeguards and the "minimum necessary" standard (see following text). Reasonable safeguards include administrative, technical, and physical measures as outlined in entity policies. Examples include: speaking quietly when discussing health information with patient or family in public areas, securing medical records in locked area, and providing password protection for computerized information.

Minimum Necessary.   This standard focuses on how much medical information is available and to whom under what circumstances. Policies or practices that allow hospital employees to have free access to medical information not necessary to perform job duties are in potential violation of this standard. The minimum necessary rule does not apply to the following disclosures:

- By a health care provider for treatment purposes,
- To the individual who in the subject of the information,
- Pursuant to an individual's authorization,
- Required for compliance with HIPAA Administrative Simplification Rules,
- HHS when disclosure of the information is required under the Privacy Rule for enforcement purposes, and
- Uses or disclosures required by other law (e.g., statute, regulation, or court orders).

§ 4.15A—HIPAA PRIVACY RULE

In some cases, it is allowable for the entity to rely on the requesting party as to what is the minimum amount of information needed. This provision, known as reasonable reliance, is permissible when the request is made by:

- a public official or agency,
- another covered entity,
- a professional who is a workforce member or a business associate of a covered entity, or
- researchers with documentation for the Institutional Research Board (IRB).

The Rule also clarifies that this standard is not intended to impede disclosures for workers' compensation cases.

Reasonable reliance is not mandated, however, and the covered entity has the ultimate right to make its own minimum necessary determination.

Personal Representatives. Provisions of this rule require that entities treat personal representatives of the individual as they would the individual themselves with respect to health information. The rule specifically outlines who must be recognized.

- Adults or emancipated minors—a person with legal authority to make health-care decisions, such as durable power of attorney or a court-appointed legal guardian.
- Deceased individuals—executor or the estate or next of kin, durable power of attorney.
- Unemancipated minors—parent, guardian, or other person acting a parent with legal authority to make decisions. This area was changed considerably during the public comment period and modifications resulted in identifying circumstances when the parent is not the personal representative for the child with respect to health information. These circumstances include:
  - ____ when state or other law doesn't require parental consent before the minor can obtain a specific health care service, such as mental health services,
  - ____ when the court determines or other law authorizes someone other than parent to make treatment decisions for a minor, and

___ when a parent agrees to the confidential relationship between the minor and physician.

Even under the above circumstances, the Privacy Rule always defers to state or other laws applicable to the subject. For both adults and children, the rule allows withholding of information from a personal representative if the provider believes that disclosure will result in harm to the individual, e.g., if abuse or neglect is suspected.

Business Associates.   As stated previously, covered entities under HIPAA are defined as health plans, health-care clearinghouses, and certain health-care providers. Typically, covered entities do not provide all services internally, but instead contract with a variety of businesses to provide specific services. HIPAA has defined these contracted individuals or agencies as "business associates." Specifically, HIPAA defines a business associate as a person or entity that performs certain functions or activities that involve the use or disclosure of protected health information on behalf of, or provides services to, a covered entity. Under this definition, a member of a covered entity's workforce is not a business associate, however a covered health-care provider, health plan, or health-care clearinghouse can be a business associate of another covered entity. See preceding § **4.3** for the specific types of functions and services that Business Associates may perform.

HIPAA allows a covered entity to disclose necessary protected health information to its business associates under the following conditions:

- The business associate provides assurances that it will safeguard protected health information it receives from the covered entity,
- The covered entity provides the business associate only information necessary to carry out health-care functions,
- The business associate does not use protected health information for its own independent use or purposes, and
- The covered entity receives satisfactory assurances in writing from the business associate in writing, either in the form of a contract or other agreement.

If a breach of contract is discovered by the covered entity, the entity must demonstrate that it took reasonable steps to cure the breach, and if unsuccessful in these efforts, terminate the contract with the offending business associate.

In some instances, there are exceptions to the business associate standard. Under the following circumstances, a covered entity is not required to have a business associate contract before protected health information is disclosed:

- Disclosures to a health care provider for treatment of the individual.
- Some (defined) disclosures to a health plan sponsor such as an employer.
- Collection and sharing of information by a health plan that is a public benefits program, such as Medicare, that is required to determine eligibility or enrollment.
- Disclosures by a health-care provider to a health plan for payment purposes.
- With persons or organizations whose functions or services do not involve the use of disclosure of protected health information, e.g., janitorial or maintenance services.
- With a person or organization that acts as a conduit for protected health information, such as courier or mail services, or their electronic equivalents.
- To disclose protected health information to a researcher for research purposes, either with patient authorization or pursuant to waiver or as a limited data set (as specifically defined by the Privacy Rule).
- When a financial institution processes consumer initiated financial transactions to facilitate payment for health care or health-care premiums.

In the final round of changes to the Rule, covered entities were given an additional year to change language in existing contracts to be in compliance.

Uses and Disclosures for Treatment, Payment, and Health-Care Operations

The intent of this provision is to establish a foundation of federal protection for personal health information, while avoiding barriers to the delivery of health care. HIPAA succinctly defines the provisions components as:

- Treatment: provision, coordination, or management of health care and related services among health-care providers, or by a health-care provider with a third party, consultation between health-care providers regarding a patient, or referral of a patient from one health-care provider to another.
- Payment: covers activities of health-care providers to obtain payment or reimbursement for services and of a health plan to obtain premiums, to fulfill coverage responsibilities and provide benefits under the plan, and to obtain or provide reimbursement for the provision of health care.
- Health-care operations: certain administrative, financial, legal, and quality improvement activities of a covered entity that are necessary to run its business and support the core functions of treatment and payment. The rule specifically defines these activities.

Within this framework, the covered entity may use or disclose the following information without the individual's authorization:

- For its own treatment, payment, and health-care operations activities,
- For the treatment activities of any health-care provider (including providers not covered by the Privacy Rule), e.g., as in a referral to a specialist who needs the information to treat the individual or as in transmission of patient health-care instructions to a nursing home.
- To another covered entity or health-care provider (including providers not covered by the Privacy Rule) for payment activities of the entity that receives the information, or
- To another covered entity for health-care operations if the entity has a relationship with the individual and if the disclosure of the protected health information is pertinent to relationship. For example, a health-care provider may disclose protected health information to a health plan for HEDIS purposes, provided the health plan has a relationship with the individual who is the subject of the information.

Additional provisions under this standard include:

Psychotherapy notes: This information still requires an individual's authorization except when used by the originator to carry out treatment. The minimum necessary standard must still apply to disclosures.

§ 4.15A—HIPAA PRIVACY RULE

Consent: A covered entity may voluntarily choose to obtain the individual's consent to disclosure of information for treatment, payment, and health-care operations, but it is not required to do so. An entity that chooses this option has the discretion to design a process that works best for its business and consumers.

Right to Request Privacy Protection: An individual may request restrictions on disclosure of health information. However, a covered entity is not required to agree to that request. The entity is, however, required to honor any restrictions to which it agrees.

Notice: Any use or disclosure of protected health information must be consistent with the covered entity's notice of privacy practices. A covered entity is required to give individuals notice of their privacy rights and the organization's privacy practices. The process for filing a complaint under the Privacy Rule must also be included in the materials. Organizations must show "good faith effort" to obtain the individual's written confirmation that this information was received.

Marketing. This portion of the Privacy Rule gives individuals control over whether and how protected health information is used and disclosed for marketing purposes. With limited exceptions, the rules requires an individual's written authorization before a use or disclosure of such information can be made for marketing. To accomplish this objective, the rule distinguishes marketing communications from those communications about goods and services that are essential for quality health care. It defines what constitutes marketing as well as exceptions to the rule.

The Privacy Rule defines marketing as making "a communication about a product or service that encourages recipients of the communication to purchase or use the product or service." In all situations meeting this definition, prior authorization must be obtained before protected health information can be released. Specific examples of this include:

- Communication to individuals on new services when the communication is not for the purpose of providing treatment advice
- Communication from a health insurer promoting a home and casualty insurance product offered by the same company
- Health plan selling member lists to companies that sell drugs or equip-

ment and those companies in turn use that information to market goods and services directly to individuals.

There are three exceptions to the marketing definition (that is, the following are not considered marketing activities under HIPAA if communication is made):

1. To describe a health-related product or service that is provided by, or included in, the benefit plan of the covered entity making the communication.
2. For treatment of the individual.
3. For case management or care coordination of the individual.

The above conditions apply to covered entities and their business associates. In all exception cases, the activity must otherwise be permissible under the Privacy Rule.

Disclosures for Public Health Activities.   HIPAA recognizes the legitimate need for public health authorities responsible for public health and safety to have access to protected health information to carry out their duties. Such authorities are legally authorized to receive reports containing protected health information for the purpose of preventing or controlling disease, injury, or disability, e.g., vital statistics, such as births or deaths, or information critical to public health surveillance or investigations. Covered entities are required to limit the information disclosed to the minimum amount necessary to accomplish the purpose of the investigation. As stated above, a public health agency may determine the minimum amount necessary under reasonable reliance. In this regard, HIPAA is not incongruent with current public health policies and procedures that address the types and amount of protected health information needed for investigation and follow-up.

Additional public health activities in which protected health information may be disclosed without specific authorization include child/elder abuse or neglect, quality or safety investigation of an FDA regulated product or activity, communication to a person at risk of contracting or spreading a communicable disease, and for the purposes of workplace medical surveillance.

Research. This portion of the Privacy Rule defines how researchers may obtain, use, and disclose protected health information. To use/disclose without authorization, a covered entity must obtain one of the following:

- Documented Institutional Review Board (IRB) or Privacy Board approval. A covered entity may disclose information provided it has obtained documentation around specific parameters defined by HIPAA.
- Preparatory to research. Documentation from the researcher that use or disclosure of protected health information is solely to prepare for research or for similar preparatory to research purposes.
- Research on protected health information of decedents. Requirements are similar to those required under Preparatory to Research.
- Limited data sets with a data use agreement. Requires a data use agreement by the covered entity and the researcher that allows the covered entity to disclose a limited data set to the researcher for research, public health, or health-care operations. A limited data set excludes specified direct identifiers of the individual or of relatives, employers, or household members of the individual.

Additional protected health information may be disclosed with individual authorization. The Rule also allows transition provisions that cover protected health information disclosed for research purposes prior to the HIPAA compliance date to prevent the disruption of ongoing research.

Disclosures for Workers' Compensation. The Privacy Rule does not apply to entities that are workers' compensation insurers, workers' compensation administrative agencies, or employers, except to the extent they are otherwise covered entities. Because of the variability of state and other laws, HIPAA defines circumstances under which information can be disclosed with and without individual authorization. Generally the law permits disclosure without authorization to the extent necessary to comply with laws relating to workers' compensation or similar programs that provide benefits to injured workers. Information disclosed with authorization must meet HIPAA requirements specified elsewhere in the Rule.

Restrictions on Government Access to Health Information. The Rule requires government-operated health plans and health-care providers, such as Medicare and Medicaid, to meet the same privacy requirements as for private plans. New authority under HIPAA includes enforcement of the protections in the Rule itself. The Rule requires that covered entities cooperate with government agency efforts by the Department of Health and Human Services (HHS) and the Office for Civil Rights (OCR) to investigate complaints and otherwise ensure compliance. Finally, the Rule outlines Administrative Requirements for covered entities that include:

- development of policies and procedures for privacy of protected health information
- designation of privacy personnel accountable for implementation of and tracking compliance to the Rule
- completion of Workforce Training
- implementation of data safeguards, including administrative, technical and physical measures

Because the HIPAA Privacy Rule compliance date for covered entities was so recent (April 2003), many questions on the impact this law will have are unanswered. Many opinions both pro and con abound in the lay news as well as in professional journals as to the effectiveness of the law. Critics maintain that HIPAA does not provide a national privacy standard, as State law pre-empts HIPAA in cases where State law is more stringent. In this sense, HIPAA only provides a minimum national standard and still allows significant variability from state to state. At issue as well are the significant implementation costs to covered entities at a time when health-care costs in America continue to escalate.

Practice Note: What impact will this law have on the legal community in obtaining medical record information from covered entities? Although it is too soon to tell, potential impacts may include the need to redesign authorizations to comply with HIPAA Privacy Rule Standards. Language may need to be modified to include:

- notice of patient rights to revoke the authorization
- the potential for disclosure of protected health information to unauthorized persons. Prior to HIPAA, medical information was routinely released to consultants and expert witnesses without specific notification to the individual.

- deletion of blanks for the persons or entities for which the information is to be provided or for the expiration date of the authorization.

Additional HIPAA Standards

Although lesser publicized, HIPPA also encompasses a set of standards aside from those of the Privacy Rule. These standards and their status as of May 2003 are as follows:

- Electronic health transactions (final rule issued)
- Unique identifier for employers (final rule issued)
- Security requirements (proposed rule issued; final rule in development)
- Unique identifier for providers (proposed rule issued; final rule in development)
- Unique identifier for health plans
- Enforcement procedures (proposed rule in development)

Additionally, although the HIPAA law called for a unique identifier for individuals, development of this standard has been indefinitely postponed.

The two standards for which final standards have been issued (in addition to the Privacy Rule standards) deserve brief mention, although the potential ramifications of these standards for the legal professional are probably minimal.

National Standards for Electronic Health-Care Transactions. The final rule for this standard was issued in August 2000. The intent of the standard was to facilitate claims processing by health plans, doctors, hospitals, and other health-care providers. The standard also establishes standard data content, codes, and formats for submitting electronic claims, which will decrease paperwork and provide better service to providers, patients, and insurers. The National Standards is also envisioned to save the health-care industry billions of dollars over the next ten years. Compliance date for this standard has been extended from October 2002 to October 2003.

Employer Identifiers. The final rule was issued May 2002. It standardizes the identification number assigned to health-care employers in the industry. In many cases, this number will be the same as the existing Employee Identification Number (EIN) already assigned and maintained by the IRS. The majority of covered entities must comply with this standard by the end of July 2004.

Page 214, replace § 4.16 with the following:

§ 4.16   Medical Information Bureau

The Medical Information Bureau (MIB) is a voluntary membership association of life insurance companies with approximately 600 members, including virtually every major insurance company issuing individual life, health, and disability insurance in the United States and Canada. Its stated purpose is the prevention of fraud.

When a member organization accepts an application for insurance, the application is sent to the underwriting department, which estimates the future cost to insure the applicant. This estimate is determined by comparing the applicant's profile as it appears in the application with the company's history in providing coverage for large numbers of other people with similar profiles. The most important pieces of information used in developing these profiles are called *risk factors* (age, health, smoker or nonsmoker, and so on).

If an applicant has a condition the insurance industry has defined as "significant to health or longevity," member companies are required to send a brief, coded report on the applicant to the MIB. The MIB currently categorizes 230 types of significant medical conditions, such as blood pressure, EKG readings, and X-rays. Additionally, there are five non-medical codes that refer to an individual's personal behavior or lifestyle— for example, participation in aviation activities, hazardous sports, or an adverse driving record.

In addition to medical information, the MIB maintains an insurance activity index that records the name of any member company that requests information on an individual and the date(s) of inquiry.

This information, along with patient identifiers (name, birth date, birth state, occupation, area of current residency) is placed in the MIB data bank, which contains over 15 million files. Social Security numbers, mailing addresses, and telephone numbers are not included. The MIB coded reports are kept for a period of seven years from date of receipt, after which they are automatically eliminated by computer edit. Insurance activity index records are retained for two years.

Any member organization that accepts an application for insurance may request information on the applicant from the MIB. This process serves to deter applicants from omitting or misrepresenting facts on an application. If the information contained in the MIB files is not consistent with the application, further investigation can be made. Information obtained from the MIB may not be used either in whole or in part to determine an applicant's eligibility for insurance. Rather, the MIB maintains that its information is intended as an "alert" to the need for further investigation. Sound underwriting practices require that coverage decisions be based not on unverified MIB reports, but on information obtained from the applicant, medical examinations, physicians, hospitals, or other medical facilities.

Individuals may access this information to determine if a personal file exists, obtain a copy of the file, or make corrections to the file. The MIB can be contacted at MIB, Inc., P.O. Box 105, Essex Station, Boston, MA 02112, telephone (617) 426-3660, fax (781) 461-8398, and e-mail at infoline@mib.com

Page 221, after § 4.21 add new sections:

§ 4.21A   The National Practitioner Data Bank (NPDB) After Ten Years

As of September 2000, the National Practitioner Data Bank (NPDB) had been in existence for 10 years and consisted of approximately 228,000 records concerning more than 146,000 practitioners, of which more than 100,000 were physicians. In 1999, the Data Bank responded to nearly 3.5 million requests for searches of the data base, more than four times the number of queries received in 1991. Those requests resulted in actual disclosures at the rate of about 3.5 per minute during a normal business day. In this 10-year period, the NPDB moved from a paper-driven system which often could not respond to a query in 30 days, to a fully electronic system which typically responds in 2 hours.

There are serious and growing concerns about the accuracy of the information contained in the NPDB. In 1990, it was estimated that hospitals would report more than 1,000 disciplinary actions every month, however, fewer than 1,000 are reported in a year. After almost ten years, more than half of all hospitals have never reported a disciplinary action.

In December of 2000, the General Accounting Office (GAO), an investigative arm of Congress, released the results of a study conducted concerning the NPDB which analyzed disciplinary reports submitted to the data bank in September 1999. The GAO study concluded:

- Approximately 80% of the disciplinary reports reviewed by the GAO concerned only medical malpractice settlements or awards. The GAO concluded that this is a result of the Health Resources and Services Administration (operator of the database) has not required or forced states and provider organizations to report disciplinary actions. For instance, in its first nine years of operation, th NPDB has received less than 10% of the expected number of reports on clinical privilege restrictions. According to the GAO study, industry experts believe these types of actions are better indicators of professional competence than medical malpractice reports.

- Critical information is often missing from actions reported to the data bank. As an example, the GAO noted that more than 95% of the reviewed medical malpractice reports did not indicate whether the standard of patient care was considered when the claim was settled or adjudicated.

- About 30% of the 252 reviewed state licensure actions were submitted late and 11% contained inaccurate or misleading information on the number of times a physician had been disciplined.

- One-third of the 79 reviewed clinical privilege restriction reports contained inaccurate information.

- 84% of managed care organizations have never reported an adverse action against a healthcare practitioner.

The Health Resources and Services Administration (HRS) acknowledges the serious problems with underreporting. In testimony before Congress in March of 2000, the Director of HRSA indicated that it would be contracting with an accounting firm to help devise and execute a plan for auditing hospital records so that required data could be efficiently collected and analyzed. The Department was also considering a recommendation by the Inspector General to seek a legislative change which would provide for monetary penalties in instances where hospitals had demonstrably failed to report actions.

§ 4.21B   Healthcare Integrity and Protection Data Bank (HIPDB)

The national Healthcare Integrity and Protection Data Bank was established by the Health Insurance Portability and Accountability Act of 1996 (HIPAA) to combat fraud and abuse in health insurance and health care delivery. The HIPDB contains information regarding civil judgments, criminal convictions, or actions by federal or state licensing agencies against a health care provider, supplier, or practitioner related to the delivery of a health care item or service. Reporting to this new data bank started on November 22, 1999. Both the HIPDB and the NPDB are operated by the same governmental agency (Health Resources and Service Administration) and share a joint web site (http://www.npdb-hipdb.com).

Information in the HIPDB consists of the following:

- Civil judgments (with the exception of malpractice judgments) against health care providers, suppliers, and practitioners in federal or state courts related to the delivery of a health care item or service
- Federal or state criminal convictions against health care providers, suppliers, and practitioners in federal or state courts related to the delivery of a health care item or service
- Actions by federal or state agencies responsible for the licensing and certification of health care providers, suppliers, and practitioners
- Exclusion of health care providers, suppliers, and practitioners from participation in federal or state health care programs
- Adverse licensure actions from August 21, 1996 through present.

Information in this data bank originates from several sources:

- State and federal law enforcement organizations
- State and federal agencies responsible for licensing or certifying any type of health care practitioner, provider, or supplier
- Federal agencies that administer or provide payment for health care

CONFIDENTIALITY OF MEDICAL RECORDS

- Private health plans (any group, organization, or company providing health benefits whether directly or indirectly through insurance, reimbursements, or otherwise. This includes insurance agents, brokers, solicitors, consultants and reinsurance intermediaries, insurance companies, self-insured employers, and health care purchasing groups).

Access to this information is strictly limited by the statute and, as with the NPDB, the general public is precluded from accessing the data bank information. Only the governmental agencies and private health plans that are required to report to the data bank are authorized to obtain data bank information. Subjects of reports may obtain access to their own report.

Information in the HIPDB is confidential and must be provided and used in a manner consistent with protecting confidentiality. Persons and organizations recieving data bank information, either directly or indirectly, must use it "solely" for the purpose for which it was desclosed. HIPDB information may be requested for privileging and employment, professional review, licensing, certification or registration, fraud and abuse investigations, certification to participate in a government program, and civil and adminstrative actions.

CHAPTER 5

UNDERSTANDING MEDICAL RECORDS

§ 5.7 —Medical Records and the Health Care System

Page 238, add new paragraph after end of first (runover) sentence:

MCO's operate with a specific framework that has been developed to control the care delivery environment. This framework assists both health plans and providers to control cost while maintaining quality and patient satisfaction. Care delivery include resources for providing care in all settings, including those outside the acute care hospital and rely heavily on the skills of a variety of healthcare disciplines, not just physician providers. There are several types of MCO structures:

1. Preferred Provider Organization (PPO). Employer health benefit plans and insurance carriers contract to provide services from a select group of providers and institutions. Unlike an HMO, the PPO does not *provide* care itself, but contracts with a group of providers and institutions that form a network to provide care. Enrollees usually may seek care outside the PPO, but typically pay greater out of pocket costs.

2. Exclusive Provider Organization (EPO). Variation of PPO, the EPO limits enrollees to providers belonging to one organization.

3. Physician-Hospital Organization (PHO). Physicians and hospitals operate under a joint agreement or contract to deliver care.

4. Health Maintenance Organization (HMO). Administers the health plan and provides care through contracted or employee providers. HMO's differ from fee for service in two key ways: they provide a wide range of comprehensive sevices at guaranteed reduced cost and their care providers accept reduced compensation for services they provide.

There are several HMO models, among the most common are:

1. Staff Model. Providers are employed by the HMO and generally receive a set salary. They deliver care out of HMO facilities.

2. Group Model. Care is provided through independent contracts with one or more multispecialty group practices that provide all physician care. Physicians are not employees of the HMO and may provide fee for service care as well.

3. Network Model. HMO contracts either single group practice. Group may or may not contract with more than one HMO.

4. Independent Practice Association (IPA). HMO contracts for services with independent specialty practice or organized association of providers that provides services at a reduced rate.

5. Point of Service (POS). Allows enrollees to choose to go out of plan for care generally pay greater out of pocket costs. POS allows care to be received from HMO, PPO, or fee for service.

The federal government funds health-care benefits to the elderly and disabled through Medicare. Benefits for certain low-income individuals and families are provided through Medicaid, which is jointly funded by the federal government and the states. The Health Care Financing Administration (HCFA), an agency within the Department of Health and Human Services, has traditionally overseen administration of benefits for both Medicare and Medicaid. In July 2001, the Health Care Financing Administration changed its name to the Centers for Medicare and Medicaid Services (CMS). Three new business centers have been formed within CMS: the Center for Beneficiary Choices, the Center for Medicare Management, and the Center for Medicaid and State Operations. The goal of the reorganization is to provide increased responsiveness to beneficiaries and providers, and support health-care quality improvement initiatives. CMS website contains many resources on a variety of topics as well as a Medicare 800 number that provides 24 x 7 service to beneficiaries.

Contact information for Center for Medicare and Medicaid Services (CMS) is:

Address: 7500 Security Boulevard, Baltimore MD 21244-1850
Toll-free number for beneficiaries: (800) 633-4227
Website address: www/cms.gov

Page 257, add after § 5.11:

§ 5.11A —Skilled Nursing Facility Records

Nursing home litigation has increased significantly over the past decade, requiring legal professionals to have detailed knowledge not only of medical records in general but also of records unique to skilled nursing or long-term care facilities.

A skilled nursing facility (SNF) is a specially qualified health-care provider with the staff and equipment to offer residents skilled nursing care or rehabilitation and other health-related services. *Skilled nursing care* is defined as 24-hour-per-day supervision and medical treatment by a registered nurse under the direction of a physician. Admission to an SNF may be on a short-term basis for rehabilitation following surgery or on a long-term, custodial basis for the elderly or individuals unable to care for themselves. An individual facility may specialize exclusively in the care and treatment of Alzheimer's patients or contain a wing within the facility to house such patients.

Each SNF must be state-licensed and in compliance with that state's standards and regulations. If a facility wishes to accept Medicaid and/or MediCare recipients and receive direct reimbursement from the government, it must also be certified, meaning the facility agrees to provide equal care to all residents, regardless of the source of payment, and consistent with the spirit of federal government regulations, which basically represent national community practice standards.

The Omnibus Reconciliation Act of 1987 (OBRA) included Nursing Home Reform Amendments covering a broad range of regulations dealing with care issues in SNFs, from patients' rights to evaluation and treatment of incontinence. The federal agency responsible for enforcing OBRA regulations is the Health Care Financing Administration (HCFA)* of the Department of Health and Human Services. HCFA inspectors conduct inspections of each SNF at least once a year but can visit more often in response to complaints. An inspector can cite a facility for violating OBRA regulations, which may result in penalties ranging from monetary fines to closure of the facility.

HCFA maintains a database containing information on every Medi-Care- and Medicaid-certified nursing home in the country. This database—Online Survey, Certification, and Reporting (OSCAR)—provides annual profiles of the resident populations of skilled nursing facilities with comparisons to state, regional, and national statistics. The data is compiled

---

Note: The Health Care Financing Administration (HCFA) was renamed the Centers for Medicare and Medicaid Services (CMS) effective July 1, 2001.

by the facility itself and completed at the time of the annual state certification study. Information includes the number or percentage of residents (1) with decubitus (pressure) ulcers, (2) receiving specialized services (occupational, speech, and physical therapy for example), and (3) showing significant weight loss. The OSCAR report also gives information on the facility's history of compliance with MediCare and Medicaid regulations and summarizes particular problems found in that SNF.

OSCAR reports can be obtained from the facility, the state agency in charge of licensing and certification surveys, or online from HCFA at http://www.medicare.gov/nursing/home.asp. The website offers a link to a directory containing the phone number for each state's long-term-care ombudsmen and survey agency. There is also a directory to each individual state Health Insurance Assistance Program, which provides information about the cost of long-term care.

The underlying premise in OBRA is that SNFs must ensure that each resident attains the "highest practicable level of physical, emotional, and psychosocial functioning." This goal is achieved by the initial and continuing comprehensive assessment and planning for all aspects of a resident's needs. The tool developed for this purpose is the Minimum Data Set (MDS).

MDS

The MDS, a standardized national resident assessment instrument unique to long-term care facilities, is designed to produce a comprehensive, accurate, and reproducible assessment of each resident's functional capacity. The MDS has two basic purposes:

1. Information is collected in a standardized fashion and submitted to the federal government for research and analysis, and individualized care plans are triggered based on the information collected for the MDS.

2. As the MDS is completed, the nursing staff is able to assess the resident's functional capability, needs, and strengths. The assessment findings are then used by an interdisciplinary team to develop individual care plans for each resident.

The MDS assessment is performed over the first seven days following admission and then at required intervals of 14, 30, 60, and 90 days. A re-assessment is also required after any noticeable change in physical or mental condition. The MDS assists the clinical nursing staff in screening for potential problems, such as wandering, dizziness, falls, risk for pressure ulcers from incontinence, immobility, peripheral vascular disease, or a history of prior pressure (decubitus) ulcers.

The MDS is completed based on information gathered by skilled nurses, nursing aides, social workers, recreational therapists, and dieticians. Interestingly, no components of the MDS require physician input, although medical diagnoses and information are used.

The specific sections included in an MDS are as follows:

- Identification and background information—name, gender, date of birth, social security and MediCare numbers, reason for assessment, responsibility/legal guardian, advanced directives.

- Demographic information—location admitted from, zip code of primary residence, lifetime occupations, education, language, cycle of daily events, etc.

- Cognitive patterns—comatose, memory, recall ability, cognitive skills for daily decision-making, indications of delirium/periodic disordered thinking, change in cognitive status.

- Communication/hearing patterns—hearing, communication devices, making self understood, speech clarity, ability to understand others, change in communication/hearing.

- Vision patterns—vision, vision limitations/difficulties, appliances.

- Mood and behavior patterns—indicators of depression, anxiety, sad mood, mood persistence, change in mood and behavioral symptoms (e.g., wandering, verbally abusive, socially inappropriate).

- Psychosocial well-being—sense of initiative/involvement, unsettled relationships, past roles.

- Physical functioning and structural problems—ADL self-performance, ADL support provided, bed mobility, transfer, walk-in room, dressing, eating, personal hygiene, bathing, change in ADL function, etc.

- Continence in last 14 days—bowel, bladder, bowel elimination pattern, appliances and programs, change in urinary continence.

- Disease diagnoses—diseases (e.g., endocrine/metabolic, heart/circulation, musculoskeletal), infections (e.g., methicillin resistant, clostridium difficile, HIV), other current or more detailed diagnoses and ICD-9 codes.

- Health conditions—problem conditions (e.g., weight gain or loss, delusions, dizziness, syncope), pain symptoms, pain site, accidents (e.g., fell in past 30 days), stability of conditions.
- Oral/Nutritional status—oral problems, height and weight, weight change, nutritional problems and approaches (e.g., parenteral/IV, feeding tube), parenteral or enteral intake.
- Oral/Dental status—oral status and disease prevention.
- Skin condition—ulcers, type of ulcer, history of resolved ulcers, other skin problems, treatments, foot problems, and care.
- Activity pursuit patterns—time awake, average time involved in activities, preferred activity settings, general activity preferences, changes in daily routine.
- Medications—number, new medications, injections, days received the following medications (e.g., anti-psychotic, antianxiety).
- Special treatments and procedures—special care (e.g., chemotherapy, dialysis, IV medication), programs (alcohol/drug treatment, Alzheimer's/dementia special care, hospice, etc.), therapies (e.g., speech, occupational, physical, respiratory, psychological), intervention programs for mood, nursing rehabilitation/restorative, devices and restraints, hospital stays, ER visits, physician visits or orders, abnormal lab values.
- Discharge potential and overall status—discharge potential, overall change in care needs.

See **Form 5–7** for an example of an MDS.

Resident Assessment Protocols

Once the MDS is completed, a second form unique to the long-term care environment is prepared. The Resident Assessment Protocol (RAP) is essentially a decision tree based on all information collected in the MDS. In other words, if certain information is contained on the MDS, this will lead to the conclusion that a problem exists, or is likely to develop, and a care plan may need to be formulated.

See **Form 5–8** for an example of a RAP.

Care Plans

After the MDS assessment has been completed and the RAP prepared, the specific plan for delivery of nursing care to a resident is developed.

114

FORM 5–7
MINIMUM DATA SET

MINIMUM DATA SET (MDS) - VERSION 2.0
Numeric Identifier _____ 000U. ..:Y
FOR NURSING HOME RESIDENT ASSESSMENT AND CARE SCREENING
FULL ASSESSMENT FORM
(Status in last 7 days, unless other time frame indicated)

SECTION A. IDENTIFICATION AND BACKGROUND INFORMATION

1.	RESIDENT NAME	a. (First) b. (Middle Initial) c. (Last) d. (Jr/Sr)
2.	ROOM NUMBER	129
3.	ASSESSMENT REFERENCE DATE	a. Last day of MDS observation period 09/24/1996 b. Original (0) or corrected copy of form (enter number of correction) **0**
4a.	DATE OF REENTRY	Date of reentry from most recent temporary discharge to a hospital in last 90 days (or since last assessment or admission if less than 90 days) / /
5.	MARITAL STATUS	1. Never married 3. Widowed 5. Divorced 2. Married 4. Separated **3**
6.	Medical Record No.	
7.	CURRENT PAYMENT SOURCES FOR N.H. STAY	(Billing Office to indicate: check all that apply in last 30 days) Medicaid per diem a. ✓ VA per diem f. Medicare per diem b. Self or family pays for full per diem g. Medicare ancillary Part A c. ✓ Medicaid resident liability or Medicare co-payment h. Medicare ancillary Part B d. Private insurance per diem (including co-payment) i. CHAMPUS per diem e. Other per diem j.
8.	REASONS FOR ASSESSMENT Note-if this is a discharge or reentry assessment only a limited subset of MDS items need be completed	a. Primary reason for assessment **1** 1. Admission assessment (required by day 14) 2. Annual assessment 3. Significant change in status assessment 4. Significant correction of prior assessment 5. Quarterly review assessment 6. Discharged-return not anticipated 7. Discharged-return anticipated 8. Discharged prior to completing initial assessment 9. Reentry 0. NONE OF ABOVE b. Special codes for use with supplemental assessment types in Case Mix demonstration states or other states where required 1. 5 day assessment 2. 30 day assessment 3. 60 day assessment 4. Quarterly assessment using full MDS form 5. Readmission/return assessment 6. Other state required assessment
9.	RESPONSIBILITY/ LEGAL GUARDIAN	(Check all that apply) Legal guardian a. Durable power attorney/financial d. Other legal oversight b. Family member responsible e. ✓ Durable power of attorney/health care c. Patient responsible for self f. ✓ NONE OF ABOVE g.
10.	ADVANCED DIRECTIVES	(For those items with supporting documentation in the record, check all that apply) Living will a. Feeding restriction f. Do not resuscitate b. Medication retrictions g. Do not hospitalize c. Other treatment restrictions h. Organ donation d. NONE OF ABOBE i. ✓ Autopsy request e.

SECTION B. COGNITIVE PATTERNS

1.	COMATOSE	(Persistent vegetative state/no discernible consciousness) 0. No. 1. Yes (If yes, skip to Section G) **0**

2.	MEMORY	(Recall of what was learned or known)
		a. Short-term memory OK-seems/appears to recall after 5 minutes **1**
		  0. Memory OK 1. Memory problem
		b. Long-term memory OK-seems/appears to recall long past **1**
		  0. Memory OK 1. Memory problem

3.	MEMORY/ RECALL ABILITY	(Check all that resident was normally able to recall during the last 7 days) Current season a. That he/she is in a nursing home c. Location of own room b. Staff names/faces c. NONE OF ABOVE are recalled e. ✓
4.	COGNITIVE SKILLS FOR DAILY DECISIONMAKING	(Made decisions regarding tasks of daily life) **3** 0. INDEPENDENT-decisions consistent/reasonable 1. MODIFIED INDEPENDENCE-some difficulty in new situations only 2. MODERATELY IMPAIRED-decisions poor;cues/supervision required 3. SEVERELY IMPAIRED-never/rarely made decisions
5.	INDICATORS OF DELIRIUM-PERIODIC DISORDERED THINKING/ AWARENESS	(Code for behavior in the last 7 days)(Note:Accurate assessment requires conversations with staff and family who have direct knowledge of resident's behavior over this time.) 0. Behavior not present 1. Behavior present, not of recent onset 2. Behavior present,over last 7 days appears different from resident's usual functioning (e.g.,new onset or worsening) a. EASILY DISTRACTED-(e.g.,difficulty paying attention; gets sidetracked) **0** b. PERIODS OF ALTERED PERCEPTION OR AWARENESS OF SURROUNDINGS-(e.g.,moves lips or talks to someone not present;believes he/she is somewhere else;confuses night and day) **0** c. EPISODES OF DISORGANIZED SPEECH-(e.g.,speech is incoherent, nonsensical, irrelevant, or rambling from subject to subject; loses train of thought) **0** d. PERIODS OF RESTLESSNESS- (e.g.,fidgeting or picking at skin, clothing, napkins, etc; frequent position changes; repetitive physical movements or calling out) **0** e. PERIODS OF LETHARGY-(e.g.,sluggishness;staring into space;difficult to arouse;little body movement) **0** f. MENTAL FUNCTION VARIES OVER THE COURSE OF THE DAY-(e.g., sometimes better, sometimes worse; behaviors somtimes present, sometimes not) **0**
6.	CHANGE IN COGNITIVE STATUS	Resident's cognitive status,skills,or abilities have changed as compared to status of 90 days ago (or since last assessment if less than 90 days) **0** 0.No change 1.Improved 2 Deteriorated

SECTION C. COMMUNICATION/HEARING PATTERNS

1.	HEARING	(With hearing appliance, if used) **0** 0. HEARS ADEQUATELY-normal talk, TV, phone 1. MINIMAL DIFFICULTY when not in quiet setting 2. HEARS IN SPECIAL SITUATIONS ONLY-speaker has to adjust tonal quality and speak distinctly 3. HIGHLY IMPAIRED / absence of useful hearing
2.	COMMUNICATION DEVICES/ TECHNIQUES	(Check all that apply during last 7 days) Hearing aid, present and used a. Hearing aid, present and not used regularly b. Other receptive comm. techniques used (e.g., lip reading) c. NONE OF ABOVE d. ✓
3.	MODES OF EXPRESSION	(Check all used by resident to make needs known) Speech a. ✓ Signs/gestures/sounds d. Writing messages to express or clarify needs b. Communication board e. American sign language or Braille c. Other f. NONE OF ABOVE g.
4.	MAKING SELF UNDERSTOOD	(Expressing information content-however able) **1** 0. UNDERSTOOD 1. USUALLY UNDERSTOOD-difficulty finding words or finishing thoughts 2. SOMETIMES UNDERSTOOD-ability is limited to making concrete requests 3. RARELY/NEVER UNDERSTOOD
5.	SPEECH CLARITY	(Code for speech in the last 7 days) **0** 0. CLEAR SPEECH - distinct,intelligible words 1. UNCLEAR SPEECH - slurred, mumbled words 2. NO SPEECH - absence of spoken words
6.	ABILITY TO UNDERSTAND OTHERS	(Understanding verbal information content-however able) **1** 0. UNDERSTANDS 1. USUALLY UNDERSTANDS - may miss some part/intent of message 2. SOMETIMES UNDERSTANDS - responds adequately to simple, direct communication 3. RARELY/NEVER UNDERSTANDS
7.	CHANGE IN COMMUNICATION/ HEARING	Resident's ability to express, understand, or hear information has changed as compared to status of 90 days ago (or since last assessment if less than 90 days) **0** 0. No change 1. Improved 2. Deteriorated

UNDERSTANDING MEDICAL RECORDS

SECTION D. VISION PATTERNS

1.	VISION	(Ability to see in adequate light and with glasses if used) 0. ADEQUATE - sees fine detail,including regular print in newspapers/books 1. IMPAIRED - sees large print, but not regular print in newspapers/books 2. MODERATELY IMPAIRED - limited vision; not able to see newspaper headlines,but can identify objects. 3. HIGHLY IMPAIRED - object identification in question, but eyes appear to follow objects 4. SEVERELY IMPAIRED - no vision or sees only light, colors,or shapes;eyes do not appear to follow objects	0
2.	VISUAL LIMITAT- IONS / DIFFICULT- IES	Side vision problems - decreased peripheral vision (e.g. leaves food on one side of tray, difficulty traveling,bumps into people and objects,misjudges placement of chair when seating self)	a.
		Experiences any of following: sees halos or rings around lights; sees flashes of light; sees "curtains" over eyes	b.
		NONE OF ABOVE	c. ✓
3.	VISUAL APPLIANCES	Glasses; contact lenses; magnifying glass 0. No 1. Yes	0

SECTION E. MOOD AND BEHAVIOR PATTERNS

1.	INDICATORS OF DEPRESSION ANXIETY SAD MOOD	(Code for indicators observed in last 30 days, irrespective of the assumed cause) 0.Indicator not exhibited in last 30 days 1.Indicator of this type exhibited up to five days a week 2.Indicator of this type exhibited daily or almost daily (6,7 days a week)	

VERBAL EXPRESSIONS OF DISTRESS			
a. Resident made negat- ive statements-e.g.. "Nothing matters", would rather be dead; What's the use; Reg- rets having lived so long; Let me die"	0	h. Repetitive health complaints, e.g.. persistently seeks medical attention, obsessive concern with body functions	0
b. Repetitive questions- e.g. "Where do I go? What do I do?	0	i. Repetitive anxious complaints/concerns (nonhealth related) e.g. persistently seeks attention/re- assurance regarding schedules, meals, laundry, clothing, relationship issues	0
c. Repetitive verbaliza- tions - e.g. calling out for help. ("God help me")	0		
d. Persistent anger with self or others - e.g. easily annoyed, anger at placement in nurs- ing home; anger at care received	0	SLEEP CYCLE ISSUES	
		j. Unpleasant mood in morning	0
		k. Insomnia/change in usual sleep pattern	0
e. Self depreciation - e.g. I am nothing; I am of no use to anyone"	0	SAD, APATHETIC, ANXIOUS APPEARANCE	
		l. Sad,pained,worried facial expressions- e.g. furrowed brows	0
f. Expressions of what appear to be unreal- istic fears - e.g. fear of being aband- oned, left alone, being with others	0	m. Crying, tearfulness	0
		n. Repetitive physical movements-e.g.,pac- ing, hand wringing, restlessness, fidge- ting, picking	
g. Recurrent statements that something terr- ible is about to hap- pen - e.g. believes he or she is about to die, have a heart attack		LOSS OF INTEREST	
		o. Withdrawal from act -ivities of intere- st,e.g.,no interest in long standing activities or being with family/friends	0
		p. Reduced social int- eraction	0

2.	MOOD PERSIS- TENCE	One or more indicators of depressed, sad or anxious mood were not easily altered by attempts to "cheer up" console, or reassure the resident over last 7 days 0. No Mood 1. Indicators present. 2. Indicators indicators easily altered present, not easily altered	0
3.	CHANGE IN MOOD	Resident's mood status has changed as compared to status of 90 days ago (or since last assessment if less than 90 days) 0. No Changes 1. Improved 2. Deteriorated	0
4.	BEHAVIORAL SYMPTOMS	(A) Behavioral symptom frequency in last 7 days 0. Behavior not exhibited in last 7 days 1. Behavior of this type occurred 1-3 days in last 7 days 2. Behavior of this type occurred 4-6 days, but less than daily 3. Behavior of this type occurred daily (B) Behavioral symptom alterability in last 7 days 0. Behavior not present OR behavior was easily altered 1. Behavior was not easily altered (A)(B)	

a.WANDERING (moved with no rational purpose, seemingly oblivious to needs or safety)	0	0
b.VERBALLY ABUSIVE BEHAVIORAL SYMPTOMS (others were threatened, screamed at, cursed at)	0	0
c.PHYSICALLY ABUSIVE BEHAVIORAL SYMPTOMS(others were hit, shoved, scratched, sexually abused)	0	0
d.SOCIALLY INAPPROPRIATE/DISRUPTIVE BEHAVIORAL SYMPTOMS(made disruptive sounds, noisiness, screaming, self-abusive acts, sexual behavior or disrobing in public,smeared/threw food/ feces, hoarding, rummaged through others' belongings)		
e.RESISTS CARE(resisted taking medications/inject- ions, ADL assistance, or eating)	0	0

5.	CHANGE IN BEHAVIORAL SYMPTOMS	Resident's behavior status has changed as compared to status 90 days ago (or since last assessment if less than 90 days) 0. No change 1. Improved 2. Deteriorated	1

SECTION F. PSYCHOSOCIAL WELL-BEING

1.	SENSE OF INITIATIVE /INVOLVE- MENT	At ease interacting with others	a. ✓
		At ease doing planned or structured activties	b. ✓
		At ease doing self-initiated activities	c.
		Establishes own goals	d.
		Pursues involvement in life of facility (e.g. makes/keeps friends; involved in group activities; responds positively to new activities, assists at religious services)	e. ✓
		Accepts invitations into most group activities	f.
		NONE OF ABOVE	g.
2.	UNSETTLED RELATION- SHIPS	Covert/open conflict with or repeated criticism of staff	a.
		Unhappy with roommate	b.
		Unhappy with residents other than roommate	c.
		Openly expresses conflict/anger with family/friends	d.
		Absence of personal contact with family/friends	e.
		Recent loss of close family member/friend	f.
		Does not adjust easily to change in routines	g.
		NONE OF ABOVE	h. ✓
3.	PAST ROLES	Strong identification with past roles and life status	a.
		Expresses sadness/anger/empty feeling over lost roles/status	b.
		Resident perceives that daily routine (customary routine, activities) is very different from prior pattern in the community	c.
		NONE OF ABOVE	d. ✓

SECTION G. PHYSICAL FUNCTIONING AND STRUCTURAL PROBLEMS

1.		(A)ADL SELF-PERFORMANCE-(Code for resident's PERFORMANCE OVER ALL SHIFTS during last 7 days-Not including setup) 0.INDEPENDENT-No help or oversight-OR-help/oversight provided only 1 or 2 times during last 7 days 1.SUPERVISION-Oversight, encouragement or cueing provided 3 or more times during last 7 days-OR-Supervision (3 or more times) plus physical assistance provided only 1 or 2 times during last 7 days 2.LIMITED ASSISTANCE-Resident highly involved in activity; received physical help in guided maneuvering of limbs or other nonweight bearing assistance 3 or more times-OR-More help provided only 1 or 2 times during last 7 days 3.EXTENSIVE ASSISTANCE-While resident performed part of activity, over last 7-day period, help of following type(s) provided 3 or more times: -Weight-bearing support -Full Staff performance during part (but not all) of 7 days 4.TOTAL DEPENDENCE-Full staff performance of activity during entire 7 days 8.ACTIVITY DID NOT OCCUR during entire 7 days		
		(B) ADL SUPPORT PROVIDED-(Code for MOST SUPPORT PROVIDED OVER ALL SHIFTS during last 7 days; code regardless of resident's self- performance classification) (A)(B) 0. No setup or physical help from staff 1. Setup help only 2. One person physical assistance 3. Two+ persons physical assist 8. ADL activity itself did not occur during entire 7 days		
a.	BED MOBILITY	How resident moves to and from lying position, turns side to side, and positions body while in bed	3	2
b.	TRANSFER	How resident moves between surfaces-to/from:bed, chair, wheelchair, standing position (EXCLUDE to/ from bath/toilet)	3	2
c.	WALK IN ROOM	How resident walks between locations in his/her room	8	8
d.	WALK IN COORIDOR	How resident walks in corridor on unit	8	8
e.	LOCOMO- TION ON UNIT	How resident moves between locations in his/her room and adjacent corridor on same floor. If in wheelchair, self sufficiency once in chair	8	8
f.	LOCOMO- TION OFF UNIT	How resident moves to and returns from off unit locations (e.g. areas set aside for dining, activi- ties, or treatments). If facility has only one floor, how resident moves to and from distant areas on the floor. If in wheelchair, self sufficiency once in chair	8	8
g.	DRESSING	How resident puts on, fastens, and takes off all items of street clothing,including donning/removing prosthesis	3	2
h.	EATING	How resident eats and drinks (regardless of skill). Includes intake of nourishment by other means (e.g.,tube feeding, total parenteral nutrition)	3	2
i.	TOILET USE	How resident uses the toilet room (or commode, bed- pan, urinal):transfer on/off toilet, cleanses, changes pad, manages ostomy or catheter, adjusts clothes	3	2
j.	PERSONAL HYGIENE	How resident maintains personal hygiene, including combing hair, brushing teeth, shaving, applying makeup, washing/drying face, hands and perineum (EXCLUDE baths and showers)	3	2

116

FORM 5–8
RESIDENT ASSESSMENT PROTOCOL

INTERDISCIPLINARY TEAM NOTE   09-24 1996   Numeric Identifier: 000000
Resident's Name:
Medical Record Number: PAGE 1

RAP GUIDELINES REVIEW
Including:
- Nature of Condition
- Complications/Risk Factors
- Need for Individualization in Care Plan
- Need for Further Assessment, Referral, Evaluation

Significant Reasons to Proceed/Not Proceed to Care Plan
   (Based on review of individualized RAPS) are as follows:

RAP PROBLEM AREA	REASONS BASED ON INDIVIDUALIZED REVIEW OF RAP
COGNITIVE LOSS/ DEMENTIA	REASON TO PROCEED TO CARE PLAN: SHORT TERM MEMORY LOSS. LONG TERM MEMORY LOSS. SEVERELY IMPAIRED SKILLS FOR DAILY DECISION MAKING. USUALLY UNDERSTANDS OTHERS. NEUROLOGIC: DEMENTIA.
COMMUNICATION	REASON TO PROCEED TO CARE PLAN: USUALLY MAKES SELF UNDERSTOOD. USUALLY UNDERSTANDS OTHERS. CHRONIC CONDITION: DEMENTIA. SHORT-TERM MEMORY PROBLEM. LONG-TERM MEMORY PROBLEM. MEMORY RECALL PROBLEM.
ADL FUNCTIONING/ REHAB POTENTIAL	REASON TO PROCEED TO CARE PLAN: NEEDS PHYSICAL HELP TO BALANCE WHEN STANDING. NEEDS PHYSICAL HELP TO BALANCE WHEN SITTING. RESID. BELIEVES THEY COULD BE MORE INDEP. IN SOME ADLS. STAFF BELIEVES THAT RESID. COULD BE MORE INDEP. IN ADLS. REHAB: NOT INDEP. IN TRANSFER. REHAB: NOT INDEP. IN WALKING IN ROOM. REHAB: NOT INDEP. IN WALKING IN CORRIDOR. REHAB: NOT INDEP. IN LOCOMOTION ON THE UNIT. REHAB: NOT INDEP. IN LOCOMOTION OFF THE UNIT. REHAB: NOT INDEP. IN DRESSING. REHAB: NOT INDEP. IN EATING. REHAB: NOT INDEP. IN TOILET USE. REHAB: NOT INDEP. IN PERSONAL HYGIENE. REHAB: NOT INDEP. IN BATHING. REHAB: RESID. BELIEVES CAPABLE OF INCREASED INDEP. IN SOME ADLS. REHAB: STAFF BELIEVES RESID. CAPABLE OF INCREASED INDEP. IN SOME ADLS.
URINARY INCONT & INDWELLING CATHETER	REASON TO PROCEED TO CARE PLAN: OCCASIONALLY INCONTINENT OF BLADDER. USES PADS/BRIEFS. DEFICIT IN ABILITY TO WALK IN ROOM. DEFICIT IN ABILITY TO WALK IN CORRIDOR. DEFICIT IN LOCOMOTION ON THE UNIT. DEFICIT IN LOCOMOTION OFF THE UNIT. DEPENDENT IN TRANSFER &.
BEHAVIOR PROBLEM	REASON NOT TO PROCEED TO CARE PLAN: BEHAVIOR HAS IMPROVED.
ACTIVITIES	REASON TO PROCEED TO CARE PLAN: DEFICIT IN WALKING IN CORRIDOR. DEFICIT IN LOCOMOTION ON UNIT. DEFICIT IN WALKING IN ROOM. DEFICIT IN LOCOMOTION OFF UNIT. REVISE PLAN: LESS THAN 1/3 TIME INVOLVED IN ACTIVITIES. REVISE PLAN: DESIRES SLIGHT CHANGE IN TYPE OF ACTIVITIES. REVISE PLAN: DESIRES SLIGHT CHANGE IN EXTENT OF INVOLVEMENT.

117

UNDERSTANDING MEDICAL RECORDS

FORM 5-8 *(continued)*

INTERDISCIPLINARY TEAM NOTE	09-2. .996	Numeric Identifier: 000000

Resident's Name:
Medical Record Number:

PAGE 2

RAP PROBLEM AREA	REASONS BASED ON INDIVIDUALIZED REVIEW OF RAP
FALLS	REASON TO PROCEED TO CARE PLAN: POTENTIAL FOR ADDITIONAL FALLS: FELL IN PAST 30 DAYS. ADL FUNCTION HAS DECLINED. ARTHRITIS. DEMETIA.
NUTRITIONAL STATUS	REASON TO PROCEED TO CARE PLAN: LEAVES 25% OR MORE FOOD UNEATEN MOST MEALS.AT RISK FOR DEHYDRATION/AT RISK FOR SIGNIFICANT WEIGHT LOSS. MECHANICALLY ALTERED DIET.CHEWING PROBLEM. STAGE 2 PRESSURE ULCER.NUTRITION HELPS IN THE HEALING PROCESS. REDUCED ABILITY TO FEED SELF. DEMENTIA.DX. OF UROSEPSIS,HX. OF DEHYDRATION. DIFFICULTY MAKING SELF UNDERSTOOD. DIFFICULTY UNDERSTANDING OTHERS.(WILL COMBINE WITH DEHYDRATION SUMMARY).
DEHYDRATION/ FLUID MAINTENANCE	REASON TO PROCEED TO CARE PLAN: UTI.DEHYDRATION DIAGNOSIS.RESIDENT LEAVES 25% AND MORE OF FOODS UNEATEN AT MOST MEALS.AT RISK FOR DEHYDRATION AND SIGNIFICANT WEIGHT LOSS.(WILL COMBINE WITH NUTRITIONAL SUMMARY AND CP). MODERATELY/SEVERELY IMPAIRED DECISION MAKING. DEFICIT IN ABILITY TO MAKE SELF UNDERSTOOD. DEFICIT IN ABILITY TO UNDERSTAND. NEEDS PHYSICAL HELP TO BALANCE WHILE STANDING. NEEDS PHYSICAL HELP TO BALANCE WHILE SITTING.
PRESSURE ULCERS	REASON TO PROCEED TO CARE PLAN: AT RISK DUE TO PROBLEM WITH BED MOBILITY.AT RISK FOR FURTHER SKIN BREAKDOWN,RESIDENT HAS IMPAIRED MOBILITY,POOR TO FAIR INTAKE. AT RISK DUE TO BOWEL INCONTINENCE. STAGE TWO PRESSURE ULCER PRESENT. DEMENTIA.DX. OF DEGENERATIVE JOINT DISEASE,ANEMIA. PRESSURE RELIEVING CHAIR. PRESSURE RELIEVING BED. NEEDS TURNING/REPOSITIONING. NUTRITION/HYDRATION PROGRAM. ULCER CARE REQUIRED. DRESSING APPLIED. PREVENTATIVE/PROTECTIVE SKIN CARE.

FORM 5–8 *(continued)*

| INTERDISCIPLINARY TEAM NOTE   09-2. .996   Numeric Identifier: 000000 |
| Resident's Name: |
| Medical Record Number: |
| PAGE 2 |

RAP PROBLEM AREA	REASONS BASED ON INDIVIDUALIZED REVIEW OF RAP
FALLS	REASON TO PROCEED TO CARE PLAN: POTENTIAL FOR ADDITIONAL FALLS: FELL IN PAST 30 DAYS. ADL FUNCTION HAS DECLINED. ARTHRITIS. DEMETIA.
NUTRITIONAL STATUS	REASON TO PROCEED TO CARE PLAN: LEAVES 25% OR MORE FOOD UNEATEN MOST MEALS.AT RISK FOR DEHYDRATION/AT RISK FOR SIGNIFICANT WEIGHT LOSS. MECHANICALLY ALTERED DIET.CHEWING PROBLEM. STAGE 2 PRESSURE ULCER.NUTRITION HELPS IN THE HEALING PROCESS. REDUCED ABILITY TO FEED SELF. DEMENTIA.DX. OF UROSEPSIS,HX. OF DEHYDRATION. DIFFICULTY MAKING SELF UNDERSTOOD. DIFFICULTY UNDERSTANDING OTHERS.(WILL COMBINE WITH DEHYDRATION SUMMARY).
DEHYDRATION/ FLUID MAINTENANCE	REASON TO PROCEED TO CARE PLAN: UTI.DEHYDRATION DIAGNOSIS.RESIDENT LEAVES 25% AND MORE OF FOODS UNEATEN AT MOST MEALS.AT RISK FOR DEHYDRATION AND SIGNIFICANT WEIGHT LOSS.(WILL COMBINE WITH NUTRITIONAL SUMMARY AND CP). MODERATELY/SEVERELY IMPAIRED DECISION MAKING. DEFICIT IN ABILITY TO MAKE SELF UNDERSTOOD. DEFICIT IN ABILITY TO UNDERSTAND. NEEDS PHYSICAL HELP TO BALANCE WHILE STANDING. NEEDS PHYSICAL HELP TO BALANCE WHILE SITTING.
PRESSURE ULCERS	REASON TO PROCEED TO CARE PLAN: AT RISK DUE TO PROBLEM WITH BED MOBILITY.AT RISK FOR FURTHER SKIN BREAKDOWN,RESIDENT HAS IMPAIRED MOBILITY,POOR TO FAIR INTAKE. AT RISK DUE TO BOWEL INCONTINENCE. STAGE TWO PRESSURE ULCER PRESENT. DEMENTIA.DX. OF DEGENERATIVE JOINT DISEASE,ANEMIA. PRESSURE RELIEVING CHAIR. PRESSURE RELIEVING BED. NEEDS TURNING/REPOSITIONING. NUTRITION/HYDRATION PROGRAM. ULCER CARE REQUIRED. DRESSING APPLIED. PREVENTATIVE/PROTECTIVE SKIN CARE.

This is called the care plan. HCFA requires that the care plan, an interdisciplinary document, be developed within seven days of the completion of the MDS.

A care plan is developed for each identified problem and consists of four main elements:

- Nursing *diagnosis* (problems, strengths, needs)
- *Outcomes/goals* to be expected with resolution of the diagnosis
- *Interventions/approaches* to be taken in order to help the resident achieve the outcome
- *Evaluation* of the effectiveness of the intervention.

The nursing notes and flow sheets will provide evidence of how the plan of care was implemented.

See **Form 5–9** for a sample care plan.

Resident Care Conferences

On a periodic basis, the interdisciplinary team will meet to discuss the status of a resident. Typical attendees include licensed nurses, CNAs, dietitians, occupational therapists, physical therapists, psychologists, the resident, and family members. Specific care planning notes, signed by all present, may be generated as a result.

Activities of Daily Living

Activities of daily living (ADL) include such tasks as bathing, grooming, eating, ambulating, and dressing. An individual's ability to perform these basic tasks help to assess the need for assistance or placement in a SNF.

The method of documenting these routine aspects of SNF care is the flowsheet. Typical flowsheets have areas for percentage of meals consumed, continence of bladder and bowel, daily hygiene activities, and so on. They may also be used to document behavior, such as wandering. Flowsheets are generally completed by CNAs and can be problematic if the information contained on the flowsheet differs from that given in the licensed nursing notes.

See **Form 5–10** for a sample flowsheet.

FORM 5–9
SAMPLE CARE PLAN

```
                              CARE PLAN                      PAGE 1
                       COMMUNICATION IMPAIRED

                     ID#:2719        DATE INITIATED: 11/11/96
```

PROBLEMS/STRENGTHS/NEEDS:

- ALTERATION IN ABILITY TO COMMUNICATE.

- RELATED TO IMPAIRED UNDERSTANDING.

- CONTRIBUTING MEDICAL DIAGNOSIS: DEMENTIA.

- DEFINING CHARACTERISTIC: SHORT-TERM MEMORY PROBLEM; LONG-TERM MEMORY PROBLEM.

- SIGNS OF DISORDERED THINKING: MEMORY RECALL PROBLEM PRESENT.

- MODES OF COMMUNICATION: USES SPEECH TO COMMUNICATE.

- LANGUAGE: . *English*

- DIFFICULTY COMMUNICATING: USUALLY MAKES SELF UNDERSTOOD; USUALLY UNDERSTANDS OTHERS.

- COGNITIVE SKILLS: SEVERELY IMPAIRED, NEVER/RARELY MADE DECISIONS.

GOAL(S):

- ABLE TO COMMUNICATE NEEDS VERBALLY USING SHORT   By: 02/97
  SENTENCES, VERBALLY BY ANSWERING "YES" & "NO"
  QUESTIONS APPROPRIATELY.

- DEMONSTRATES UNDERSTANDING OF VERBAL   By: 02/97
  COMMUNICATION BY RESPONDING APPROPRIATELY.

APPROACHES: Discipline

- OBSERVE FOR DIFFICULTY IN COMMUNICATING. WATCH   N SS A
  FOR GESTURES, WATCH FOR POINTING, WATCH FACIAL
  EXPRESSION.

- ANTICIPATE NEEDS FOR RESIDENT: KEEP SIGNAL CORD   N SS A
  WITHIN REACH AT ALL TIMES, HELP TO FIND THE
  BATHROOM, HELP TO FIND THE DINING ROOM, HELP TO
  FIND OWN ROOM, HELP TO USE TELEPHONE, GUIDE TO
  ACTIVITIES.

UNDERSTANDING MEDICAL RECORDS

```
┌─────────────────────────────────────────────────────────────────┐
│                        CARE PLAN                         PAGE 2   │
│                  COMMUNICATION IMPAIRED                           │
│                                                                   │
│                 ID#:2719        DATE INITIATED: 11/11/96          │
├───────────────────────────────────────────────────────────────── │
```

APPROACHES: Discipline

· OBSERVE FOR SIGNS OF DISCOMFORT. WATCH FOR   N SS A
  FACIAL GRIMACE, WATCH FOR MOANING, WATCH FOR
  INCREASED AGITATION.

· USE GOOD EYE CONTACT WHEN TALKING TO RESIDENT.   N SS A D
  ALLOW TIME TO RESPOND.

· USE SHORT SIMPLE PHRASES WHEN SPEAKING TO   N SS A D
  RESIDENT.

· ENCOURAGE TO RESPOND BY NODDING HEAD, TURN   N SS A
  TOWARD THE SPEAKER WHEN BEING ADDRESSED.

· USE TOUCH THERAPEUTICALLY: HOLD HAND, TOUCH FACE   N SS A
  IF WILLING.

· PROVIDE SENSORY STIMULATION PER TV, RADIO, 1:1   N SS A
  VISITS.

· ALWAYS ANTICIPATE RESIDENT'S NEEDS AT ALL TIMES.   N

EVALUATION:

FORM 5–10
SAMPLE FLOW SHEET: ACTIVITIES OF DAILY LIVING

NIGHT SHIFT   DATE
- Positioned q 2 hours as needed (P)
- Fluids offered
- Slept well (S);   Restless (R)
- Bladder: Incont. (I);   Cont. (C);   Foley (F)
- Bowel: Incont. (I);   Cont. (C) | # of BMS
- Alert (A);   Oriented (O);   Confused (C)
- Soft restraints | Postural supports checked q 2 hours
- AM Care: Teeth brushed, dentures in
- Side rails: Up (↑);   Down (↓)
- NURSE ASSISTANT'S INITIALS

DAY SHIFT   DATE
- Breakfast   Diet: % Eaten:
- Eats Indep. (I);   Assist (A);   Fed
- Pers. Hygiene: Indep. (I);   Assist (A);   Total (T)
- Dressing: Indep. (I);   Assist (A);   Total (T)
- Bowel: Incont. (I);   Cont. (C) | # of BMS
- Bladder: Incont. (I);   Cont. (C);   Foley (F)
- Bath: Shower (S);   Tub (T);   Bed (B)
- Ambulate (I);   Assisted (A);   Walker (W)
- Wheelchair (W);   Chair (C);   Bed (B)
- Positioned q 2 hours as needed (P)
- Nourishments given
- Lunch   Diet: % Eaten:
- Eats Indep. (I);   Assist (A);   Fed
- Soft restraints | Postural supports checked q 2 hours
- Side rails: Up (↑);   Down (↓)
- Participated in activities
- Alert (A);   Oriented (O);   Confused (C)
- R.O.M. given
- Fluids offered q 2 hours
- NURSE ASSISTANT'S INITIALS

P.M. SHIFT   DATE
- Dinner   Diet: % Eaten:
- Eats Indep. (I);   Assist (A);   Fed
- Bowel: Incont. (I);   Cont. (C) | # of BMS
- Bladder: Incont. (I);   Cont. (C);   Foley (F)
- Ambulate (I);   Assisted (A);   Walker (W)
- Up in Wheelchair (W);   Chair (C);   Bed Pt. (B)
- Positioned q 2 hours as needed (P)
- Alert (A);   Oriented (O);   Confused (C)
- R.O.M. given
- Fluids offered q 2 hours
- Soft restraints | Postural supports checked q 2 hours
- HS nourishment offered
- PM Care; Oral Hygiene
- Side rails: Up (↑);   Down (↓)
- Participated in activities
- Shower
- NURSE ASSISTANT'S INITIALS

INITIAL	SIGNATURE	INITIAL	SIGNATURE	INITIAL	SIGNATURE	INITIAL	SIGNATURE

LAST NAME	FIRST NAME	ROOM NO.	PATIENT NO.	AGE	MONTH
		124C			Sept. '96

CEN - 18 (4/86)   NURSE ASSISTANT RECORD   000260

123

CHAPTER 6

OBTAINING MEDICAL RECORDS

§ 6.1   Determining Which Medical Records to Obtain

Page 268, replace § 6.1 with the following:

A common problem faced by legal teams is determining which medical records to obtain. For plaintiffs, this can be a financial consideration, and the tendency may be to keep costs down by obtaining only those records that concern the subject incident. For the pre-accident medical history, attorneys often depend solely on their client's recollection, which can be a disadvantage. It is essential for the attorney to be aware of and familiar with the client's entire medical status and history prior to the incident in order to understand how the accident or incident impacted the client's life, if at all. It is also vital to identify any prior medical conditions that could affect the allegations made in the case. Deciding not to order prior medical records initially can save money, but in the long run it could prove costly as defense counsel will always subpoena all medical records and the plaintiff's attorney must then scramble to determine the relationship of a pre-existing condition to the subject incident. As a general guideline, plaintiff's counsel should always obtain a complete set of records prior to filing suit.

Page 268, add the new § 6.1A:

§ 6.1A   —Initial Client Interview

One of the most useful tools in obtaining a complete medical history is the initial client interview. At the time of the interview, the legal team will identify the client's problem and ultimate goal. The attorney and paralegal should prepare the client for the future conduct of the case, including the anticipated duration of the case, the steps the attorney will take prior to and during litigation, the status and role of the paralegal, and the invasive nature of a lawsuit. A potential plaintiff rarely has any concept of the time and emotional involvement inherent in a lawsuit, nor of the degree of privacy he or she may sacrifice. A client unprepared or unwilling to endure the invasion into his or her personal and business life or the "hurry up and wait" nature of a lawsuit may be advised to reconsider initiating the action. Similarly, early settlement of a matter may be advised in order to avoid the commitment of time or loss of privacy that a party may be unwilling or unable to tolerate.

Cases related to death or significant personal or psychological injuries are especially emotionally charged. Economic damage, loss of physical or mental well-being, and the impact on a marriage and family involve serious stress. A client can be angry and depressed, and may be grieving. Some clients are demanding, abusive, aggressive, absent-minded, or emotional. They may lack normal behavioral constraints due to their losses and stress, and their judgment and concentration may be impaired. The client interview is the time during which the attorney and paralegal can establish trust and focus on the client's problem. Gathering complete information regarding the incident is extremely important, but collecting necessary information can occur over time and during the course of the litigation.

Practice Note: A client is often accompanied to meetings by a relative or friend who may influence the client by their presence, emotional response to the questioning, or contributions to the interview. It is not uncommon, for example, for a spouse or parent to answer questions posed to the client or to interject his/her opinions, thereby preventing the client from telling his or her own story.

When this situation occurs, it may be necessary to ask the companion to wait outside the interview room or reschedule the interview for a time when the client is alone.

The following categories of inquiry are typically used to obtain information during the interview. They also enable the attorney to lay a good foundation for discovery responses when interrogatories are propounded or the client's deposition is taken. Conversely, the categories are good starting points for discovery to be propounded to the plaintiff, and for questioning during deposition. The categories for personal information, incident descriptions, injuries, and damages are applicable to most cases, although the specific questions propounded will vary depending on the client and the basis of the case. The remaining categories relate to particular types of cases and must be combined as appropriate with the more general topic categories.

General Information

Personal

- Full name
- Other names used and when
- Address (current and past five years)
- Telephone number, facsimile, e-mail
- Name of parent or guardian (if minor)
- Name and address of conservator (if incapacitated person)
- Marital status
- Spouse's name(s) and dates of marriage
- Children's names and ages
- Name, address, phone number of person who will always know witness's location
- Social Security number
- Date and place of birth
- Driver's license number and restrictions
- Felony or misdemeanor conviction(s)
- Education—high school through graduate or technical training
- Prior claims and lawsuits—circumstances, names of parties, names of attorneys, case names and numbers, resolution

Employment

- Military service and dates, type of discharge received
- Current employer, address, and phone number
- Date employment started
- Position, job description, responsibilities, and duties
- Employer information for five years prior to incident

- Wages and benefits
- Supervisor identification

Incident (act or omission)

- When incident occurred
- Identification of each party involved (including address and phone number)
- Content of conversations with parties
- Location of incident
- Description of incident or conduct
- Identification of each medication (prescription or otherwise), drug, or alcohol consumed in 24 hours prior to incident
- Identification of each witness (name, address, phone, and specific location at site)
- Content of conversations with witnesses
- Comments made by any party or witness at scene
- Location and description of any statements, incident reports, photographs, videotapes, diagrams
- Connection of accident, if any, to employment
- Contact with insurance company regarding accident
- Contact with investigator regarding incident
- Identification of any statements given
- Media reports

Injuries

- Loss of consciousness or shock
- Immediate first aid administered
- Description of injuries sustained and treatment (chronological)
- Complete description of all health-care providers: name; address; phone number; dates and type of service provided, i.e. ambulance; physician; hospital; clinic; psychologist; dentist; radiologic or other diagnostic service; nursing; physical, speech, or occupational therapy, vocational rehabilitation; pharmacy; convalescent facility

- Diagnostic testing (laboratory work, x-rays, CT scans, MRI, etc.)
- Medications taken since accident
- Psychological or psychiatric counseling
- Home care required (name, address, and phone number; dates of service; types of service)
- Length of time bedridden
- Medical equipment (description, provider, and costs)
- Period of disability
- Current physical and mental condition
- Description of permanent disability, disfigurement, or psychological disability
- Necessary structural changes to residence to accommodate disability (description, name of contractor, cost)
- Prognosis
- Future health-care/treatment required (name of provider recommending care, approximate timeframe and cost)
- Prior health-care providers (at least 10 years prior to incident)
- Prior accidents or industrial injuries
- Prior complaints of a similar nature

Insurance coverage

- Type of policy (homeowners, business, automobile, umbrella, errors and omissions)
- For each applicable policy: insurance company, address, policy number, policy limits, location of policy
- Knowledge of reservation or rights or policy dispute
- For health or disability policies: insurance company, policy number, right of reimbursement, current location of policy

Medical and related expenses

- All medical expenses incurred (ambulance, physician, hospital, clinic, diagnostic studies, medication, durable medical equipment, etc.)
- Copies of medical bills

- Use of Medicare or Medicaid benefits
- Incidental costs related to medical care (travel, hotel, car rental, mileage, parking, tolls)
- Home care costs
- Assistance required for household (cleaning, shopping, childcare, other): type of assistance, name and address of provider, type of service provided, length of time services required, total costs, receipts

Loss of income/earning capacity

- Employer at time of incident
- Name of supervisor
- Position at time of incident
- Duties
- Date employment began
- Special education or training required for position
- Length of time with company
- Salary and benefits at time of incident
- Salary and benefit changes since incident
- Number of hours worked per week (regular and overtime) at time of incident
- Overtime hours during year prior to incident
- Expectations regarding promotion
- If terminated, date and reason for termination
- Dates off work due to incident
- Impact on job, if any, from incident including accommodations made to work place and hours of work
- Employment history for at least five years prior to incident
- Eligibility for disability or unemployment benefits
- Disability or unemployment benefits applied for and received

Other economic damages

- Consequential damages: repair, replacement, or cleaning costs; rental expenses

- Loss in real or personal property value
- Fees for and description of services
- Vocational rehabilitation expenses

Non-economic damages

- Description of damage to personal or business reputation; humiliation suffered; loss of consortium
- Loss of use and enjoyment of property
- Potential future health risks (identify physician or other medical provider with knowledge)
- Fear related to future health risks

Special Categories

Animals

- Description of animal
- Name and address of owner of animal
- Where incident occurred
- Description of incident including any provocation, whether animal was on leash, enclosed in a cage or fence, or under control of a person
- Previous incidents and warnings
- Status of vaccinations

Motor vehicle accident

- Date, day of week, time of accident
- Police on scene, accident report prepared, citations issued, police opinion as to fault and reason for fault
- Name, address, and phone number of each driver involved
- If driver not registered owner, identify person giving permission to driver, including address and phone number
- Name, address, and phone number of each registered owner of each vehicle involved
- License plate numbers for all vehicles involved

- Name, address, and phone number of pedestrian or bicyclist involved
- Insurance information for each involved party (and vehicle owner, if different)
- Identification of all passengers in each vehicle: name, address, and phone number; location in vehicle
- Whether vehicle use was personal or related to employment
- Injuries sustained by all other persons involved
- Alcohol or drug use during 24 hours prior to accident
- Physical or mental disabilities at time of accident
- Use of seat belts while operating or riding in vehicle; presence of bruising or abrasions from seat belt use
- Deployment of air bags, injuries as a result of deployment
- Use of cellular phone while operating or riding in vehicle
- Description of each vehicle involved
- Modifications to standard vehicle equipment with identification of specific modification, dates completed, person(s) completing modification
- Recent repairs to vehicle and name of repair service; location of operation and repair records, service and repair records
- Use of headlights or turn signals
- Observation of brake lights
- Defects or malfunctions in any of the involved vehicles
- Previous motor vehicle accidents
- Weather and road conditions
- Lighting (natural light, streetlights, lights from surrounding buildings)
- Traffic conditions
- Traffic controls and speed limit
- Street construction, repair work, or obstruction in immediate area
- Description of scene at the time of the accident, including: number of traffic lanes; type of lane markers; traffic signs and signals; warning or caution signs, markers, barriers; road condition signs; pedestrian crosswalks and signals; pavement surface; terrain, curves; sight distance limitations; type of area—rural, residential, business, etc.; buildings in immediate area
- When other party first sighted (vehicle, pedestrian, cyclist)
- Intended destination and route taken

- Activities in vehicle just prior to incident (talking on phone, viewing videos, argument, changing CD or radio station, etc.)
- Direction each party traveling
- Evasive action taken by any party
- Estimated speed of each vehicle
- Point of impact
- Point of rest of each vehicle, person, or bicycle
- Skid marks, gouges, and debris
- Damage to each vehicle involved, repairs performed, total cost of repairs, estimates and receipts
- Current location of each vehicle involved
- Repair of vehicles: estimates, cost, location of documentation
- Personal property damaged, value of property
- Payments received from any insurance carrier

Premises liability

- Owner of subject property
- Rental or lease agreement
- Current monthly rent
- Date moved in
- Name and address of property manager
- Description of unsafe or defective condition
- Date unsafe or defective condition first noticed
- Complaints made regarding subject condition
- Person/entity to whom each complaint made
- Date of each complaint
- Response to each complaint; maintenance or repairs performed as a result
- Exterior incident: weather, lighting, physical conditions
- Slip or trip and fall: shoes worn, clothing, lighting, physical conditions, foreign substance or object on surface, familiarity with location, route taken
- Construction site incident: name and address of contractor, name and address of each subcontractor, description of construction site, OSHA inspections and citations

OBTAINING MEDICAL RECORDS

Product liability

- Description of product involved: model, year, serial number, size
- Description of how and where product was used
- Purpose of product
- Where and when product obtained
- Manufacturer of product
- Current location of product
- Description of product defect
- Training received on use of product
- Prior use and problems with product
- Prior maintenance or repair of product: identification of repair, warranty, cost
- Warnings on product: labels, brochure, consumer use information
- Safety standards associated with product
- Location of: maintenance and repair records, warranties, use and repair manuals, brochures or advertisements, warnings
- Photographs of product

Professional malpractice

- Description of relationship
- Dates of relationship, chronology of relationship
- Agreements involved
- Identification of parties to each agreement
- Location of written contract
- Services performed
- Identity and location of any executed release or consent form
- Identity and location of pertinent files
- Arbitration or mediation agreement
- License, board certification, registration held by professional

Professional malpractice—medical

- Condition for which the medical practitioner was seen
- Treatment given for condition

- Procedures performed by the medical practitioner
- Facility in which treatment was provided
- Discussions regarding consent for treatment
- Discussions regarding risks of procedure, side effects of medication
- Staff members or employees on duty at the time consent for subject treatment was obtained, subject treatment given or procedure performed, follow-up care that was provided
- How often seen by the medical practitioner
- Length of each visit
- All health or psychological care providers involved in treatment at time malpractice committed and subsequent to injury
- Recommendations of any other health-care provider seen before the incident regarding the same condition
- Statement(s) made as to possible malpractice: date, identification of speaker, content of statement(s)
- Opinions expressed by any medical practitioner as to: whether or not correct procedures used, prognosis, future medical treatment
- Names and addresses of authorities in the field
- All collateral source benefits for which eligible: health insurance, workers compensation
- Social Security or state disability, veterans benefits, private disability insurance

Toxic tort liability

- Address of real property involved
- Name, address, and phone number of each owner
- Business involved
- Identification of each prior owner
- Description of current property use
- History of property use
- Current permits or licenses
- Clean-up or abatement orders, citations or cease and desist orders
- Type of contamination
- Duration of problem

- Public agencies involved
- Estimated clean-up costs
- Anticipated duration of clean-up and required date of completion
- Injuries: current physical injuries, anticipated future health problems
- Agreements involved and parties to agreements

§ 6.7 —General Authorization

Page 274, replace the Practice Note at the end of 6.7 with the following:

Practice Note: Having the client sign several general authorizations in advance without dating them allows records to be requested without having to contact the client each time a new authorization is needed. In some cases, an original authorization can also be copied and the copy used to obtain the records. If the records are voluminous and are to be sent to a copy service, the service does not have to be directly identified because it is acting as the agent for the law firm.

The new HIPAA regulations specifically identify what must be included in an authorization:

- A description of the protected information to be used and disclosed;
- The identification of the person authorized to make the disclosure;
- The person to whom the covered entity (provider) may disclose the records;
- The purpose for which the information may be used (in some cases).

The authorization in revised Form 6-1, below, clearly meets these requirements. Please note that the sentence "The disclosed health information will be used for purposes of litigation, etc." is included on this form.

FORM 6–1
SAMPLE AUTHORIZATION FOR RELEASE OF MEDICAL INFORMATION

AUTHORIZATION FOR RELEASE OF RECORDS

To: [name of provider]   Re: [name of individual]

Date of birth: _____

Social Security Number: _____

Medical Record Number: [if applicable]

This authorizes you, [name of provider], to release the following documents to my attorneys, [name and address of attorneys] (or to their designated representative, [e.g., copy service, deposition officer, etc.]):

[see categories below]

The disclosed health information will be used for purposes of [litigation, etc.].

All prior authorizations are hereby canceled. This authorization does not allow the further disclosure of this information to any other person or party. Photocopies of this authorization shall be deemed as valid as the original. This authorization will become effective immediately and shall remain in full force and effect until [e.g., specific date or until rescinded].

Date: [date authorization signed]

_____
[signature of client]

§ 6.12   —Custodian's Response to Request

Page 277, replace the Practice Note at the end of § 6.12 with the following:

OBTAINING MEDICAL RECORDS

Practice Note: If you suspect you have not been provided with a complete chart, call the provider's office immediately and request that it comply with your request. The HIPAA Privacy Rule allows providers to release a complete medical record, including portions that were created by another provider. The "Minimum Necessary" provision [see § **4.15** for discussion] is not imposed when records are disclosed pursuant to an authorization.

CHAPTER 7

SUMMARIZING MEDICAL RECORDS

§ 7.45 —Poor Copies

Page 324, add at end of § 7.45:

It is becoming increasingly common for plaintiff's attorneys to request color copies of a medical chart, particularly if the case involves allegations of medical malpractice or nursing home litigation. Anyone who has reviewed a medical record knows that the original is far from the clean, black-and-white set of records provided by a copy machine. Inks of all colors may be used when charting. Originals may be pink, yellow, or green. Highlighting of entries, often found on the original, may not show up on copies.

Color copies of medical records are expensive, ranging from $1 to $1.50 per page. However, the clarity achieved using this technology is often superior to that from standard photocopies or records photographed and then copied from film.

§ 7.67 —The Internet

Page 349, add at end of § 7.67:

Here are some additional Internet-related terms you will encounter:

Domain name—Internet site identifier that comes after the "@" in an Internet address. The main domain name extensions include:

.com—commercial entities

.edu—educational institutions, limited to four-year schools or universities

.gov—government, reserved for federal government branches and agencies

.mil—reserved for the U.S. military

.net—network, identifying those entities and computers that are part of the Internet infrastructure

.org—organization, often nonprofit but not always so

.country—country of website origin denoted by a two-letter code

Browser—a software program used to access websites or documents on the WWW. Netscape, Yahoo, Microsoft Internet Explorer, are browsers.

Case-sensitive—refers to upper- and lower-case letters; some browsers are case-sensitive and it will make a difference in the relative success of a search to know this.

GIF—graphic interchange format, a type of image file.

Homepage—the main web page for a business, organization, or individual. Usually introduces the user to the site and contains directions for navigating through the site.

JPEG—joint photographic experts group, a type of image file that stores photographic images better than a GIF file.

Keyword—word or phrase used to search a database or search engine by subject.

Link—a connection to another document or site, can be internal (connects to document or page within the website) or external (connects to document or page at a different website). Links are generally indicated by a different color; when the cursor is moved over a link, it will turn into a hand shape.

CHAPTER 8

USE OF MEDICAL CONSULTANTS

§ 8.18 —National Committee for Quality Assurance

Page 367, add at end of section:

The National Committee for Quality Assurance (NCQA) continues to collect data on existing Health Plan Employer Data and Information Set (HEDIS) indicators as well as develop new ones. The HEDIS comparative data provides one of the most comprehensive views of managed care plans (HMOs) available to purchasers and consumers. In 2004, HEDIS will have over 50 measures across the 8 domains of care (see § **8.19,** page 368 of main text). As of this writing, newly proposed 2004 measures are in draft. These measures are designed to address gaps in existing measures, specifically overuse and misuse, while maintaining consistency in measurement. Eleven new measures are proposed:

- Three service measures: claims timeliness, call answer timeliness, call abandonment that will apply to both HMOs and PPOs,
- Two antibiotic prescribing practice measures covering appropriate treatment of children with URI and antibiotic treatment of children with pharyngitis,
- Outpatient management of heart failure,
- Colorectal cancer screening,
- Management of urinary incontinence in older adults,
- Osteoporosis management in women with fractures, and
- Two substance abuse measures: identification and treatment of alcohol abuse and other drug abuse.

When approved in their final form, these measures will become part of the HEDIS data set.

Partnership for Human Research Protection

In January 2003, a partnership was formed between JCAHO and NCQA to develop a new program for accrediting human research programs. This program, the Partnership for Human Research Protection (PHRP), will develop standards designed to protect safety and rights of participants in clinical trials and research programs in public and private hospitals, academic medical centers, and other research centers. The program's set of national standards and voluntary review process will complement current regulatory efforts. Release of final standards is expected in April 2003, and reviews will begin shortly after. Components of the accreditation standards include

- organization responsibilities,
- Institutional Review Board structure and operations,
- consideration of risks and benefits, and
- informed consent.

It is envisioned that this program will fill an identified need for additional human research protection for subjects participating in research programs; a need that is driven by dramatic increases in biomedical research, drug trials, and other studies.

§ 8.19 —HEDIS Indicators

Page 368, add to § 8.19:

HEDIS indicators are revised frequently; data collection methodology changes, new indicators are developed, existing indicators are deleted. Although indicators may differ slightly according to product line (Medicare, commercial, or Medicaid), many are common to all. Six additional outcome measures are being developed for HEDIS 2000. The new measures, which expand the focus on areas that affect the health of large numbers of Americans, include:

- Controlling hypertension—to measure the percentage of plan members whose blood pressure is brought within a target range

- Appropriate use of medications for people with asthma—to evaluate the appropriate use of drug regimes for asthmatics, especially anti-inflammatory medications

- ED visits for asthma—to identify people with asthma receiving emergency room care
- Chlamydia screening—to assess screening for sexually active women ages 15 to 25
- Menopause measure—to assess health plans' efforts to counsel women about hormone replacement therapy
- Comprehensive diabetes care—to look at comprehensiveness of diabetes care, including blood sugar testing and control, cholesterol screening and control, frequency of retinal examinations, and monitoring for kidney disease

§ 8.20—Foundation for Accountability (FACCT)

Page 369, add at the end of the first paragraph:

FACCT evaluates the utility of their indicators and measurement tools on an ongoing basis. As of 2003, FACCT has organized current measurement tools on their website in the Consumer Information Framework. The framework contains five categories that reflect how consumers think about their care. Comparative information is contained within each category. The five categories and information they contain are

1. The basics—access to care, customer service, and satisfaction.
2. Staying healthy—preventative care, reduction of health risks, early detection of illness, and education.
3. Getting better—recovery through appropriate treatment and follow-up.
4. Living with illness—for ongoing, chronic conditions: self-care, symptom control, complication avoidance, and maintenance of activities of daily living. Information is available on the following conditions: asthma, diabetes, heart care, and HIV.
5. Changing needs—coping skills needed as a result of dramatic changes in lifestyle due to disability or terminal illness.

Child and Adolescent Health Measurement Initiative

FACCT is also coordinating the work of the Child and Adolescent Health Measurement Initiative (CAHMI). This group's goal is to improve health-care and quality measurement for children and adolescents. It is a collaborative effort among consumer and health-care provider organizations, public and private sector purchasers, and policymakers.

FACCT and the Leapfrog Group

Another major FACCT initiative has been their partnership with the Leapfrog Group. The Leapfrog Group is a non-profit coalition of more than 90 public and private organizations that provide health-care benefits. The group began in 2000, with the backing of many large employer groups that were concerned about the safety of health-care delivery in hospitals and the impact of medical mistakes on employee health. This concern was driven by the findings in a 1999 Institute of Medicine publication, "To Err is Human: Building a Safer Health System," on hospital safety in America. This comprehensive study found that many medical mistakes made in hospitals were preventable. The study also included a series of recommendations designed to minimize the occurrence of mistakes. See § **8.2** for a more detailed summary of study findings.

The Leapfrog group's purpose is to help consumers make more informed decisions about their health care, with a major emphasis on choosing hospitals utilizing three practices that have demonstrated reduction in *preventable* mistakes. The three identified hospital practices are:

1. Use of computerized physician order entry system.
2. Have proven outcomes or extensive experience with specific procedures.
3. Have adequately staffed Intensive Care Units by MDs and other staff trained in critical care.

Although there are many additional practices that can reduce preventable mistakes, Leapfrog has chosen the above three as their initial areas of focus. The group estimates that these three steps together could prevent approximately 60,000 hospital deaths and more than half a million serious medication errors annually.

§ 8.21 HEALTH CARE INSTITUTION STANDARDS

FACCT, in partnership with a communications firm, has developed a toolkit for Leapfrog Group members to use in the marketing of healthcare services to prospective purchasers. Use of the toolkit materials is voluntary and designed to assist group members in their communications with potential healthcare purchasers.

Clearinghouse for Consumer-Centered Health

The FACCT website also contains a page for the *Clearinghouse for Consumer-Centered Health Care.* The page has five icons representing the following different interest groups:

- Consumers
- Health-care providers
- Health-care purchasers
- Health plans and insurers
- Policymakers and researchers

Within each section is a wealth of resources including additional websites, tools, and other resources. The site is very user-friendly and easy to navigate. More detailed information on all FACCT activities is available on their website: http://www.facct.org.

§ 8.21 —Health Care Institution Standards

Page 370, add to end of § 8.21:

JCAHO also sponsors the ORYNX® initiative, a program that integrates outcomes and other performance measurement data into the accreditation process. Introduced in 1997, ORYNX was designed to implemented in phases, ultimately using nationally standardized performance measures that allow for comparative data for outcome measures. In February 2000, JCAHO approved the first five core measure sets and a plan for introducing them into the accreditation process. Core measure set areas are:

- acute myocardial infarction, including coronary artery disease
- heart failure
- pneumonia

145

- surgical procedures and complications
- pregnancy and related conditions, including newborn and maternal care

Pilot testing in selected states began in 2001, focusing on acute myocardial infarction, heart failure, and pneumonia measures. Information gained from the pilot will used to develop the plan for full implementation. Ultimately, organizations seeking accreditation will be required to utilize a database to compare their outcomes and other clinical data through national benchmarking established under the ORYNX program.

JCAHO continues its work with ORYNX data collection and revisions for health-care institution accreditation standards. Additionally, in July 2002 the organization added patient safety as an accreditation focus. Driven by the National Institute of Medicine study on medical mistakes in hospitals cited in the following text, JCAHO developed the following framework for patient safety goals:

- No more than six goals established for any given year.
- No more than two recommendations/goals.
- Yearly evaluation of goal effectiveness—some may continue while others may be replaced because of new priorities.

Sentinel Event Identification and Reporting

Ensuring patient safety has always been within the purview of JCAHO accreditation standards. In the 1990s the organization, through its Sentinel Event Policy, began to require in-depth review of cases of medical errors that resulted in severe patient harm or death. Types of Sentinel Events include:

- medicine errors,
- wrong site surgery,
- restraint related deaths,
- blood transfusion errors,
- inpatient suicides,
- infant abductions, and
- fatal falls.

§ 8.21   HEALTH CARE INSTITUTION STANDARDS

Organizations are required to report all Sentinel Events to JCAHO. The report must include findings of an in-depth case review using root cause analysis methodology on why the incident occurred as well as an action plan designed to prevent similar incidents. Information gained from Sentinel Events is shared with member organizations through JCAHO's "Sentinel Event Alerts" newsletters.

National Institute of Medicine Study

In 1999, concern over patient safety reached new levels with the publication of a National Institute of Medicine (IOM) study, "To Err is Human: Building a Safer Health System." Findings from study included the following:

- Every year, between 44,000 and 98,000 people die in America's hospitals as a result of medical errors.
- Medical mistakes cause more deaths annually than car accidents, breast cancer, and AIDS.
- Medication errors alone, in or out of the hospital, are estimated to account or over 7,000 deaths annually.

The study concluded that a comprehensive approach to patient safety was needed and developed recommendations in four broad areas:

- Establishing a national focus to create leadership, research, tools, and protocols to enhance the knowledge base about safety,
- Identifying and learning from errors through immediate and strong mandatory reporting as well as encouragement of voluntary reporting, both with the aim of making systems safer for patients. The group strongly recommended that peer review protection from disclosure be extended to information in the system.
- Raising standards and expectations for improvements in safety through oversight organizations, group purchasers, and professional groups, and
- Creating safety systems inside health-care organizations through the implementation of safe practices at the delivery level.

These study recommendations created the impetus for organizations

147

such as JCAHO and FACCT to incorporate patient safety into their goals. For JCAHO, the Sentinel Event Alert Advisory Group undertook this work.

JCAHO Sentinel Event Alert Advisory Group

The Sentinel Advisory Group was formed February 2002 and charged with conducting thorough review of all past JCAHO Sentinel Event Alert recommendations to assess:

1. face validity and evidence for the recommendations, and
2. practicality and cost effectiveness of implementing them.

Utilizing this process and their framework cited above, JCAHO finalized six patient safety goals for 2003 accreditation.The goals include specific implementation practices that are designed to standardize the risk-reduction strategies hospitals use.

Surveys will include evidence for implementation of JCAHO recommendations or acceptable alternatives. The organization must demonstrate that alternatives are at least as effective as published recommendations in achieving the specific patient safety goal. Failure to implement patient safety goals will result in a Type 1 (most serious) recommendation. Although more goals are expected to be added in the future, the 2003 goals focus on 6 areas:

Goal 1—Improve accuracy of patient identification.

- Use at least two patient identifiers when taking blood, giving meds or blood products.
- Prior to start of surgery or invasive procedure, verify identification information with active communication.

Goal 2—Improve communication effectiveness among caregivers.

- Implement process that requires "read back" to verify verbal and telephone orders.
- Standardize organization abbreviations, acronyms, and symbols. In-

148

clude list of what not to use. Refer to § **5.20** for more information on potential pitfalls of abbreviations.

Goal 3—Improve safety of using high-alert meds.

- Remove concentrated electrolytes from patient floors, e.g., potassium and sodium chloride > 0.9%.
- Standardize/limit numbers of drug concentrations available in the organizations.

Goal 4—Eliminate wrong-site, wrong-patient, wrong-procedure surgery.

- Create/use pre-op verification process to confirm all necessary information is available.
- Implement a process for the marking of the surgical site and involve the patient in the process.

Goal 5—Improve safety of using infusion pumps.

- Ensure free flow protection on all infusion and PCA pumps.

Goal 6—Improve effectiveness of clinical alarm systems.

- Regular preventive maintenance and testing of alarm systems.
- Alarms activated with appropriate setting and sufficiently audible.

Approval for alternative goal implementation approaches must be requested from JCAHO. Requests submitted reviewed by the JCAHO Sentinel Event Advisory Group and approved or denied.

Office of Quality Monitoring

JCAHO's Office of Quality Monitoring evaluates and tracks complaints and concerns about health-care organizations involving quality-of-care issues. Information about these concerns comes from many sources, including patients, families, public, and an organization's own staff. Concerns may be reported in many ways, including the phone Hot Line (800) 994-6610, email, or written reports.

JCAHO reviews the organization's most recent accreditation information and depending on nature of the concern, can take any of following actions:

- Incorporate into quality database to track over time (ID trends)
- Ask organization to provide written response
- Review with related standard at time of accreditation
- Conduct unannounced site visit

Regardless of the type of action taken, JCAHO requires that all incident investigation responses submitted by the organization must demonstrate an effective system to address

- identification of errors,
- root cause analysis,
- compilation of data on error frequency,
- dissemination of findings to allow redesign of systems, and
- assessment of effectiveness of actions to reduce errors over time.

Data collection began in July 2002. Over time, results will be used by JCAHO to focus on site survey evaluation.

§ 8.22 —Clinical Practice Guidelines

Page 372, replace last paragraph of § 8.22 with:

As of 1996, AHCPR stopped internal development of clinical practice guidelines, but now helps groups in the private sector develop them. This work occurs at regional evidence-based practice centers around the country. The Institute of Medicine defines *evidence-based clinical practice guidelines* thus: "Clinical practice guidelines are systematically developed statements to assist practitioner and patient decisions about appropriate health care for specific clinical conditions."

Evidence-based medicine collects information that is patient-reported, clinician-observed, and research-derived. This information is synthesized and the strength of the evidence evaluated and used to develop guidelines. In 1999 the Department of Health and Human Services, AHCPR launched an Internet-based repository for evidence-based clinical guidelines. Known as the National Guideline Clearinghouse (NGC), this site is operated in partnership with the American Medical Association (AMA) and the American Association of Health Plans (AAHP). The NCG gives clinicians easy access to the latest clinical information on a wide range of diagnoses, including standardized abstracts and tables that allow comparison of different guidelines. It also has discussion groups and annotated bibliographies on guideline development methodologies, implementation, and use. The information is intended primarily for health professionals, but can also be useful to other audiences, including patients. Links to patient resources include, in part:

- Consumer pages for AAHP, AMA, AHCPR
- Consumer magazine of the FDA
- MedlinePlus (U.S. National Library of Medicine)
- PDG—National Cancer Institute database
- Consumer information from the National Institutes of Health (NIH)

Consider the utility of the NGC when performing medical research. Its website address is www.guidelines.gov.

Case law for failure to follow clinical practice guidelines does exist. In *Lowry v. Henry Mayo Newhall Memorial Hospital* (185 Cal.App.3d 188) a malpractice suit was brought against a physician for treatment administered during CPR. The physician administered atropine instead of epinephrine as recommended under American Heart Association guidelines.

The decedent was admitted to the hospital following an auto accident. While hospitalized, she sustained a cardiac arrest. A Code Blue was called and the defendant physician responded as designated head of the hospital's team. Resuscitation efforts were not successful.

The trial court granted summary judgment to the physician; the decision was appealed and upheld based on the following:

1. Statutory immunity to physicians responding to hospital emergency applied as designated, nonvolunteer, non-Good Samaritan member of the hospital resuscitation team.
2. The physician did not engage in malpractice by administering atropine instead of epinephrine as recommended under American Heart Association guidelines.

§ 8.49 —State Jury Verdict Reports

*Page 401, replace **Table 8–1** with:*

Table 8–1
Jury Verdict Reporters

State	Reporting Service
Alaska	*Jury Verdicts Northwest, Inc.* P.O. Box 1165, Seattle, WA 98111 Phone: (425) 774-0530 Fax: (425) 778-4502 E-mail: jurynw@aol.com
Arizona	*The Trial Reporter of Central and Northern Arizona* *The Trial Reporter of Southern Arizona* Verdict Summaries and Research P.O. Box 8187, Phoenix, AZ 85066-8187 Phone: (800) 266-7773 Fax: (800) 266-3131; (602) 276-5133
California	*Confidential Report for Attorneys* 503 Vista Bella, Suite 12, Oceanside, CA 92057-7006 Phone: (800) 237-6525; (760) 721-3622 Fax: (760) 721-3683 E-mail: editor@caljury.com *Jury Verdicts Weekly* 738 Montecito, Santa Rosa, CA 95409-2997 Phone: (707) 539-5454 Fax: (707) 539-1839 *Tri-Service Weekly Jury Verdict Report* P.O. Box 270770, San Diego, CA 92198-2770 Phone: (619) 487-6194 Fax: (619) 487-0083 *Trials Digest* 1144 65th Street, Suite D, Oakland, CA 94608-2000 Phone: (510) 420-1800 [CHECK OUT AREA CODE] Fax: (510) 420-8006 E-mail: wolfe@trialsdigest.com *Verdictum Juris* P.O. Box 270770, San Diego, CA 92198-2770 Phone: (619) 487-6194 Fax: (619) 487-0083

Table 8–1 *(continued)*

State	Reporting Service
Colorado	*Jury Verdict Reporter of Colorado* 7396 South Garfield Court, Littleton, CO 80122-2201 Phone: (303) 779-4073 Fax: (303) 779-5311
Connecticut	*Connecticut Verdict Reporter* P.O. Box 709, Crestwood, KY 40014-0709 Phone: (800) 445-3165 Fax: (502) 241-6161 E-mail: solarity@ka.net
District of Columbia	*Metro Verdicts Monthly* P.O. Box 709, Crestwood, KY 40014-0709 Phone: (800) 445-3165 Fax: (502) 241-6161 E-mail: solarity@ka.net
Florida	*Florida Jury Verdict Reporter* P.O. Box 3730, Tallahassee, FL 32315-3730 Phone: (800) 446-2998, (850) 224-6649 Fax: (850) 222-6266 E-mail: fljury@aol.com *Jury Trials and Tribulations* 9100 South Dadeland Blvd., Suite 400 Miami, FL 33156-7819 Phone: (305) 670-9735 Fax: (305) 670-6146 E-mail: verdicts@gate.net
Georgia	*JAS Publications* P.O. Box 709, Crestwood, KY 40014-0709 Phone: (800) 445-3165 Fax: (502) 241-6161 E-mail: solarity@ka.net
Hawaii	*Jury Verdicts Weekly* 738 Montecito, Santa Rosa, CA 95409-2997 Phone: (707) 539-5454 Fax: (707) 539-1839

Table 8–1 *(continued)*

State	Reporting Service
	Personal Injury Judgments Hawaii 47-378 Hui Koloa Place, Kaneohe, HI 96744 Phone: (808) 239-9639 Fax: (808) 531-0053
Idaho	*Jury Verdicts Northwest, Inc.* P.O. Box 1165, Seattle, WA 98111 Phone: (425) 774-0530 Fax: (425) 778-4502 E-mail: jurynw@aol.com
	Rocky Mountain Verdicts and Settlements P.O. Box 571261, Murray, UT 84157-1261 Phone: (801) 268-2321 Fax: (801) 263-0338
Illinois	*Cook County Jury Verdict Reporter* 415 North State Street, Chicago, IL 60610-4674 Phone: (312) 644-7800 Fax: (312) 644-5990 E-mail: kirkton@lawbulletin.com
	Jury Verdict Reporting Service 2440 S. Brentwood Blvd., Suite 102, St. Louis, MO 63144-2327 Phone: (314) 962-7500 Fax: (314) 962-6864
Kansas	*Greater Kansas City Jury Verdict Service* 4418 West 72nd Terrace, Prairie Village, KS 66208-2822 Phone: (913) 362-2909 E-mail: fsmithkc@gte.net
Louisiana	*Blue Sheet of Louisiana* 8323 Southwest Freeway, Suite 370, Houston, TX 77079 Phone: (800) 783-0313 Fax: (713) 772-1935 E-mail: bluesht@bluesheet.com
Maryland	*Metro Verdicts Monthly* P.O. Box 709, Crestwood, KY 40014-0709 Phone: (800) 445-3165 Fax: (502) 241-6161 E-mail: solarity@ka.net

Table 8–1 *(continued)*

State	Reporting Service
Massachusetts	*Massachusetts Verdict Reporter* P.O. Box 709, Crestwood, KY 40014-0709 Phone: (800) 445-3165 Fax: (502) 241-6161 E-mail: solarity@ka.net
Michigan	*Michigan Trial Reporter* P.O. Box 709, Crestwood, KY 40014-0709 Phone: (800) 445-3165 Fax: (502) 241-6161 E-mail: solarity@ka.net
Missouri	*Greater Kansas City Jury Verdict Service* 4418 West 72nd Terrace, Prairie Village, KS 66208-2822 Phone: (913) 362-2909 E-mail: fsmithkc@gte.net *Jury Verdict Reporting Service* 2440 S. Brentwood Blvd., Suite 102 St. Louis, MO 63144-2327 Phone: (314) 962-7500 Fax: (314) 962-6864
Nevada	*Jury Verdicts Weekly* 738 Montecito, Santa Rosa, CA 95409-2997 Phone: (707) 539-5454 Fax: (707) 539-1839
New Mexico	*Blue Sheet of New Mexico* 8323 Southwest Freeway, Suite 370, Houston, TX 77079 Phone: (800) 783-0313 Fax: (713) 772-1935 E-mail: bluesht@bluesheet.com
New York	*New York Jury Verdict Reporter* 128 Carleton Avenue, East Islip, N.Y. 11730 Phone: (800) 832-1900; (516) 581-1930 Fax: (516) 581-8937 E-mail: info@moranlaw.com
Ohio	*Ohio Trial Reporter* P.O. Box 709, Crestwood, KY 40014-0709 Phone: (800) 445-3165 Fax: (502) 241-6161 E-mail: solarity@ka.net

Table 8–1 *(continued)*

State	Reporting Service
Oregon	*Jury Verdicts Northwest, Inc.* P.O. Box 1165, Seattle, WA 98111 Phone: (425) 774-0530 Fax: (425) 778-4502 E-mail: jurynw@aol.com
Rhode Island	*Rhode Island Verdict Reporter* P.O. Box 709, Crestwood, KY 40014-0709 Phone: (800) 445-3165 Fax: (502) 241-6161 E-mail: solarity@ka.net
Tennessee	*Tennessee Litigation Reporter* 901 Church Street, Nashville, TN 37203-3411 Phone: (615) 255-6288 Fax: (615) 255-6289 E-mail: llaska@verdicts.com
Texas	*Blue Sheet of Texas* 8323 Southwest Freeway, Suite 370, Houston, TX 77079 Phone: (800) 783-0313 Fax: (713) 772-1935 E-mail: bluesht@bluesheet.com *East Texas Trial Reports* P.O. Box 342, Scurry, Texas 75158 Phone: (214) 452-8590 *North Texas Reports* 3332 Harwood Road, Suite 360, Bedford, TX 76021-3904 Phone: (800) 600-2015; (602) 395-9141 Fax: (800) 600-2025 *Texas Reporter-Soele's Trial Report* 12500 San Pedro, Suite 410, San Antonio, TX 78216-2858 Phone: (210) 496-1750 (210) 496-1751 E-mail: jeff@texasreporter.com *Trial Report Service, Inc.* 5405 Hidalgo Court, Garland, TX 75043-5517 Phone: (972) 686-8080 Fax: (972) 686-4141 E-mail: verdicts@airmail.net

Table 8–1 *(continued)*

State	Reporting Service
Utah	*Rocky Mountain Verdicts and Settlements* P.O. Box 571261, Murray, UT 84157-1261 Phone: (801) 268-2321 Fax: (801) 263-0338
Virginia	*Metro Verdicts Monthly* P.O. Box 709, Crestwood, KY 40014-0709 Phone: (800) 445-3165 Fax: (502) 241-6161 E-mail: solarity@ka.net
Washington	*Jury Verdicts Northwest, Inc.* P.O. Box 1165, Seattle, WA 98111 Phone: (425) 774-0530 Fax: (425) 778-4502 E-mail: jurynw@aol.com
Wisconsin	*Wisconsin Jury Verdict* 621 16th Street, Racine, WI 53403 Phone: (414) 635-0400 Fax: (414) 635-0416
Wyoming	*Rocky Mountain Verdicts and Settlements* P.O. Box 571261, Murray, UT 84157-1261 Phone: (801) 268-2321 Fax: (801) 263-0338

§ 8.52   —Areas of Litigation Against Managed Care

Page 407, add before first full paragraph:

In deciding cases of vicarious liability, the determination of employer-employee relationship is critical as it relates to control of care delivery. If the MCO controls care delivered by their providers, finding of vicarious liability under respondeat superior is likely. Critical issues to determine are:

1. right of employer to control work performed
2. method of provider payment for work performed
3. skill required in specific provider occupation

4. determination of whether employer supplies or equipment

5. belief of parties as to the nature of the employer-employee relationship.

Page 407, add after bulleted list:

One key strategy to minimizing risk of corporate liability is thorough documentation of providers' credentials, including:

1. definition of credentialing process in organization bylaws

2. development of credentialing processes and procedures

3. detailing credentialing requirements in all practitioner contracts.

In *Hughes v. Blue Cross of Northern California* (215 Cal.App.3d 832) corporate liability for utilization management procedures was at issue in the complaint for breach of good faith and fair dealing from coverage denial for psychiatric hospitalization of plaintiff's son.

The case involved a 21 year old male who overdosed on aspirin and stabbed himself in the abdomen with a screwdriver. He was admitted to a psychiatric hospital where he received treatment for approximately 6 weeks. During the period of hospitalization, the patient did not respond well to treatment, and expressed grandiose delusions characteristic of schizophrenia to his psychiatrist. Eventually, the patient was discharged to a half way house when his symptoms improved, although his "instability was always apparent." Shortly after his discharge to the half-way house, the patient ran away, returning to his mother's house and repeating overdose attempts that precipitated his first hospitalization. He was readmitted to the psychiatric hospital and again discharged after treatment, but rehospitalized five times over the next 7 month period because of repeated outpatient treatment failures. He was finally admitted to a long-term psychiatric care facility.

Plaintiff's action concerned two periods of hospitalizations. The insurer only paid only a small portion of the submitted costs, disallowing the balance on the grounds that the hospitalizations were not medically necessary. At trial, it was determined that during the utilization review process by the physician reviewer, no attempt was made to secure all pertinent medical information relevant to the claim, nor was there any attempt to communicate with the treating physician before denying the claim. Based on this testimony, the jury could reasonably infer that the insurer em-

158

ployed a standard of medical necessity markedly at variance from that of the psychiatric community in California. Therefore, there was not good faith effort on the part of the insurer to properly investigate the claim.

The court entered judgment in favor of plaintiff. The case was appealed and decision affirmed. The courts held that:

1. Insurer breached covenant by employing a standard of medical necessity that was significantly at variance with community and by failing to properly investigate insured's claim
2. Evidence supported award of punitive damages
3. Insurer waived issue of ERISA preemption by failing to raise it as affirmative defense.

Page 407, add before last full paragraph:

The goal of all utilization management programs should be to render quality medical care in a cost effective manner and ensure that all members receive this care in line with their benefit plan. Utilization management programs typically use the following types of review to accomplish these goals:

1. Prospective. Requires prior approval before a treatment can be rendered. This type of review has the potential to create liability if the patient believes treatment is denied solely on the basis of cost.
2. Concurrent. Monitors hospital length of stay and evaluates the necessity for continued hospitalization.
3. Retrospective. Performed after services have been rendered. Usually this review method does not impact actual delivery of service, but may affect provider reimbursement for the service.

In all cases, utilization management programs must demonstrate that policies, procedures, and practices are in place that protect the right of the patient to receive medically necessary care.

In *Wickline v. State of California* (192 Cal.App.3d 1630) plaintiff brought action against her insurer Medi-Cal (State of California) after undergoing amputation of her leg as a result of alleged premature discharge for the hospital. The case involved a female patient admitted to the hospital with severe vascular disease resulting from occlusion of her aorta. This condition was treated surgically with removal of the occluded portion of the aorta and insertion of aortic graft. The patient had a stormy post-operative course requiring two additional operations, one to remove a clot in the graft and a second to relieve spasms in the blood vessels that were impeding blood flow to her lower extremities. After the second surgery, the patient's physicians felt it was medically necessary for the patient to stay in the hospital eight days beyond the number of days initially authorized, and this request was submitted to Medi-Cal. Medi-Cal reviewers authorized four additional days, a decision not questioned by the treating physicians. The patient was discharged four days later, with the agreement of her attending physicians, medically stable.

Within the first few days after discharge to home, the patient began experiencing color changes and increased pain in her right lower extremity. Nine days after discharge, the patient was emergently readmitted to the hospital and found to have wound infection and color changes in her right leg. Eventually, the patient underwent an amputation of her right leg for a clot and infection in her graft.

At the trial court level, the jury verdict in favor of the plaintiff, and the State appealed. The Court of Appeals reversed the lower court's decision, based on the following arguments:

1. Patient who is harmed when care that should have been provided and is not should recover from all responsible, including, when appropriate, health care payor.
2. Third party payors of health care services can be held legally accountable when medically inappropriate decisions result from design or implementation defects in cost containment mechanisms.
3. Physicians who comply without protest with payor decisions cannot escape responsibility for the patient's care.
4. Medi-Cal was not liable for the discharge decision. (The treating physicians did not dispute the four day extension by Medi-Cal.)

In *Wilson v. Blue Cross of Southern California* (222 Cal.App3d 660) the mother of a patient brought action against her health insurer and the contractor who performed utilization review. She sought to recover for her son's suicide after he was discharged from a psychiatric hospital following notification that his insurance benefits had been discontinued.

The decedent was admitted to the hospital suffering from major depression, drug dependency, and anorexia. His physician determined that three to four weeks of hospitalization were medically indicated. After 10 days of hospitalization, the insurer denied further payment. The patient was discharged and committed suicide shortly thereafter. The *Wickline* case was used by plaintiff's bar as precedent for the insurer's liability.

The trial court entered summary judgment in favor the defendant; this decision was appealed. The appellate court reversed the decision and remanded the case for retrial, holding that:

1. Contractor could be partially liable if their conduct was a substantial factor in bringing about the suicide, and
2. Whether conduct was substantial factor in causing suicide was question of fact precluding summary judgment.

The court ruled that the *Wickline* decision pertained to discharge under Medi-Cal and did not apply to those insured under a policy issued in the private sector. In remanding the case for retrial, the court determined the critical question to answer was whether or not the decision to discharge was a substantial factor in the patient's suicide. The above cases illustrate the liability potential of utilization review programs. Managed Care Organization can however, mitigate this risk potential through development of programs that:

- Allow providers to exercise independent clinical judgment.
- Require providers to document and communicate plan of care (to both patient and UM reviewer) and medical necessity for treatment.
- Encourage patient communication regarding the appeals process when MCO denies care as recommended by the provider.

Page 409, delete last paragraph and insert the following:

In 2000, the House passed a Patient's Bill of Rights which, among other provisions, gives Americans the right to challenge medical decisions made by insurers and HMO's. As of this printing, the bill is currently in the Senate, but has not yet been passed. At issue is the language that would give patients the right to sue their HMO. In an attempt to reach Senate approval of a Patient's Bill of Rights, two competing bills are being considered: one sponsored by Senators John McCain, R-Ariz, Edward Kennedy, D-Mass, and John Edwards D-NC; the second sponsored by Senators John Breaux D-La and Bill Frist R-Tenn. While both have language that allows patients to sue their HMO, there are major differences in the scope of the right to sue provision. The McCain-Kennedy-Edwards bill permits suit in both state and federal courts and caps damages at $5 million. In contrast, the Breaux-Frist bill allows suits only in federal courts and caps damages at $500,000. Both bills have severe opposition from the insurance industry and corporate America. American business concerns are greatest for companies that are self-insured and manage their own health plans. These companies make final decisions on medical care for their employees. Opponents to this provision contend that it is vague and ambiguous and this language could potentially extend to other companies.

In addition to the right to sue provision in the national Patient's Bill of Rights, 38 states have passed bills that allow patients to appeal medical decisions to external review boards; 7 states have passed bills allowing patients to sue HMO's; and 26 more are considering them. To date, the states with right to sue bills have not shown massive increases in litigation. Problems that do arise in states with right to sue bills center on determining which groups or individuals are permitted to sue HMO's and which are prevented. The principle cause of this disparity is the 26 million workers nationally who are not covered by state laws and the 55 million who are excluded from state laws by ERISA (see **§ 8.51, page 404**).

For states that have passed bills allowing patients to appeal medical decisions to external review boards, overall experience to date demonstrates that external review processes can work smoothly. While these review processes differ from state to state, many have similar requirements:

1. State selects an independent review organization to review all appeals.
2. Patients requesting appeals inform the provider who made the decision, which then sends pertinent medical information to the external review board.
3. Specialists employed by the board review the medical information and reach a decision within a specified time from claim filing date, often 15–30 days for nonurgent claims and 24–72 hours for urgent care claims.

To date decisions reached by external review boards are running 50-50 between health plans and patients, but the volume of appeals is relatively low. Low volume may be due to the newness of many laws and/or public unawareness of existing appeal rights.

MEDICAL RECORDS IN LITIGATION AND AT TRIAL
[New]

*Page 411, replace **Chapter 9** with the following:*

§ 9.1   Introduction—Independent Medical Examinations

Litigation is propelled by discovery and when discovery is completed, the case is ready either for settlement of the matter through mediation or arbitration, or for trial. One of the more important discovery devices is the independent medical examination.

§ 9.2   Criteria for Independent Medical Examinations

Federal Rules of Civil Procedure (Fed. R. Civ. P.) 35 permits the use of a physical or mental examination as a means of discovery. Examinations are appropriate in actions in which the mental or physical condition of a person is in controversy. This can include actions in which an individual's blood group is at issue. This type of examination is commonly referred to as an independent medical examination (IME) or defense medical examination (DME).

§ 9.3   History

The foundation for the use of medical examinations in litigation in California was laid in *Johnston v. Southern Pacific* (1907) 150 Cal. 535. Plaintiff sued for a skull fracture and brain hemorrhage she sustained when the train from which she was exiting made a sudden, violent movement. The defense asked that she undergo a physical examination by two physicians. The trial court denied the motion because it felt that it lacked the power to make such an order.

On review, the California Supreme Court determined that courts did have the power to order examinations of this type and should exercise this power with "sound discretion." The court held that the denial of such power to the trial court would leave the defendant completely at the mercy of the plaintiff's medical witnesses and would constitute an injustice so gross and intolerable that it must be avoided, even at some cost to the "refined and delicate feelings of the plaintiff."

§ 9.4   When Examinations Are Appropriate

The medical examination as a discovery tool is appropriate only on a showing that the physical or mental condition of the individual is actually *at issue or in controversy* in the case and that *good cause* exists for the examination. Fed. R. Civ. P. 35(a). Often these requirements are interwoven.

In general practice, medical examinations are most frequently used by the defense in personal injury cases. The filing of a personal injury complaint by the plaintiff places his or her physical condition at issue and provides the defense with good cause to seek a physical examination.

A plaintiff who is making a claim for emotional distress or other psychological condition *suffered as a result of the incident* has placed his or her mental condition at issue. Under these circumstances, the defense is entitled to a mental examination of the plaintiff. However, the act of filing a personal injury action seeking general damages for pain and suffering does not put the plaintiff's general mental condition at issue and does not make pre-injury and post-injury records discoverable. (See *Houghton v. M&F Fishing, Inc.* (S.D. Cal. 2001) 198 F.R.D. 666, 669.) Generally speaking, an additional element is required, e.g. a separate cause of action for negligent or intentional infliction of emotional distress or plaintiff's designation of an expert witness to testify to the distress. (See *Turner v. Imperial Stores* (S.D. Cal. 1995) 161 F.R.D. 89, 92-97.)

§ 9.5   Who May Be Examined

Fed. R. Civ. P. 35 and the California Code of Civil Procedure §2032(a) allow a physical or mental examination of the following categories of individuals:

- Any party to the action.
- A natural person in the "custody or legal control" of a party. Parties are required to make a "good faith effort" to produce persons over whom they have control, for example, minor children. This may also extend, upon proper showing, to a executor being required to produce the body of a decedent. *In re Certain Asbestos Cases* (N.D. Tex. 1986) 112 F.R.D. 427, 433. See, however, *Holm v. Superior Court* (1986) 187 Cal. App. 3d 1241, 232 Cal. Rptr. 432, in which the court held that even though the physical or mental condition of a decedent may be in controversy, the exhumation of a corpse for an autopsy was not allowed.

Some jurisdictions will allow an agent or employee of a named party to be ordered to undergo a medical examination. For example, the court may order a defendant corporation, sued as a result of the alleged negligence of its driver, to produce that employee for a compulsory medical examination, even though the driver has not been named as a party. There is no sanction, however, against a nonparty agent or employee who refuses to undergo a court-ordered medical examination. Any sanctions awarded would run against the party who has custody or control of the individual, or who employs the individual whose examination has been ordered. The sanction can be avoided by demonstrating an inability to produce that person for examination (California Code of Civil Procedure § 2032(f)).

§ 9.6   Examination of Party

The most obvious candidate for a medical examination is the personal injury plaintiff who is asking the court to resolve issues concerning his or her medical condition. Some jurisdictions do not limit examination of a "party" solely to the plaintiff, however. California Code of Civil Procedure § 2032 allows that the medical examination of a defendant may be obtained where that party's physical or mental condition is the suspected cause of the incident. For example, the plaintiff may allege that the defendant's physical condition (such as poor eyesight) acted, or should have acted, as a bar to operating a vehicle. In this case, an ophthalmologic examination of the defendant could be obtained.

In paternity determination cases, one or both of the parents may be directed to undergo blood tests. Where a libel case is based on defamatory assertions concerning the medical condition of the plaintiff, the defendant is entitled to a medical examination of the plaintiff to aid in the establishment of the affirmative defense of truth.

Keep in mind that "good cause" is the benchmark standard. In *Sacramona v. Bridgestone/Firestone, Inc.* (D. Mass. 1993) 152 F.R.D. 428, 431, the court denied a motion to compel the plaintiff to submit to a blood test to determine his HIV status. Defendant argued that plaintiff led a lifestyle exposing him to the risk of contracting HIV. The court held that despite the fact that Plaintiff was seeking future damages and AIDS would shorten his life expectancy, this did not rise to the level of placing his HIV status "in controversy."

In *Reuter v. Superior Court* (1979) 93 Cal. App. 3d 332, 155 Cal. Rptr. 525, the court held that in order to qualify for an examination, the person to be examined must be more than a *nominal* party. The defendant wanted the mother (and guardian ad litem) of a minor plaintiff to undergo a battery of mental tests collateral to those tests to be administered to her son. The court held that the requirement that a minor have an adult representative was no justification for ordering the guardian to submit to the invasion of her body or mental processes. In effect, the mother's mental condition was *not* in controversy and therefore she could not be subjected to an examination.

§ 9.7 Number of Examinations

Fed. R. Civ. P. 35(a) does not limit the number of examinations that may be ordered so long as "good cause" is shown for each examination requested, including mental examinations. In *Peters v. Nelson* (N.D. Iowa 1994) 153 F.R.D. 635, 638, the court allowed multiple mental examinations based on the fact that a substantial time lag occurred between the first examination and the trial.

Multiple medical examinations have been allowed under the following circumstances:

- Plaintiff alleges separate injuries requiring examination by different specialists (e.g., orthopedic and neurological);
- The examining physician requests the assistance of other consultants in making a diagnosis;

- It can be shown that the initial examination was incomplete or inadequate.

In California, the Code of Civil Procedure § 2032(c)(1) allows "any defendant" to demand one physical examination of the plaintiff or cross-complainant in a personal injury case. This would seem to allow each individual defendant and co-defendant the right to demand a separate physical examination on his or her own behalf. This section specifically allows third-party cross-defendants access to this discovery procedure as well.

§ 9.8 Examiner

A physical examination may be conducted by any "suitably licensed or certified" health care practitioner. Fed. R. Civ. P. 35(a). In the past, only licensed physicians could conduct examinations. However, the definition of licensed health care practitioner has been significantly expanded to include psychologists, chiropractors, dentists, physical therapists, speech pathologists, osteopaths, podiatrists, optometrists, and acupuncturists.

When determining the appropriate individual to perform an examination, the following should be considered.

Professional Qualifications and Experience. The nature and severity of the injury will determine the level of experience required. For example, if the plaintiff is alleging a closed head injury with cognitive and emotional residuals, a board-certified neurologist or neuropsychiatrist would be an appropriate choice.

Credibility. Medical practitioners who work exclusively for either plaintiff or defendant, or practitioners who do not have an active practice may have less credibility than individuals who are actively engaged in the care and treatment of patients and who have experience "on both sides of the fence."

Ability to Communicate. A medical examiner must be able to formulate his or her ideas on paper and in testimony in a manner that can be easily understood by all persons involved, including members of the jury, because the reality is that the IME physician will probably act as the defense medical expert.

In federal practice, the party seeking the medical examination chooses the person who will conduct it and the court generally appoints the examiner requested by the moving party. Trial courts have broad discretion to determine whether good cause exists for refusing to accept the examining party's choice of an examiner. However, a party's unsupported objections to a particular doctor conducting the examination should be given little weight. *Edwards v. Superior Court* (1976) 16 Cal. 3d 905, 913, 130 Cal. Rptr. 14; *Looney v. National Railroad Passenger Corp.* (D. Mass. 1992) 142 F.R.D. 264, 265, in which the court found it "immaterial" that the physician was "prodefendant."

§ 9.9   Time Frame

Although examinations may be set soon after the first appearance of a defendant, there are reasons to wait to schedule an examination. Most medical professionals who perform medical-legal examinations require a complete set of medical records and x-rays before or during the examination. It is reasonable therefore to wait until after discovery of the plaintiff's medical care or condition has progressed and copies of medical records have been obtained.

Because one of the objectives of a medical examination is to determine the extent of residual damage from the initial injury, it may be more appropriate to wait to schedule an examination until the plaintiff has achieved the maximum recovery that can be anticipated.

§ 9.10   Obtaining an Examination by Stipulation

In cases where the medical condition of the litigant is so obviously and importantly an issue that both sides recognize the need for an examination, Fed. R. Civ. P. 35(b)(c) allows the use of stipulations. More often than not, medical examinations are arranged in this manner between counsel. In fact, local federal rules require that, before moving for a court-ordered examination, the parties must first try to arrange for the examination by agreement. See N.D. Cal. Rule 37-1(a).

Examination by stipulation is most appropriate when:

§ 9.10   OBTAINING AN EXAMINATION BY STIPULATION

_____ The case is an action for personal injuries.

_____ The examinee is the plaintiff.

_____ The type of examination sought is physical.

_____ No previous examination has been obtained.

_____ The examination will be routine in nature with no diagnostic test or procedure that is painful, protracted, or intrusive.

Examination by stipulation is often arranged informally by telephone between counsel and confirmed by letter. However, confirming the stipulation formally in writing is strongly advised. (See **Form 9–1**—Stipulation for Medical Examination.) At this time, counsel can set forth the conditions for the medical examination, including a description of each test or procedure to be done as well as the conditions of the examination. Unless the stipulation expressly states otherwise, however, it will be deemed to incorporate all provisions of FRCP 35, including the requirements concerning the exchange of medical reports and the waiver of privileges. Fed. R. Civ. P. 35; California Code of Civil Procedure § 2032(h); *Grover v. Superior Court* (1958) 161 Cal. App. 2d 644, 327 P.2d 212.

FORM 9–1
STIPULATION FOR MEDICAL EXAMINATION

[Date] _____

[Name of Plaintiff's Attorney] _____

[Address] _____

[City, State, Zip] _____

Re:_____[name of case]_____

Dear Plaintiff's Attorney:

This letter is in confirmation that your client [name] will appear for a neurological medical examination to be conducted on [date] at [time] at the medical office of [identity of examiner]. The address and phone of Dr. [name] are [address and phone]. This examination may include the following: taking of oral history by Dr. [name]; physical examination including range of motion, gait and other tests; an electromyogram study.

Thank you for your cooperation in arranging this examination.

Very truly yours,

[Name of attorney]

Practice Note: Whether the examination is arranged by agreement or demand, determine as soon as possible the dates on which the plaintiff is available. Having a list of possible dates is helpful because it is difficult to obtain medical appointments, cancellations can result in significant charges, and most examination have to be set well in advance of the appointment date.

§ 9.11   Examination by Noticed Motion

When the medical examination involves more than the routine physical examination of a plaintiff, the likelihood of an examination by stipulation diminishes and it becomes more likely that the plaintiff will resist the examination. If the initial informal attempt to schedule the examination fails, leave of court must be obtained.

In federal court, if the parties have been unable to stipulate to the examination, a physical or mental examination may be obtained only by court order on noticed motion showing good cause. Fed. R. Civ. P. 35(a). Pursuant to that rule, the notice of motion must be directed to all parties and the potential examinee, showing with specificity the following:

- The date, time, place, and location of the examination;
- The manner, conditions, scope, and nature of the examination;
- The identity and specialty, if any, of the physician or other licensed health care provider who will perform the examination.

The showing of "good cause" requires that specific facts be set forth justifying this type of discovery, the need for the examination, and the inability or lack of means to obtain the information elsewhere. Be prepared to submit declarations in support of the motion indicating that the physical or mental condition to be examined has been placed in controversy, the facts constituting good cause, and explaining all attempts made at informal resolution/stipulation to the examination. Attach copies of the examiner's curriculum vitae for the court to review. See **Form 9–2** for a sample Notice of Motion for Physical Examination.

FORM 9–2
NOTICE OF MOTION FOR PHYSICAL EXAMINATION

[CAPTION]   Case No. _____

NOTICE OF MOTION FOR
PHYSICAL EXAMINATION

To: Plaintiff [name], [his or her or its] attorney, to each other party, and to the attorney of record for each other party in this action:

PLEASE TAKE NOTICE that on [date], at [time], or as soon thereafter as the matter can be heard, in Department _____ of the above-entitled Court, located at [address], Defendant [name] will move the Court under [Fed. R. Civ. P. 35(a); California Code of Civil Procedure § 2032(d); your specific authority] for an order directing Plaintiff, [name], to submit to a physical examination, on [date] and at [time] by Dr. [name], whose specialty is [specify, for example, neurology, pediatric, psychology], at [his or her] office at [address].

This examination will consist of: [state the scope, nature, manner, and conditions of the examination, including the diagnostic tests and procedures that will be used].

This motion is made after unsuccessful attempts to arrange for the examination by agreement, and on the ground that the following factors constitute good cause for a physical examination of the Plaintiff conducted at the instance of the Defendant as part of [his or her or its] pretrial discovery:

171

MEDICAL RECORDS IN LITIGATION AND AT TRIAL

1. Plaintiff seeks by this action the recovery of damages for personal injuries claimed to have been sustained in the occurrence described in the Complaint.

2. It is anticipated that Plaintiff will offer at trial in support of this claim for damages the testimony of one or more doctors who have had the advantage of conducting a physical examination of the type sought by this motion.

3. Expert opinion on the nature, extent, and duration of the injuries alleged by Plaintiff is essential to a determination of the amount of damages, if any, to which Plaintiff may be entitled for the cause of action alleged in the Complaint.

4. Defendant cannot safely proceed to trial without having the benefit of an independent medical evaluation of the actual nature, extent, and duration of any physical injuries sustained by Plaintiff.

This motion is based on the attached memorandum of points and authorities, and [specify any documents, exhibits, or declarations that accompany the motion].

Dated: _____

_____
[Name of Attorney]

_____
Attorney for Defendant

Practice Note: This form represents the most common situation in which the examination of the plaintiff is sought by the defendant. It may be adapted to cover more unusual situations in which the examinee is a defendant, or a nonparty. It may also be adapted to fit the requirements for any type of medical examination for which a motion is required by statute.

Practice Note: Some jurisdictions, including California, require that in the absence of a stipulation, a formal Demand for Medical Examination be served on the examinee with a required response within 20 days. California Code of Civil Procedure § 2032 *et seq.*

§ 9.12   Scope of Examination

In many jurisdictions, leave of court is required if the examination will include any diagnostic test or procedure that is "painful, protracted, or intrusive." CCP § 2032(d); *Klein v. Yellow Cab Co.* (N.D. Ohio 1944) 7 F.R.D. 169, 170, where the court ordered plaintiff to undergo a cystoscopy. If a potentially dangerous or painful procedure is to be part of the examination, the burden of proof is shifted to the examinee's attorney to show the danger or pain involved. At the very least, a declaration or affidavit from an expert is required. *Pena v. Troup* (D. Col. 1995) 163 F.R.D. 352, 355.

If counsel for the examinee wishes to limit the scope of the examination this must be stated at the time of the opposition to the noticed motion. It is not advisable to object to the scope of the exam during the process itself as this might expose the client and his or her attorney to sanctions including the costs of further hearings on the issue and those associated with a continued examination.

Specific oppositions should be succinctly stated, for example:

- If the motion requests that plaintiff undergo x-rays of the cervical spine, the court should be referred to the specific number of cervical x-rays that have been taken to date and ask that additional x-rays not be taken by the examining physician except by court order for good cause.

- If the plaintiff has specific religious or cultural mores that would argue against disrobing for a physician, request that the examiner respect the examinee and conduct the examination through the individual's clothing.

- Limitation of examination to specific part(s) of the body—e.g., shoulder injury may not require examination of lower extremities.

§ 9.13   Order for Physical Examination

The order granting the motion is subject to the same specificity requirements as the motion. It must specify the designation of the examiner, the time and place of the examination, and the manner, conditions, and scope of the examination. Fed. R. Civ. P. 35(a). An order that does not do so is defective. *Harabedian v. Superior Court* (1961) 195 Cal. App. 2d 26, 15 Cal. Rptr. 420, 89 ALR 2d 994.

See **Form 9–3** for a sample Order on Motion for Physical Examination.

FORM 9–3
ORDER FOR PHYSICAL EXAMINATION

[CAPTION]

Case No. _____

ORDER ON MOTION FOR
PHYSICAL EXAMINATION

TO ALL PARTIES AND TO THEIR ATTORNEYS OF RECORD:

PLEASE TAKE NOTICE that on [date of hearing], the duly noticed motion of [moving party] to compel the physical examination of [examinee] came on regularly for hearing, the Honorable [name], judge presiding. [Name of attorney] appeared on behalf of [Defendant or Plaintiff] and [identify moving party], and [attorney] appeared on behalf of [Plaintiff or Defendant].

After consideration of the moving papers and oral argument, the court [set forth the court's findings made at the hearing **making sure to fully set forth all rulings made on the scope of the examination, e.g. no further x-rays, examinee allowed to remain fully clothed, examinee to undergo non-contrast CT scan of spine, etc.**].

Dated:_____   _____
                                 JUDGE OF THE SUPERIOR COURT

§ 9.14   Mental Examination

If a party stipulates that (1) no claim is being made for mental and emotional distress over and above that usually associated with the claimed physical injuries and (2) that no testimony regarding this usual mental and emotional distress will be presented at trial in support of the claim for damages, courts will generally not order a mental examination in the absence of exceptional circumstances.

A defendant cannot place the plaintiff's mental condition in controversy by alleging that the plaintiff's injuries are the result of mental problems. See *Houghton v. M&F Fishing, Inc.* (S.D. Cal. 2001) 198 F.R.D. 666, 669.

Where the injury pleaded is entirely or primarily to an individual's emotional status, these allegations alone have been deemed good cause to permit the defendant to obtain a mental examination of the plaintiff. *Vinson v. Superior Court* (1987) 43 Cal. 3d 833, 239 Cal. Rptr. 292. This does not mean, however, that the plaintiff forfeits all rights to privacy. The court recognizes that plaintiff is not compelled "as a condition to entering the courtroom, to discard entirely her mantle of privacy." At the same time, plaintiff cannot be allowed to make serious allegations without affording defendants an opportunity to put their truth to the test. *Vinson, supra*, at 840.

See **Form 9–4** for sample Notice of Motion for Mental Examination.

FORM 9–4
MOTION FOR MENTAL EXAMINATION

[CAPTION]

Case No. _____

MOTION FOR
MENTAL EXAMINATION

To: Plaintiff [name], [his or her or its] attorney, to each other party, and to the attorney of record for each other party in this action:

PLEASE TAKE NOTICE that on [date], at [time], or as soon thereafter as the matter can be heard, in Department _____ of the above-entitled Court, located at [address], Defendant [name], will move the Court under [cite appropriate authority] for an order directing Plaintiff, [name], to submit to a mental examination, on such date and at such time as the Court shall specify, by Dr. [name], whose specialty is [specify], at [his or her] office at [address].

This examination will consist of: [state the scope, nature, manner, and conditions of the examination, including the diagnostic tests and procedures that will be used].

This motion is made after unsuccessful attempts to arrange for the examination by agreement, and on the ground that the following factors constitute good cause for a mental examination of the Plaintiff conducted at the instance of the Defendant as part of [his, her, its] pretrial discovery:

1. Plaintiff seeks by this action the recovery of damages for mental and emotional pain over and above that normally associated with the personal injuries claimed to have been sustained in the occurrence described in the Complaint.

2. It is anticipated that Plaintiff will offer at trial in support of this claim for mental and emotional damages the testimony of one or more psychiatrists or psychologists who have had the advantage of conducting a mental examination of the type sought by this motion.

3. Expert opinion on the nature, extent, and duration of the injuries alleged by Plaintiff is essential to a determination of the amount of damages, if any, to which Plaintiff may be entitled for the cause of action alleged in the Complaint.

4. Defendant cannot safely proceed to trial without having the benefit of an independent [psychiatric or psychological] evaluation of the actual nature, extent, and duration of any mental or emotional injuries sustained by Plaintiff.

This motion is based on the attached memorandum of points and authorities, and [specify any documents, exhibits, or declarations that accompany the motion].

Dated: _____

[Name of Attorney]
Attorney of Defendant

§ 9.15 Defense Preparation

Once the decision is made to require a medical examination, the appropriate specialty for the examiner should be determined. For example, if plaintiff alleges nerve damage resulting from an orthopedic injury, the defense will choose as an examiner either a neurologist or a neurological surgeon.

After the specialty has been determined, it will be necessary to locate an appropriate examiner. Many offices have established relationships with physicians and other medical providers. Teaching hospitals and medical school faculty are often excellent sources for an examiner. Current and prior years' jury verdicts publications can also identify potential examiners. The next step is to contact the medical provider, obtain an up-to-date curriculum vitae, and make arrangements for the examination, keeping in mind the statutory requirements. Plaintiff's counsel is then notified of the arrangements by letter or demand.

Before the examination date, copies of the medical records should be forwarded to the examiner. Consider also sending a copy of the examinee's deposition transcript if available. Arrange for existing copies of x-rays and other diagnostic studies to be brought to the examination or sent to the examiner beforehand. Many facilities will forward original radiology studies directly to a medical provider for review. Generally speaking, copies of radiology studies (x-rays, MRIs, CT scans) are acceptable substitutes.

§ 9.16 Plaintiff Preparation and Role of Paralegal

When the agreement or demand for examination arrives, it is important to perform a background check on the proposed examiner to determine his or her specialty and experience in legal actions. This can be done through various jury verdicts services and other sources.

The client must be notified immediately of the arrangements for the examination. Close to the date of the examination, the client's attorney should meet with and prepare the client for the examination process. It is important for the client to understand who the examiner is and what the purpose of the examination is. The client should be cautioned as to his or her conduct at the examination.

§ 9.17   Attendance at Examination

Arrangements should be made for the attorney or other representative to attend and record the entire examination by audiotape. Some plaintiff's attorneys feel that allowing a client to attend a medical examination without representation is tantamount to malpractice. The theory is if the examinee is without legal representation, the medical examiner is free to inquire into areas of the client's past or present condition unrelated to the subject incident and injuries.

However, the majority of federal courts have consistently denied the examinee's right to have counsel or other legal representative witness a physical examination. Some federal courts have made an exception and allowed third parties to be present with a showing of good cause. See *Vreeland v. Ethan Allen, Inc.* (S.D. N.Y. 1993) 151 F.R.D. 551-552, attorney attended; *Klein v. Yellow Cab Co.* (N.D. Ohio 1944) 7 F.R.D. 169, 170, plaintiff's physician attended. Under these circumstances, it does not seem reasonable that a court would exclude the presence at an examination of a parent or custodian of a minor child, a debilitated elder, or a plaintiff who is developmentally or physically disabled.

California allows observers to attend a physical examination, including the examinee's attorney or designated representative and a court reporter. (California Code of Civil Procedure § 2032(g)(1).) It generally is assumed that the term "designated representative" includes a paralegal or an interpreter and could also permit the attorney to be represented by a medical consultant. Although no California case has dealt directly with the matter, the trial court probably retains discretion to permit a spouse, relative, or friend to attend a physical examination. This is advisable where the examinee is a minor or incompetent, and may be appropriate where the examining physician is of the opposite sex. Hogan, *Modern California Discovery* (4th), § 8:13.

An examination normally will include detailed questioning of the examinee regarding the history of his or her condition. This questioning poses the possible danger that it will enter into the area of liability, producing statements about the circumstances of the event causing the injury which are or might be construed as harmful to the examinee. In a 1955 case, the California Supreme Court held that a lay person "should not be expected to evaluate the propriety of every question at his peril. The plaintiff, therefore, should be permitted to have the assistance and protection of an attorney during the examination." *Scharff v. Superior Court* (1955) 44 Cal. 2d 508, 282 P.2d 896. Thus, the most significant reason for having an observer attend the medical examination is to prevent improper questioning.

A physician conducting a physical examination pursuant to Fed. R. Civ. P. 35(a) may ask the examinee questions which are necessary to reach an opinion about the person's medical condition and the "cause of the alleged injury." See *Romano v. II Morrow, Inc.* (D. Oreg. 1997) 173 F.R.D. 271, 273, in which the court refused to limit the physician to questions propounded in advance of the examination.

In those jurisdictions in which third parties may attend and observe physical examinations, the realm of the mental exam remains off limits. In *Vinson v. Superior Court* (1987) 43 Cal. 3d 833, 239 Cal. Rptr. 292, the court denied the plaintiff an unqualified right to the company of counsel during a psychiatric interview. The court reasoned that given the "sensitive" nature of the psychiatric examination itself and the need for a "special and private rapport between examiner and examinee," mental examinations were best conducted on a one-to-one basis. The court found that a psychiatric examination was almost wholly devoted to a "careful probing of the examinee's psyche for the purpose of forming an accurate picture of his mental condition" and the presence of a third party might impair this process.

§ 9.18   Notification Requirements

In the interest of cooperation, it is advisable to let all involved parties know that an observer will be present. The authorization can be made by a letter to the medical examiner with a copy to the opposition attorney, either sent beforehand or brought to the examination.

Practice Note: While certain jurisdictions allow the presence of third parties, many doctors do not. If the plaintiff has indicated that an observer will be present, ensure that the physician selected to perform the examination knows and agrees. The examining physician may refuse to perform the examination but bill the attorney for the time anyway.

§ 9.19   Role of Observer

It is extremely important that any person attending a medical examination be aware of his or her role as an observer. The attorney's representative often attends the examination to provide emotional support to the client. The representative should:

- Accurately document the information the client gives the examiner, the type of tests performed, and a description of the examination itself, including the client's verbal and physical responses, in order to allow an objective assessment of the accuracy of the medical report and of the client's version of the examination. An audiotape can provide much of this information.
- Refrain from offering any information to the examiner concerning the examinee's history and symptoms, even though the observer may be able to remember more than the client, and even though the examiner may ask the observer questions.

The role of the observer is to monitor the examination, not to participate in or disrupt it. The observer should be sensitive to appropriate and inappropriate areas of questioning by the physician. For example, questions concerning the subject's injury are acceptable, as may be questions concerning prior related injuries. However, questions regarding the use of alcohol or other controlled substances, personal relationships, or unrelated physical conditions may not be appropriate.

If, in the opinion of the observer, the examiner becomes abusive to the examinee, or tries to perform unauthorized tests or procedures, the examination can be brought to a halt. Counsel for the examinee can then move for a protective order.

On the other hand, if the observer disrupts the examination by directing the examinee how to answer a question, for example, the physician may suspend the examination. The party requesting the examination can thereafter move for a protective order and a monetary sanction in order to control the conduct of the examinee and observer.

Practice Note: Some medical examiners ask plaintiffs to complete "Client History" forms before the examination. Many plaintiff's attorneys believe it is not appropriate for the client to fill out any papers for the examining physician. At the very least, the attorney should completely review the forms. The reasoning is that the physician can obtain this information from the defense, and medical history forms represent inquiry into inappropriate areas by the examining physician.

§ 9.20   Recording the Examination

Because of the intrusive nature of video equipment, an examination may not be videotaped. In *Edmiston v. Superior Court* (1978) 22 Cal. 3d 699, 150 Cal. Rptr. 276, the trial court authorized the videotaping of a discovery physical examination. Its order provided that the operator be a disinterested person, that the taping be conducted in a nondisruptive way, and that the tape itself be made available for viewing by the other side. A divided Supreme Court ruled that the trial court lacked the power to order even such a carefully regulated attempt to obtain a visual record of the examination. The court said that "videotaping with its heavy equipment and necessary additional personnel would unnecessarily create a sideshow atmosphere at which taping was the main attraction."

A federal court has found that videotaping of an examination by a professional videographer (or even an unattended video camera) would give the plaintiff/examinee an "unfair advantage"because defendant cannot tape the examination or treatment by the plaintiff's doctors. See *Holland v. United States* (D. S.C. 1998) 182 F.R.D. 493, 495.

Either party may record a medical examination with audiotape. See California Code of Civil Procedure § 2032(g)(1). Prior notice of intent to audiotape is not required.

Practice Note: Examinations can last from one to four hours, depending on the complexity of the injuries alleged. Make sure that there are adequate batteries and blank tapes available for a long examination.

§ 9.21   Failure to Appear

If the examinee fails to appear for or submit to an examination, monetary sanctions may be imposed on that individual or on the party required to produce him or her for examination. In addition, the court may preclude the party from introducing expert testimony as a sanction for failure to attend the court-mandated examination. See *Mraovic v. Elgin, Joliet & Eastern Ry. Co.* (7th Cir. 1990) 897 F.2d 268, 271.

181

Practice Note: In addition, doctors almost uniformly require payment for the scheduled visit if the examination is not canceled 24 to 48 hours in advance.

It may be the case that the examiner is late for the examination. Although no authority appears to address this issue, 45 minutes is an adequate time to wait for the examiner to appear. If, after this length of time, the examiner has not appeared, the examinee may be advised to leave.

§ 9.22 Exchange of Written Reports

On request, the examinee is entitled to receive a copy of any report generated as a result of the examination. The report must be "a detailed written report of the examiner setting out the examiner's findings, including results of all tests made, diagnoses, and conclusions together with like reports of all earlier examinations of the same condition." Fed. R. Civ. P. 35(b)(1); California Code of Civil Procedure § 2032. See **Form 9–5** for a sample request.

FORM 9–5
DEMAND FOR MEDICAL REPORTS

[CAPTION]

Case No. _____

DEMAND FOR REPORT OF
MEDICAL EXAMINATION

To: [Defendant or Plaintiff], [his or her or its] attorney, to each other party, and to the attorney of record for each other party in this action:

[Plaintiff or Defendant] demands under Code of Civil Procedure § 2032(h) that you furnish to [Plaintiff's or Defendant's] counsel on or before [date no sooner than 30 days after service of demand or, if service is by mail, 35 days], a copy of the written report(s) of the examination of [Plaintiff, Defendant, or nonparty examinee], [name],

§ 9.22   EXCHANGE OF WRITTEN REPORTS

conducted by [examiner] on [date], in which [examiner] sets forth [his or her] findings, including the results of all tests made, diagnoses, prognoses, and conclusions, as well as the examinee's history and the nature of the examination(s) done.

It is also demanded that you furnish a copy of all reports of earlier examination; by [examiner] or any other [physician or psychiatrist or psychologist or other examiner], relating to the same condition for which [name] was examined by [name].

Dated: _____   [Name of Attorney]
                               Attorney for [Plaintiff or Defendant]

A plaintiff's demand for copies of the defense medical report has the following significant consequences:

_____ The defendant is entitled to receive, upon request, copies of all medical reports by the plaintiff's doctors and experts.

_____ The plaintiff must exchange any *future reports* relating to the same condition by the same or any other examiner.

_____ The plaintiff waives any claim of privilege or work product that would otherwise protect such reports from discovery.

This requirement for the exchange of reports does not apply to consultants who have reviewed the medical records but have not examined the plaintiff personally. These reports are protected by the work product privilege until that consultant is declared an expert witness, at which point all of the expert's reports are discoverable.

Practice Note: Generally speaking, plaintiffs' attorneys should ask any examining doctor they have retained to contact them before preparing a written report. If the results of the examination are to plaintiff's disadvantage, or if the examiner is acting as a consultant only and not an expert, the examiner may be asked not to prepare a written report. The examiner's identity or the unfavorable evaluation remains protected as work product.

183

If a party fails to make a timely delivery of the reports demanded, the demanding party may move for an order compelling their delivery and for sanctions. If a party then fails to obey the order compelling deliverance of the reports, the court may impose harsher sanctions, including an evidence or terminating sanction. In addition, an examiner whose report has not been provided will not be allowed to testify at trial. Fed. R. Civ. P. 35(b)(1); California Code of Civil Procedure § 2032(h).

§ 9.23   Using Medical Records at Trial

All of the work that has been done in reviewing medical records comes to fruition at this time. One of the more important functions of a legal professional is preparing the documents to be used at trial. When preparing for trial, arbitration, or settlement conference, one of the most important tools used by the attorney will be the trial book. This book (or books if the case is complex and involves many parties) will present in an organized and easily accessible format the pertinent information needed by the attorney in order to present the case.

There is no standard method for preparing a trial book. Its format will depend upon the size of the case and the attorney's individual needs. One method is to create a working trial book (see **§ 9.24**) and an evidence book (see **§ 9.25**), using as many three-ring binders as needed.

§ 9.24   Working Trial Book

The working trial book contains the formal and procedural legal material preceeded by the attorney to present the case. As an example, separate sections pertaining to each of the following categories might be included.

Trial Plan.   This section contains the attorney's "road map" for the presentation of the case, i.e., the order of witnesses, exhibits, and so on.

Pleadings.   This section contains the basic pleadings—the complaint, any cross-complaints, and answers to them.

Settlement Offers.   This section contains written settlement offers including statutorily proposed offers to compromise.

Legal Research.   This section should include any research memoranda, plus copies of case law and statutes regarding key questions of law or evidence to be presented or raised at trial.

Motions.   A significant portion of any trial can involve motion work, for example, motions to sever or bifurcate certain causes of action or issues, motions in limine regarding evidentiary questions, motions to exclude witnesses or to disclose their identities, and so on.

Voir Dire and Jury Selection.   This section will contain the list of voir dire questions to be directed at the jury panel (unless the jurisdiction requires that the judge conduct the voir dire), any notes that have been made regarding particular panel members, and any other information concerning the jury selection process.

Opening Statements.   This section will generally include a chronology of significant events in the case, notations regarding points made by opposing counsel in opening remarks, and so on.

Trial Notes.   Notes made by the attorney during testimony and following the completion of each day's session are placed here.

Exhibits.   This section will contain a list of exhibits offered by all parties as evidence. The actual documentary evidence does not appear in this section, however.

Closing Arguments.   This section contains the attorney's notations regarding statements by opposing counsel and her draft of closing arguments.

Jury Instructions.   Place copies of jury instructions as given by the court, notations regarding changes and/or additions, and copies of special verdicts utilized in this section.

§ 9.25   Evidence Book

This book contains all the investigative and documentary evidence to be used at trial. The following categories of information could be included.

MEDICAL RECORDS IN LITIGATION AND AT TRIAL

Witness/Party List. This sheet, located at the front of the binder, contains the phone numbers (office, home, cell) and addresses (home, office) of all individuals who are germane to the case and/or who might be called to testify. This includes the trial team members (partner, associate, paralegal, secretary, jury research), client(s), the insurance company claims representative (if a defense case), attorneys for each party, lay witnesses, expert witnesses, investigators, court personnel, and support staff (copy service, attorney services, etc.)

To-Do List. Depending upon the time frame of the case, this list can include such items as depositions to be taken (or summarized), witnesses to be contacted or interviewed, experts to be retained or deposed, tests to be performed, and subpoenas to be issued.

Investigation. This section includes investigative police agency reports, reports made by your private investigator, and photographs of the location of the accident and/or the vehicles involved. (Photographs of injuries to a party would be located in the medical records section.)

Discovery. This section contains all documents related to discovery conducted in the case, including interrogatories and answers (or the summary of answers), requests for production of documents and responses, and requests for admissions and responses.

Witness Testimony. Each witness should be assigned a subsection, which contains copies of statements made prior to litigation, summaries of deposition testimony, both narrative and page-line, excerpts from applicable answers to interrogatories, or responses to requests for production of documents.

Expert Witness Testimony. Designate a separate section for the testimony of each expert witness. This section includes a copy of the expert's curriculum vitae, any report generated by the expert, a summary of his or her deposition testimony, and copies of any technical articles the expert relied upon in rendering the opinion.

Wage Loss. If the case involves allegations of wage loss or loss of earning capacity, this section will contain information concerning the party's employment history, including summaries of employment records, W-2 and other tax related information, and statements made by the party in answers to interrogatories or during deposition that concern wage loss.

§ 9.26 —Medical Records

All of the summaries that have been prepared throughout the life of the case that document the medical care and treatment received by a party are placed in this section. Included with the summaries are copies of significant entries from the record, for example, admission history and physical examinations, operative reports, results of diagnostic tests, discharge summaries, and consultations.

If the medical treatment rendered is complex, include any information that assists in understanding the nature of the disease and/or its treatment. This includes well-labeled anatomical diagrams, excerpts from medical resource texts explaining a particular injury or surgical procedure, and diagrams illustrating the injury or condition.

This section will contain the itemization of medical bills as illustrated in **Chapter 7,** along with copies of the pertinent medical bills.

Practice Note: For plaintiffs, it is advisable to delete any references made to insurance coverage or payments by using correction fluid on a copy of the bill, keeping the original available in case it is needed at trial.

§ 9.27   Preparation of Evidence Book

Ideally, the evidence book is prepared in the months prior to the commencement of trial, as the case moves through discovery. It is a convenient method of keeping all of the significant material in one place, making it easily accessible to the attorney for use during depositions and settlement conferences. As new information is obtained (witnesses or treating physicians, additional medical bills), the binder is reviewed and updated.

§ 9.28   Medical Records Allowed at Trial

In personal injury, workers' compensation, and medical malpractice cases, the medical record as used at trial can be crucial to the presentation or defense of a case. Federal Rules of Evidence 101 *et seq.* set the standards for admissibility of medical records as evidence at trial. Rule 401 defines *relevant evidence* as that which has "any tendency to make the existence of any fact that is of consequence to the determination of the action more probable or less probable than it would be without the evidence." Accordingly, all relevant evidence is admissible (Rule 402).

Hearsay, defined at Rule 801(c) as "a statement offered in evidence to prove the truth of the matter asserted," is not relevant as evidence. Medical records, however, fall within one of the widely known exceptions to the hearsay rule as defined by Rule 803(6). This exception defines certain records as "a . . . report, record . . . in any form, of acts, events, conditions, opinions, or diagnoses, made at or near the time by, or from information transmitted by, a person with knowledge, if kept in the course of a regularly conducted business activity . . . ." Records kept by hospitals and all medical providers fall within this exception and are admissible as evidence.

§ 9.29 Original Records versus Duplicates

Federal Rule 1003 states that a duplicate is admissible to the "same extent as an original unless (1) a genuine question is raised as to the authenticity of the original or (2) in the circumstances it would be unfair to admit the duplicate in lieu of the original."

Practice Note: Check applicable state rules regarding use of duplicates in lieu of original records. As late as the mid-1980s, for example, California required that the original record be produced for trial. However, this requirement has since been dropped and subpoenaed copies are now acceptable.

If duplicate records have been obtained by subpoena, these documents are accompanied by a statement from the custodian of records that they constitute a true and complete copy of those in the custody and control of the provider.

Although notice requirements vary from state to state, generally each party is notified that particular records have been placed under subpoena. Each party is entitled, upon request, to a complete copy of all records provided to the party filing the subpoena. In this manner, subpoenaed records offered as evidence at trial have been made available to all parties.

For this reason, and in order to avoid compromising the integrity of the record, no markings should be made on subpoenaed documents.

Practice Note: Copy the subpoenaed documents and use the copied duplicate for making any markings or notations directly on the record.

§ 9.30   Demonstrative Evidence at Trial

In actions involving medical malpractice, personal injury, or workers' compensation, demonstrative evidence (photographs, models, charts, video or motion pictures) is used to illustrate and supplement the testimony of witnesses. Testimony becomes clearer to the jury when it is accompanied by visual aids. Visual images, whether photographs or charts, provide jurors with points of reference that tie important concepts together. In short, people remember what they see. Good exhibits must also reflect an understanding of all of the processes involved in jury decision-making. Clear, concise graphic communication is required if attorneys are to stimulate the visual imaginations of jurors.

Generally speaking, any item that serves to explain or aid the jury in its understanding of an issue is relevant and admissible upon a foundational showing that the item is an accurate portrayal of the matter depicted and that it fairly illustrates the witness testimony.

Most trials utilize some form of demonstrative evidence, from simple copies of documents to enlargements of photographs to sophisticated video reconstructions of accidents. Clearly, anything that will assist a jury in understanding the nature of an injury, its impact on an individual's life, or the manner in which it was received can be significant.

Enlargements of Chart Entries

At the time the medical records were first reviewed and summarized, certain documents were no doubt identified as being of extreme importance to proving or disproving the main issues of the litigation. It is those documents that should be chosen for enlargement and use at trial. For example, in any case in which it appears that the medical record has been altered, an enlargement of the altered records should be prepared. It can then be used by the attorney, by expert physicians, or other individuals who may be called upon to testify about the alterations.

189

MEDICAL RECORDS IN LITIGATION AND AT TRIAL

Practice Note: Enlargements of medical record entries must be large enough that details can be clearly seen. Plan to have each page enlarged to poster size (2 × 3 feet).

Still Photographs

Still photographs can be very persuasive exhibits at trial, depicting anything from the plaintiff's injuries to the kinds of medical devices used during rehabilitation (halo braces, full body casts, and so on). In motor vehicle accident cases, photos showing the damage to the vehicles involved can be helpful.

Practice Note: Photographs must also be large enough that details can be clearly seen. Plan to have photographs enlarged to at least an 8 × 10-inch or 11 × 17-inch format. In some cases, it may be valuable to have photos enlarged to poster size (2 × 3 feet).

Videotapes

Videotapes are a dramatic method of demonstrating medical evidence and can have a profound effect at trial. They make the impact of the consequences of a catastrophic event come alive for the jury, especially in a "day in the life" format. Conversely, surveillance films can be used to impeach testimony regarding the effect of injuries on an individual's life.

Practice Note: Make sure that a video recorder and monitor (or projector and screen) have been obtained for the screening, along with spare batteries and extension cords. Confirm the availability and location of electrical plugs in the courtroom itself, prior to the start of trial, and check with the judge's clerks to determine the judge's particular preferences in use of video equipment.

Prosthetic and Surgical Devices

Often, the most telling piece of evidence will be the actual rod that was placed in a plaintiff's femur, the plate and screws used to stabilize a fracture, the artificial limb worn by the plaintiff, or the halo brace that was anchored into the plaintiff's skull and worn for months. These devices should be retained throughout the duration of the litigation for potential use at trial.

Anatomical Models, Drawings, or Diagrams

Models are three-dimensional representations used to demonstrate the functioning of a body part or the skeleton as a whole. They are useful in demonstrating the location of an injury. Medical drawings and diagrams are often used in opening remarks and closing arguments and to illustrate the testimony of expert witnesses.

X-Rays

X-rays and scans (MRI, CT, bone scan) are used to illustrate and assist an expert or treating physician in describing the plaintiff's condition.

Practice Note: Make sure that any necessary aids are available to the witness: light screens for viewing x-rays (larger is better than smaller, two to three sections are better than one), laser or collapsible pointers, and so on.

Other Demonstrative Aids

At the time the medical records were first summarized, various formats may have been used in order to present the medical information to the attorney or other individuals in the most easily absorbed fashion. Those different types of summaries—chronologies, break-out, charts—should now seriously be considered as the basis for trial demonstrative aids. As with the general, initial summary of the records, the specific issues that must be proven will need to be presented to the jury as well. For example, consider the following potential issues and aids:

_____ Weight loss: prepare a graph of the patient's weights over a period of months or years to demonstrate the gradual (or sudden) decline in weight.

_____ Medical history: for individuals with complex medical histories, consider an anatomical drawing of the human body with bullet points illustrating each and every illness, disease, injury, or surgery that person experiences in his or her lifetime.

——— Touch charts: for a 24-hour period of time, illustrate every incident in which an individual was interacted with, or "touched" by a staff member. (This can be significant in skilled nursing facility cases in which plaintiff alleges that their loved one was "abandoned.")

The type of demonstrative aid is limited only by one's imagination and budget.

§ 9.31 —Sources for Demonstrative Aids

Treating physicians and experts often have charts, models, and other teaching aids that can be utilized at trial. Local medical schools and colleges often have models that can be borrowed or rented.

In addition, with the availability of highly efficient computers and software, many demonstrative aids can be formulated and printed within the law office itself. Medical images downloaded from the Internet or from purchased software can be integrated into exhibits using PowerPoint display systems. Many junior or community colleges offer one-day courses in the use of PowerPoint and legal professionals would be well-advised to become proficient in its use. With the use of scanners and laptop computers, some law firms have the ability to place their entire trial presentation on a CD-ROM for incredible ease of presentation.

§ 9.32   Guide to Resources and Services

*Life*ART™ is a company that provides quality medical illustrations for various medical content areas, including anatomy, physiology, physical therapy, surgery, pediatrics, 3-D anatomy, neurology, cardiology, and orthopedics. The images can be ordered on-line through their MediClip™ service or as packages on CD-ROM.

*Life*ART™ Professional Medical Computer Illustrations
Lippincott Williams & Wilkins
351 West Camden Street
Baltimore, MD 21201-2436

Telephone: 800-LIFEART (800-543-3278)
Fax: 800-447-8438
E-mail: custserv@wwilkins.com
Web: www.lifeart.com or www.mediclip.com

Anatomical Reproductions and Charts

Medical Plastics Laboratory
P.O. Box 38
Gatesville, TX 76528
Telephone: (800) 433-5539

Anatomical Chart Company
8221 Kimball Avenue
Skokie, IL 60076-2956
Telephone: (800) 679-4700
E-mail: accinfo@anatomical.com

Medical Illustrators

Association of Medical Illustrators
2692 Huguenot Springs Road
Midlothian, VA 23113
Telephone: (804) 794-2908

The Medical College of Georgia
Graduate Program in Medical Illustration
Augusta, GA 30912-0300
Telephone: (706) 721-3266
Fax: (706) 721-7855
Web: http://www.mcg.edu/SAH/MedIll/index.html

University of Illinois at Chicago
Department of Biomedical Visualization
1919 W. Taylor Street, Room 213, M/C 527
Chicago, IL 60612
Telephone: (312) 996-7337
Fax: (312) 996-8342
Web: http://www.bvis.uic.edu

MEDICAL RECORDS IN LITIGATION AND AT TRIAL

The Johns Hopkins School of Medicine
Department of Art as Applied to Medicine
1830 E. Monument Street, Suite 7000
Baltimore, MD 21205
Telephone: (410) 955-3213
Fax: (410) 955-1085
Web: http://www.med.jhu.edu/medart

The University of Michigan
M.F.A. Program in Medical and Biological Illustration
Northern Brewery, Suite 102B
1327 Jones Drive
Ann Arbor, MI 48105-1899
Telephone: (313) 998-6270
Fax: (313) 998-6273
Web: http://www.umich.edu/~medill/index.html

The University of Texas Southwestern Medical Center at Dallas
Department of Biomedical Communications—Exchange Park
5323 Harry Hines Boulevard
Dallas, TX 75235-8881
Telephone: (214) 648-4699
Fax: (214) 648-5353
Web: http://www.swmed.edu/medillus

APPENDIXES

*Page 425, replace **Appendix A** with the following:*

APPENDIX A

LIST OF ROOT WORDS
AND COMBINING FORMS

---

*Note: Terms that are listed in **bold** italics are new additions as of 2002 Supplement.*

TERM	PERTAINS TO
ab-	***away from***
acro-	extremity, end
actin-	***ray, radius***
aden-	gland
adren-	adrenal gland
aer-	gas, air
alb-	***white***
alg-	***pain***
all-	different, another
alve-	***trough, channel***
ambi-, ***amphi-***	both, both sides
angi-	vessel
ankyl-, ancyl-	***crooked, looped***
ano-	anus
ante, anter-	before, in front of
arteri-	artery
arthr-	joint
anti-	against
aur-	***ear***
aux-	***increase***
ax-	***axis***

APPENDIXES

TERM	PERTAINS TO
bacill-	*small staff, rod*
bacteri-	bacteria
bar-	*weight*
bi-	*life (bios), two*
bil-	*bile*
blep-	*look, see*
blephar-	eyelid
bol-	*ball*
brachi-	*arm*
brachy-	*short*
brady-	slow
bronch-	windpipe
bry-	*full of life*
bucc-	*cheek*
cac-	*bad, abnormal*
calc-	*stone, limestone, heel*
calor-	*heat*
cancr, chancr-	*crab, cancer*
capit-	head
caps-	*container*
carbo-	*coal, charcoal*
carcin-	*crab, cancer*
cardi-	heart
carp-	wrist
caud-	*tail*
cav-	*hollow*
-cele	*tumor, hernia*
cente-	*to puncture*
centr-	*point, center*
cephal-	head
cer-	*wax*
cerebr-	brain
cervic-	neck
chlor-	*green*
chol-	bile
chondr-	cartilage

198

TERM	PERTAINS TO
chyl-	lymph
-cid(e)	*cut, kill*
circum-	*around*
cleid-	collarbone
coccyg-	coccyx
colo-	colon
colp-	*hollow, vagina*
con-	*with, together*
contra-	against, opposite
cost-	rib
crani-	skull, head
cry-	*cold*
cult-	*tend, cultivate, culture*
cune-	*wedge*
cut-	*skin*
cyan-	*blue*
cycl-	*circle, cycle*
cyst-	bladder
cyt-	cell
dacry-	tear
dactyl-	*finger, toe*
de-	*down from*
dent-, dont-	tooth
derm-	skin
dextr-	right side
di-	*two*
dia-	*through, apart*
didym-	*twin*
digit-	*finger, toe*
diplo-	*double*
dis-	*apart from*
disc-	*disk*
dors-	*back*
duoden-	duodenum
dur-	*hard*
dys-	abnormal, bad, painful

APPENDIXES

TERM	PERTAINS TO
e-	out from
ec-	out of
ect-	outside
ede-	swell
encephal-	brain
end-	inside
enter-	intestine
ep, epi	upon, after, in addition
erg-	work
erythr-	red
eso-	inside
esophag-	esophagus
esthe-	perceive, feel
eu-	good, normal
ex-	out of
exo-	outside
extra-	outside of, beyond
faci-	face
-facient	make
fasci-	band
febr-	fever
-ferent	bear, carry
fibr-	threadlike, fiber
fil-	thread
fiss-	split
flav-	yellow
-flect-	bend, divert
flu-	flow
for-	door, opening
-form	shape
fract-	break
front-	forehead, front
funct-	perform, serve, function
fund-	pour

APPENDIX A

galact-	milk
gangli-	*swelling, plexus*
gastr-	stomach
gen-	*become, be produced*
genu-	knee
gest-	*bear, carry*
gingiv-	gums
gloss-, *glott-*	tongue
gluc-, glyc(y)-	*sweet*
gnath-	jaw
gno-	*know, discern*
grad-	*walk, take steps*
graph-	*scratch, write, record*
grav-	*heavy*
gyn(ec)-	*woman*
hem(a, o, to)-	blood
hemi-	half
hepat-	liver
hidr-	*sweat*
hist-	tissue
hom-	*common, same*
horm-	*impetus, impulse*
hydat-, hydr-	water
hyper-	above, beyond, *extreme*
hypn-	*sleep*
hypo-	*under,* below, less
hyster-	uterus, *womb*
iatr-	*physician*
idi-	*peculiar, separate, distinct*
ile-	*ileum*
ili-	*lower abdomen, intestines*
ilium-	upper hip bone
infra-	beneath
insul-	*island*

APPENDIXES

202

TERM	PERTAINS TO
malac-	*soft*
mamm-	*breast*
man-	*hand*
mani-	*mental aberration*
mast-	*breast*
medi-	*middle*
mega-, *megal-*	great, large
mel-	*limb, member*
melan-	black
men-	*month*
mening-	membrane
ment-	*mind*
mes-	*middle*
meta-	*after, beyond*
metr-	*measure, womb*
micr-	*small*
mne-	*remember*
mon-	*only, sole*
morph-	*form, shape*
mot-	*move*
my-	muscle
myel-	marrow
myring-	eardrum
myx-	*mucus*
narc-	*numbness*
nas-	*nose*
ne-	*new, young*
necr-	*corpse*
nephr-	kidney
neur-	nerve
nutri-	*nourish*
ocul-	eye
-ode	*road, path*
odont-	tooth

APPENDIXES

TERM	PERTAINS TO
-odyn	*pain, distress*
-oid	*form*
ole-	*oil*
olig-	*few, small*
onc-	*bulk, mass*
onych-	*claw, nail*
oo-	*egg*
oophor-	ovary
-orb	*circle*
orchi-	testicle
opth-	eye
orth-	*straight, right, normal*
oss-, ost(e)-	bone
ot-	ear
ov-	*egg*
oxy-	*sharp*
pachy(n)-	*thicken*
pag-	*fix, make fast*
par(t)-	*bear, give birth*
para-	*beside, beyond*
path-	*sickness, that which one undergoes*
pec-	*fix, make fast*
ped-	*child*
pell-	*skin*
pen-	*need, lack*
pend-	*hang down*
peps-, *pept*	*digest*
per-	*through*
peri-	*around*
pet-	*seek, tend toward*
pha-	*say, speak*
phac-	*lens*
phag-	*eat*
pharmac-	*drug*
pharyng-	*throat*
phen-	*show, be seen*

APPENDIX A

pher-	*bear, support*
phil-	*like, have affinity for*
phleb-	*vein*
phleg-	*burn, inflame*
phob-	*fear, dread*
phon-	*sound*
phot-	*light*
phrag-	*fence, wall off, stop up*
phthi-	*decay, waste away*
phy-	*beget, bring forth, produce*
phylac-	*guard*
physe-	*blow, inflate*
pil-	*hair*
pituit-	*phlegm*
plas-	*mold, shape*
platy-	*broad, flat*
pleg-	*strike*
plet-	*fill*
pleur-	*rib, side*
plex-	*strike*
plic-	*fold*
pne-	*breathing*
pneum(at)-	*breath, air*
pneumo(n)-	lung
pod-	*foot*
poie-	*make, produce*
pol-	*axis of a sphere*
poly-	*much, many*
pont-	*bridge*
por-	*passage*
post-	*after, behind in time or place*
pre-, pro-	*before in time or place*
proct-	anus
prosop-	*face*
pseud-	*false*
psych-	*soul, mind*
pto-	*fall*

APPENDIXES

TERM	PERTAINS TO
pub-	*adult*
pulmo(n)-	*lung*
puls-	*drive*
punct-	*prick, pierce*
pur-	*pus*
py-	*pus*
pyel-	*trough, basin*
pyl-	*door, orifice*
pyr-	*fire*
re-	*back, again*
ren-	kidney
retro-	*backwards*
rhag-	*break, burst*
rhaph-	*suture*
rhe-	*flow*
rhex-	*break, burst*
rhin-	nose
rot-	*wheel*
rub(r)-	*red*
sacr-	sacrum
salping-	tube
sanguin-	*blood*
sarc-	*flesh*
schis-	*split*
scler-	*hard*
scop-	*look at, observe*
sect-	*cut*
semi-	*half*
sens-	*perceive, feel*
sep-	*rot, decay*
sept-	*fence, wall off, stop off*
ser-	*whey, watery substance*
sial-	*saliva*
sin-	*hollow, fold*
sit-	*food*

206

TERM	PERTAINS TO
solut-	*loose, dissolve, set free*
somat-	*body*
spas-	*draw, pull*
spectr-	*appearance, what is seen*
sperm(at)-	*seed*
spers-	*scatter*
sphen-	*wedge*
spher-	*ball*
sphygm-	*pulsation*
spin-	*spine*
spirat-	*breathe*
splanchn-	*entrails, viscera*
splen-	spleen
spor-	*seed*
squam-	*scale*
sta-	*make stand, stop*
stal-	*send*
staphyl-	*bunch of grapes, uvula*
stear-	*fat*
sten-	*narrow, compressed*
ster-	*solid*
stern-	sternum
stol-	*send*
stom(at)-	mouth, opening, orifice
strep(h)-	*twist*
strict-	*draw tight, compress, cause pain*
stroph-	*twist*
struct-	*pile up against*
sub-	*under, below*
super-	*above, beyond, extreme*
syn-	*with, together*
tac-	*order, arrange*
tachy-	rapid
tact-	*touch*
tars-	instep of foot, ankle
tect-, teg-	*cover*

APPENDIXES

TERM	PERTAINS TO
tel-	*end*
tele-	*at a distance*
tempor-	*time, timely or fatal spot, temple*
ten(ont)-	*tight stretched band,* tendon
tens-	*stretch*
test-	*testicle*
the-	*put, place*
thel-	*teat, nipple*
therap-	*treatment*
therm-	*heat*
thorac-	chest
thromb-	*lump,* clot
thym-	*spirit*
thyr-	shield
toc-	*childbirth*
tom-	*cut*
ton-	*stretch, put under tension*
top-	*place*
tors-	*twist*
tox-	*poison*
trache-	windpipe
trachel-	neck
tract-	*draw, drag*
traumat-	*wound*
trich-	*hair*
trip-	*rub*
trop-	*turn, react*
troph-	*nuture*
tuber-	*swelling, node*
typ-	*type*
typh-	*fog, stupor*
typhl-	*blind*
ur-	urine, urinary
ureter-	ureter
urethr-	urethra
utero-	uterus

APPENDIX A

TERM	PERTAINS TO
vacc-	*cow*
vagin-	*sheath*
vas-	vessel
ven-	vein
ventricul-	ventricle, of heart or brain
ventr-	belly, abdominal
vesic-	*bladder*
viscer-	viscera
vit-	*life*
vuls-	*pull, twitch*
xanth-	*yellow, blond*
zo-	*life*
zyg-	*yoke, union*
zym-	enzyme, ferment

*Page 430, replace **Appendix B** with the following:*

APPENDIX B

PREFIXES

*Note: Terms that are listed in **bold** italics are new additions as of 2002 Supplement.*

PREFIX	MEANING
a-, an-	without, absent
ab-	away from
ad-	to, toward
aden-	***gland***
al-	***like, similar***
amyl-	***starch***
angi(o)-	vessel, duct (usually blood vessel)
ankyl-	***crooked, looped***
ante-	***before***
anti-	against
arterio-	***artery***
arthro-	***joint***
asthen-	***weakness, lack***
aud-, aur-	***ear, hearing***
auto-	self
bacter-	bacteria
bar-	***weight***
bi-	***both, two***
bi(o)-	life
brachio-	***arm***
brachy-	short

APPENDIX B

PREFIX	MEANING
brady-	slow
bronch(i)(o)-	*bronchial*
buccal-	*cheek*
carcin-	*cancer*
cardio-	*heart*
carpo-	*wrist*
caud-	*tail*
centi-	hundred
cephalo-	*head*
cerebro-	*brain*
cervic-	*neck*
chiro-	*hand*
chole-	*bile*
cholecyst-	*gallbladder*
chondro-	*cartilage*
circum-	*around*
co-	with, together
col-	*colon*
colp-	*vagina*
com-, con-	with, together
contra-	*against*
cort-	*covering*
costo-	*ribs*
cranio-	*skull*
crypto-	hidden
cubitus-	*elbow, forearm*
cut-	*skin*
cyano-	blue
cysto-	*bladder, sac*
cyt(e)(o)-	cell
de-	away, not
deci-	*tenth*
demi-	half
dent-	*tooth*
derma-	*skin*

APPENDIXES

PREFIX	MEANING
dextro-	right
di-, dis-	twice, doubly
diplo-	double
dors-	*back*
dys-	*painful, abdominal*
e-	out
ecto-	*outside*
edem-	*swelling (fluid)*
encephal-	*brain*
endo-	*inside, within*
entero-	*intestine*
epi-	*upper, above*
erythro-	red
eu-	good, normal
ex-	away from, out
faci-	*facies, face*
fascia-	*band (fibrous)*
gastro-	*gastro*
genu-	*knee*
gingiva-	*gums*
gloss-	*tongue*
glyco-	*sugar*
gravid-	*pregnant*
gyn-, gyneco-	female
hemi-	half
hepato-	*liver*
hetero-	other, different
homeo-	unchanged
homo-	same
hydra-, hydro-	water
hyper-	high
hypo-	low
hyster-	*uterus, womb*

212

PREFIX	MEANING
idio-	peculiar to the individual
ile-	*intestine (part)*
ili-	*hipbone*
in-, im-	in, inside, not
inter-	*between*
intra-	*inside*
ir-	against, into, toward
iri-	*iris, eye*
iso-	equal, same
kerat-	*cornea, scaly*
kilo-	*thousand*
labia-	*lip*
lacto-	*milk*
lapar-	*abdomen*
laryng-	*larynx*
leuko-	white
lingua-	*tongue*
lip-	*fat*
lith-	*stone*
lymph-	*fluid*
macro-	large
mal-	bad
mamm-	*breast*
mast-	*breast*
mega-	large
melan-	*black*
mening-	*membrane*
meno-, mens-	*menstruate*
meso-	*middle*
metro-	*uterus, womb*
micro-	small
milli-	*thousand*
mono-	*one, single*
multi-	many

<u>PREFIX</u>	<u>MEANING</u>
myelo-	*bone marrow, spinal cord*
myo-	*muscle*
myx-	*mucus*
nares-, nas-	*nose, nostrils*
natus-	*birth*
neo-	new
nephro-	*kidney*
neuro-	*nerve*
non-	not
normo-	normal
null(i)-	none
ocul-	*eye*
odont-	*teeth*
olig(o)-	little, small, scant
onych-	*finger or toenail*
oophoro-	*ovary*
ophthal-	*eye*
or-	*mouth, bone*
orchid-	*testes*
ortho-	straight
osteo-	*bone*
oto-	*ear, hearing*
ovario-	*ovary*
ovi-	*egg*
pan-	all
para-	*beside, along side of*
part-	*birth, labor*
path(o)-	disease
ped-	*foot*
ped-	*child*
per-	through
peri-	*around*
pharyng-	*pharynx*

APPENDIX B

PREFIX	MEANING
phleb-	*vein*
phrenic-	*diaphragm*
pleur-	*pleura of lung*
pneumo-	*lung*
pod-	*foot*
poly-	many
post-	*behind*
pre-	*before*
pro-	forward, anterior
pseudo-	false
psycho-	*mind, soul*
pulm-	*lung*
pyelo-	*kidney*
pyo-	*pus*
re-	back, again
ren-	*kidney*
retro-	behind, backward
rhin-	nose
salpingo-	*tube*
sclero-	hard
semi-	half
semin-	*seed*
sial-	*saliva*
sinistr(o)-	left
soma-	*body*
splen-	*spleen*
spondyl-	*spine*
squam-	*scaly*
steno-	narrow, contracted
stoma-	*mouth*
stric-	*narrowing*
sub-	*below*
super-	*above*
supra-	*above*

APPENDIXES

PREFIX	MEANING
tachy-	fast
thel-	*nipple*
therap-	treatment
therm-	heat, warmth
thorac-	*thorax*
thrombo-	*clot*
trache-	*trachea*
trachel-	*neck*
trans-	*across*
toxi-	poison
tri-	three
uni-	one
vas-	*vessel*
vesic-	*bladder, sac*
viscera-	*organ*

*Page 433, replace **Appendix C** with the following:*

APPENDIX C

SUFFIXES

---

*Note: Terms that are listed in **bold** italics are new additions as of 2002 Supplement.*

SUFFIX	MEANING
-ac	pertaining to
-ad	toward, in direction of
-al, -an, -ar(y)	pertaining to
-algia	pain
-ase	enzyme
-atresia	abnormal closure
-cele	swelling, tumor
-centesis	***puncture***
-cide	killer
-crine	***to secrete within***
-cyst	bladder-like sac
-dactyl	***finger, toe***
-dema	***swelling (fluid)***
-deses	fusion, binding
-desis	***surgical fixation***
-duct	***opening***
-dynia	pain
-ectasis	***enlargement***
-ectomy	excision, cutting out

217

APPENDIXES

SUFFIX	MEANING
-ema	swelling, distension
-emia	blood
-form	structure, shape
-ful	full of, characterized by
-gen	production of
-genic	***source, origin***
-gram, -graphy	act or method of recording, ***picture***
-ia, -iasis	diseased condition
-ic	pertaining to
-ious	capable of, causing
-ism	condition, process of
-itis	inflammation
-less	without, not capable
-lysis	setting free, dissolution
-malacia	***softening***
-megaly	large, ***enlarged***
-oid	like
-ology	science of, ***study of***
-olysis	***breakdown***
-oma	tumor
-osis	action, state, condition, ***disease***
-ostomy	***surgical opening***
-otomy	cutting into, ***incision***
-ous	pertaining to
-pathy	suffering, disease
-penia	deficiency, lack of
-pexy	***fixation***
-phagia	***swallowing***
-phasia	***speech disorder***
-philia	love of

218

APPENDIX C

SUFFIX	MEANING
-phobia	fear
-phrenia	*mental disorder*
-physis	*growth (physical)*
-plasty	molding, shaping
-plegia	*paralysis*
-ptosis	drooping
-rraphy	repair or closure of, *suture*
-rrhage, -rrhagia	*hemorrhage*
-rrhea	flow, discharge
-rrhexis	*rupture*
-sarcoma	*tumor, cancer*
-sclerosis	*hardening*
-scope, -scopy	look at, examine
-spasm	*contraction*
-stasis	at a standstill, *stoppage*
-tonia	stretching, putting under tension
-tripsy	*crushing*
-uria	*urine*
-vert	turn

*Add new **Appendix N:***

INTERNET RESOURCES

This appendix consists of all Internet websites and resources referenced in the body of the text. The following addresses have been verified as of the date of publication. However, readers are cautioned that addresses and individual websites on the Internet change frequently.

Accreditation/Regulation of Health Care Entities
Joint Commission on Accreditation of Health Care Organizations
   (JCAHO)—http://www.jcaho.org

Ancillary Medical Specialties
American Academy of Physician Assistants—http://www.aapa.org
Association for Professionals in Infection Control and Epidemiology—
   http://www.apic.org

QA & Clinical Standards
Agency for Health Care Policy and Research (AHCPR)—
   http://www.nnlm.nlm.nih.gov/sec/etc/factahcp.html
Clinical Practice Guidelines for Chronic Pain Management (American
   Ass'n of Anesthesiologists)—http://www.ASAhq.com
Foundation for Accountability—http:www.facct.org/
National Committee for Quality Assurance (NCQA)—
   http://www.ncqa.com
National Guideline Clearinghouse—http://www.guidelines.gov/

Federal Government Sites
Centers for Disease Control & Prevention—http://www.cdc.gov
Centers for Medicare and Medicaid Services (formerly Health Care Financing Admin (HCFA)—http://www.cms.gov/
COBRA Online—http://www.medlaw.com
Consumer Product Safety Commission—http://www.consumer.gov
Food & Drug Administration—www.fda.gov

APPENDIX N

Health Insurance Portability and Accountability Act (HIPAA)—http://www.hhs.gov/ocr.hippa
Human Genome Project—http://www.nhgri.nih.gov/
MediCare—http://www.medicare.gov
MediCare/Skilled Nursing Home information—http://www.medicare.gov/nursing/home.asp
National Institutes of Health—http://www.nih.gov
National Library of Medicine—www.nlm.nih.gov

Forensic Document Review
American Academy of Forensic Sciences—http://www.aafs.org

Expert Witnesses
American Academy of Facial Plastic and Reconstructive Surgery—http://www.facialplasticsurgery.org
American Medical Association—http://www.ama-assn.org
Centers for Disease Control & Prevention—http://www.cdc.gov
National Institutes of Health—http://www.nih.gov

Health Care Plans
American Association of Health Plans—http://www.aahp.org

Litigation
Federation of State Medical Boards—http://www.fsmb.org/b_action.htm
The Johns Hopkins School of Medicine Department of Art as Applied to Medicine—http://www.med.jhu.edu/medart
Judicial Statistical Inquiry Form—http://www.healthfinder.gov
Legal Resource Network—http://www.witness.net
*Life*Art™ Professional Medical Computer Illustrations—http://www.lifeart.com (or) http://www.mediclip.com
The Medical College of Georgia Graduate Program in Medical Illustration—http://www.mcg.edu/SAH/MedIll/index.html
The Medical Malpractice Home Page—http://www.vcilp.org/~psand/medmal/open.html
The Medical School for Trial Lawyers—http://www.seak.com
Medi-Net—http://www.healthfinder.gov

The University of Michigan M.F.A. Program in Medical and Biological Illustration—http://www.umich.edu/~medill/index.html

The University of Texas Southwestern Medical Center at Dallas Department of Biomedical Communications—http://www.swmed.edu/medillus

Medical Illustration

The Johns Hopkins School of Medicine Department of Art as Applied to Medicine—http://www.med.jhu.edu/medart

The Medical College of Georgia Graduate Program in Medical Illustration—http://www.mcg.edu/SAH/MedIll/index.html

The University of Illinois at Chicago Department of Biomedical Visualization—http://www.bvis.uic.edu or http://rs6000.bvis.uic.edu/

The University of Michigan M.F.A. Program in Medical and Biological Illustration—http://www.umich.edu/medill/index.html

The University of Texas Southwestern Medical Center at Dallas Department of Biomedical Communications—http://www.swmed.edu/medillus

Medical Research

Agency for Health Care Policy and Research (AHCPR)—http://www.nnlm.nlm.nih.gov/sec/etc/factahcp.html

EurekAlert!—www.eurekalert.org

Greater Midwest Regional Library—http://www.nnlm.nlm.nih.gov/gmr/

Hardin Meta Directory of Internet Health Sources—http://www.arcade.uiowa.edu/hardin-www/md.html

Health Industry Manufacturers Association—http://www.himanet.com

Health on the Net Foundation—http://www.hon.ch

Healthfinder—http://www.healthfinder.org

HealthGate—http://www.healthgate.com

HealthWorld—http://www.healthworld.com/library/search/medline.htm

Infotrieve—http://www.infotrieve.com

Internet Grateful Med: New User's Survival Guide—http://www.igm.nlm.nih.gov/splash/igm_20/IGM.survivial.guide.html

Internet Literacy Consultants™—http://www.matisse.net/files/glossary.html.

Mayo Clinic—http://www.mayoclinic.com

APPENDIX N

MedGate—http://www.healthgate.com
MEDguide—http://www.medguide.net/index.asp
Medi-Net—http://www.healthfinder.gov
Medical Abbreviations:—http://www.neilmdavis.com
The Medical List—http://www.kumc.edu:80/mmatrix
Medical Matrix—http://www.slackinc.com/matrix
The Medical School for Trial Lawyers—http://www.seak.com
MedicineNet—http://www.medicinenet.com
Medscape—http://www.medscape.com
MedWeb—http://www.cc.emory.edu/WHSCL/medweb.html
Midcontinental Regional Library—http://www.nnlm.nlm.nih.gov/mcr/
Middle Atlantic Regional Library—http://www.nnlm.nlm.nih.gov/mar/
National Library of Medicine—www.nlm.nih.gov
New England Journal of Medicine—http://www.nejm.org
New England Regional Library—http://www.nnlm.nlm.nih.gov/ner/
OncoLink—http://www.oncolink.upenn.edu
Ovid—http://www.ovid.com/
Pacific Northwest Regional Library—
    http://www.nnlm.nlm.nih.gov/pnr/
Pacific Southwest Regional Library—
    http://www.nnlm.nlm.nih.gov/psr/
PaperChase—http://www.paperchase.com
Pharmaceutical Research and Manufacturers of America—
    http://www.phrma.org
PharmInfo Net—http://www.pharminfo.com
PharmWeb—http://www.mcc.ac.uk/pharmacy
Physicians' Online—http://www.po.com
South Central Regional Library—http://www.nnlm.nlm.nih.gov/scr/
Southeastern Atlantic Regional Library—
    http://www.nnlm.nlm.nih.gov/sar/
Thrive@pathfinder—http://www.pathfinder.com/thrive

Medical Specialties
American Academy of Facial Plastic and Reconstructive Surgery—
    http://www.facialplasticsurgery.org
American Academy of Physical Medicine and Rehabilitation—
    http://www.aapmr.org
Medi-Net—http://www.healthfinder.gov

APPENDIXES

Medline—Fee
Dialog—http://www.dialog.com
MedGate—http://www.healthgate.com
Ovid—http://www.ovid.com/
PaperChase—http://www.paperchase.com
SilverPlatter—http://www.silverplatter.com

Medline—Free
Healthfinder—http://www.healthfinder.org
HealthGate—http://www.healthgate.com
HealthWorld—http://www.healthworld.com/library/search/medline.htm
Infotrieve—http://www.infotrieve.com
Medline—Medlineplus.gov
Medscape—http://www.medscape.com

Nursing
American Association of Critical Care Nurses—http://www.aacn.org
Association of Operating Room Nurses—http://www.aorn.org

Pharmacology
Medscape—http://www.medscape.com
OncoLink—http://www.oncolink.upenn.edu
Pharmaceutical Research and Manufacturers of America—
    http://www.phrma.org
PharmInfo Net—http://www.pharminfo.com
PharmWeb—http://www.mcc.ac.uk/pharmacy

Regional Medical Libraries
Middle Atlantic Region—http://www.nnlm.nlm.nih.gov/mar/
Southeastern Atlantic Region—http://www.nnlm.nlm.nih.gov/sar/
Greater Midwest Region—http://www.nnlm.nlm.nih.gov/gmr/
Midcontinental Region—http://www.nnlm.nlm.nih.gov/mcr/
South Central Region—http://www.nnlm.nlm.nih.gov/scr/
Pacific Northwest Region—http://www.nnlm.nlm.nih.gov/pnr/
Pacific Southwest Region—http://www.nnlm.nlm.nih.gov/psr/
New England Region—http://www.nnlm.nlm.nih.gov/ner/

APPENDIX N

Skilled Nursing Facilities
COBRA Online—http://www.medlaw.com
Health Care Financing Administration (HCFA)—http://www.hcfa.gov
MediCare site for nursing home information—
http://www.medicare.gov/nursing/home.asp.

APPENDIX O (REVISED)

STATE STATUTES REGARDING USE OF GENETIC TESTS/ INFORMATION

STATE	STATUTE	DISCUSSION
Alabama	Ala. Code § 27-53-2	Health benefit plans (insurance issuers, self-insured plans, HMOs, PPOs) may not use the results of a genetic test to determine insurability or to otherwise discriminate against the person in rates or benefits based on the results; a plan may not require a genetic test as a condition of insurability.
Alaska	—	No relevant statutes.
Arizona	Rev. Stat. § 12-2802	Tests may not be performed without specific written consent of the subject. Results are privileged and confidential and may not be released without the express consent of the subject.
Arkansas	Ark. Code Ann. §§ 11-5-400, *et seq.;* 23-66-320	An insurer may not require or request a genetic test and condition the provision of insurance on the test. The results of a genetic test are confidential and may not be

STATE	STATUTE	DISCUSSION
		disclosed without the patient's informed written consent; informed consent may not be included with consent for treatment, admission to a hospital or clinic. Genetic information may be disclosed per subpoena or in civil discovery in cases where the genetic information is the basis of the suit.
California	Civ. Code § 56.17; Ins. Code §§ 742-407, 10123.35, 10146	Insurers may not discriminate on the basis of a person's genetic characteristics. Written authorization required for release of genetic information. Life and disability insurers may require individuals to take a genetic characteristic test to determine insurability where the policy is contingent on review or testing for other diseases and medical conditions. Right to sue for improper disclosure of genetic test results.
Colorado	Rev. Stat. Ann. § 10-3-1104.7	Information derived from testing is confidential and privileged. Any release of patient-identifying information requires specific written consent of the subject. Disclosure of information without consent is allowed for diagnosis, treatment, or therapy. Disclosure for scientific research is allowed as long as the subject's identity is not released to a third party.
Connecticut	Gen. Stat. § 46a-60A	An employer, employment agency, or labor organization may

STATE	STATUTE	DISCUSSION
		not request or require genetic information from an employee, person applying for employment, or labor organization member, or otherwise discriminate against an individual on the basis of genetic information.
Delaware	Code Ann. tit. 16 § 1220 *et seq.*	Upon request, an individual may inspect, request the correction of, and obtain genetic information from his own records. No person may obtain or retain an individual's genetic information without informed consent. Informed consent not required pursuant to court order, to determine paternity, to identify deceased individuals, etc.
District of Columbia	—	No relevant statutes.
Florida	Stat. Ann. § 760.40	DNA analysis may only be performed with the informed consent of the subject (except for three specific purposes). The results are confidential and may not be disclosed without the consent of the subject. If the information is used to deny insurance, the subject must be notified, the analysis repeated, and any denial must be reviewed if the first analysis is found to be inaccurate.
Georgia	Code § 33-54-3 *et seq.*	Information is confidential and may be released only to the subject tested and to persons specifi-

STATE	STATUTE	DISCUSSION
		cally authorized by such subject. Insurers may not seek information derived from genetic testing; any insurer in possession of such information may not release it to a third party without the explicit written consent of the subject.
Hawaii	Rev. Stat. §§ 431:10A-101 and 10A-118	Insurers and HMOs may not request or require collection or disclosure of an individual's or his family member's genetic information. Written consent required for disclosure.
Idaho	—	No relevant statutes.
Illinois	410 Comp. Stat. 513/15; 513/30	The fact that someone has undergone genetic testing, and the results, are confidential and may only be released to the individual and to persons specifically authorized in writing by the individual to receive the information. The results are not admissible as evidence and not discoverable in in any court or proceeding. Disclosure without authorization may be made where necessary by facilities. Civil penalties for violations.
Indiana	Code Ann. § 27-8-26-1 *et seq.*	An insurer may not ask questions designed to ascertain the results of genetic testing or for the results of such testing, or use such information to cancel, refuse to issue or renew, or limit benefits.

STATE	STATUTE	DISCUSSION
		Disclosure requires written consent.
Iowa	—	No relevant statutes.
Kansas	—	No relevant statutes.
Kentucky	—	No relevant statutes.
Louisiana	Rev. Stat. Ann. §§ 40:1299.6; 22:213.7(C)(2, 5)(D)	Results of any tests are confidential, excluded from state reporting requirements, and may not be disclosed without the express written consent of the subject. The authorization must be in writing, and adhere to the requirements of the statute. Results can be released without consent to determine paternity, identify a deceased person, or for anonymous research.
Maine	Rev. Stat. Ann. tit. 24-A, § 2159-C; tit. 25, § 1577	Insurers and employers may not discriminate on the basis of genetic tests. An employer may not discriminate against an employee or applicant for employment because of the individual's refusal to submit to a test or make the results available, or because the individual was subject to a test. DNA records are confidential and may be disclosed to limited individuals in specified circumstances.
Maryland	Code Ann. Ins. § 27-909	Restricts the use and disclosure of genetic information by insurers, nonprofit health service plans, and

STATE	STATUTE	DISCUSSION
		HMOs. Information may not be released without prior written authorization, each release requires a separate authorization.
Massachusetts	Gen. Laws. Ch. § 76 151B	Information is confidential and not accessible to anyone other than the Department and the Commissioner of Public Health. Release of genetic information requires informed written consent. An employer may not collect, solicit, or require disclosure of genetic information as a condition of employment. Genetic testing requires prior written consent except for certain exceptions.
Michigan	Comp. Laws §§ 37.1202; 333.17020	Informed written consent required for testing. An employer may not require an applicant or a member or their dependents to undergo genetic testing before issuing, renewing, or continuing health-care coverage.
Minnesota	Stat. § 72A.139	Prohibits health plan companies from requiring, requesting, or inquiring if an individual has a genetic testing history. Written informed consent must be obtained for testing and disclosure.
Mississippi	—	No relevant statutes.
Missouri	Rev. Stat. §§ 375.1300 through 1309	All testing results and personal information are held as a confidential medical record subject to re-

STATE	STATUTE	DISCUSSION
		lease only on informed written consent. Disclosure without consent is allowable for health research, pursuant to legal or regulatory process, or for body identification. Civil penalties for violations.
Montana	Code Ann. § 38-18-901 *et seq.*	An insurer, health service corporation, HMO, or benefit society may not require an individual to submit to a genetic test unless required by law. Neither may these entities see an individual's genetic information for purposes unrelated to assessing or managing his/her current health, if inappropriate in an asymptomatic individual, or unrelated to research.
Nebraska	Rev. Stat. §§ 236, 44-7, 100	Employers may not require an employee or applicant for employment to submit to a genetic test or provide genetic information as a condition of employment or promotion, or use genetic information unrelated to the individual's ability to perform job. Insurers may not require any covered person or dependent, or asymptomatic applicant to undergo genetic test before issuing or renewing policy.
Nevada	Rev. Stat. § 396.521, 523; 629.141-161	Results of genetic tests are confidential and require informed consent of the individual or his/her legal guardian. Disclosure without consent is allowable for health re-

STATE	STATUTE	DISCUSSION
		search, pursuant to legal or regulatory process, or for body identification. Insurers prohibited from requiring an insured or any member of his family to take a test or disclose results (insurers providing long-term care or disability are not covered by this provision). Civil penalties for violations.
New Hampshire	Rev. Stat. § 141-H:2	Restrictions on the instances in which genetic testing may be done without the prior written informed consent of the individual. No person may disclose to another that an individual has undergone testing; no person may disclose the results without prior written informed consent. Disclosure without consent is allowed to establish paternity, for newborn tests on metabolic disorders, criminal investigations, and prosecutions.
New Jersey	Stat. § 10:5-47 to 49	A person may not disclose or be compelled to disclose the identity of an individual who has been the subject of tests or the results of the test with any identifying information. Disclosure is required for paternity or as authorized by a court. Civil penalties for violations.
New Mexico	Stat. Ann. § 24-21-3 to 6	No tests or information may be taken or obtained without informed written consent from the

STATE	STATUTE	DISCUSSION
		subject. Information may be used without consent to establish paternity, for criminal investigation, to identify deceased persons, to screen newborns. Insurers are exempt from these provisions if their use of the information for underwriting purposes is based on "sound actuarial principles or related to actual or reasonably anticipated experience." Civil penalties for violations.
New York	Civ. R. Law § 79-1 *et seq.*	No tests may be performed without prior written informed consent of the individual except pursuant to court order or as required by public health law. Genetic tests are confidential and may not be disclosed without written informed consent. Insurers must obtain an individual's written informed consent prior to a genetic test, and the consent form must specify the name of the persons or categories of persons or organizations to whom the test results may be disclosed.
North Carolina	Gen. Stat. §§ 95-28.1A and 58-3-215.	Employers may not deny or refuse to employ or discharge any person based on the person's request for genetic testing or the results of genetic testing. Insurers may not raise premiums or refuse to issue a health benefit plan on the basis of genetic information obtained about an individual.

STATE	STATUTE	DISCUSSION
North Dakota	—	No relevant statutes.
Ohio	Code Ann. § 3729.46	Information is confidential and may not be released without the individual's consent. Civil penalties for violation of statute.
Oklahoma	Stat. tit. 36, § 3614.1-3	Genetic information is not discoverable in any judicial, legislative, or administrative proceeding, with the exception of court-ordered paternity tests or for use in a law-enforcement proceeding or investigation. Insurers and employers are prohibited from requiring an insured, employee, potential employee, or any member of his/her family to take a genetic test.
Oregon	Rev. Stat. 659.720	No person may disclose or be compelled to disclose the identity of an individual who has undergone testing or the results of the testing in a manner that permits identification of the individual without that person's written, signed, specific consent. Disclosure without consent is allowed: when authorized by criminal laws, in accordance with rules adopted for civil actions; to establish paternity; to furnish genetic information relating to a decedent for medical diagnosis of relatives of the decedent; and for identifying bodies. These prohibitions apply to any re-disclosure by the recipient of any genetic information.

STATE	STATUTE	DISCUSSION
Pennsylvania	—	No relevant statutes.
Rhode Island	Gen. Laws 28-6.7-1	No person may sell or interpret a genetic test of a current or prospective employee or licensee for an employer, employment agency, or licensing agency.
South Carolina	Code 38-93-30	All genetic information is confidential and must not be disclosed to a third party in a manner that allows identification of the individual tested without obtaining the written informed consent of that individual. Genetic information may be disclosed without consent for the purpose of a criminal or death investigation, or a criminal or judicial proceeding; to determine the paternity, pursuant to an order of a court, where genetic information concerning a deceased individual will assist in medical diagnosis of blood relatives of the decedent; to identify a person or a dead body; or as specifically authorized or required by a state or federal statute. An insurer may not require a person to consent to the disclosure of genetic information to the insurer as a condition for obtaining accident and health insurance.
South Dakota	Codified Laws §§ 34-14-22 and 58-1-25	No one may order or perform a genetic test without the written informed consent of the test subject. Insurers may not require or re-

STATE	STATUTE	DISCUSSION
		quest an individual or a blood relative to submit to a genetic test or consider the refusal to submit to a genetic test in determining eligibility for coverage.
Tennessee	Code Ann. 56-7-2702-04	Prohibits an insurer from disclosing genetic information without the prior written authorization of the individual or legal representative of the individual. An authorization must include an identification of the person to whom the disclosure would be made and is required for any subsequent disclosure. Additionally, an insurer may not request or require an individual to disclose to the provider genetic information about the individual or family member of the individual.
Texas	—	No relevant statutes.
Utah	Code Ann. §§ 58-75-502, 26-45-103 to 104	It is unprofessional conduct for a genetic counselor to disclose any information received from a client unless released by the client or otherwise authorized or required by law. Employers may not take into consideration private genetic information about an individual, request or require an individual to consent to release such information, or request or require an individual or blood relative to submit to a test. An employer may seek an order compelling disclosure of

STATE	STATUTE	DISCUSSION
		private genetic information in certain circumstances. Health insurers are permitted to ask about, use, and disclose private genetic information in a number of circumstances.
Vermont	18 Vt. Stat. Ann. §§ 9331 to 9333	No person can be required to undergo genetic testing, with exceptions for paternity, for remains identification, for criminal investigation. Results of genetic test or the fact that an individual has requested genetic services or undergone genetic testing may be disclosed only by written authorization. An insurer, employer, or labor organization may not require genetic testing as a condition of insurance, employment, or membership.
Virginia	Code Ann. §§ 38.2-508.4 and 613, 40.1-28.7:1	Employers may not request, require, solicit, or administer a genetic test to any person as a condition of employment, nor may they refuse to hire, fail to promote, discharge, or otherwise adversely affect any terms or conditions of employment solely on the basis of the results of a genetic test. All information obtained from testing is confidential and may not be made public or used in any way to cancel, refuse to issue or renew, or limit benefits under any health insurance plan. Insurers are specifically prohibited from disclosing

STATE	STATUTE	DISCUSSION
		any genetic information obtained in connection with an insurance transaction without the written authorization of the individual.
Washington	—	No relevant statutes.
West Virginia	—	No relevant statutes.
Wisconsin	Stat. Ann. §§ 111.372, 631.89, and 942.07	Insurers or entities that provide health-care services may not require or request of an individual directly or indirectly if that individual or member of his/her family has obtained a genetic test or the results of the test. A genetic test may not be required by an employer or labor organization as a condition of employment. Prior written and informed consent by the test's subject is required for disclosure.
Wyoming	Stat. Ann. § 14-2-109	Where genetic testing is undertaken to establish paternity, the testing of genetic material for any other purpose is prohibited without the individual's written consent. Any information obtained in this manner is confidential, to be used solely for the purposes of determining paternity.

BIBLIOGRAPHY

AACN Clinical Reference for Critical Care Nursing. 4th ed. Marguerite Kinney & Sandra B. Dunbar. St. Louis: Mosby-Yearbook, Inc., 1998.

Anatomy Coloring Book, 2d ed. Wynn Kapit & Lawrence M. Elson. New York: HarperCollins, 1997.

Chiropractic Standards of Practice and Quality of Care. Herbert J. Vear. Gaithersburg, Md.: Aspen Publishers, Inc., 2001.

Consent Manual—A Reference for Consent and Related Health Care Law. 20th ed. California Hospital Association, 1993.

Control of Communicable Diseases Manual, 20th ed. James Chin, ed., Baltimore MD: United Book Press Inc., 2002.

Current Medical Diagnosis and Treatment, 42nd ed. Lawrence J. Tierney, Jr., Stephen J. McPhee, and Maxine A. Papadakis. Norwalk, Conn.: Appleton & Lange, 2003.

Diagnostic and Statistical Manual of Mental Disorders and *Quick Reference to the Diagnostic Criteria from DSM-IV.* 4th ed. Washington, D.C.: American Psychiatric Association, 1994.

Dorland's Illustrated Medical Dictionary and *Dorland's Pocket Medical Dictionary.* 28th ed. Philadelphia: W.B. Saunders, 1994.

Drug Facts and Comparisons. 57th ed., Facts & Comparisons, 2002.

Drugs and Nursing Implications. 8th ed. Margaret T. Shannon & Billie A. Wilson. Norwalk, Conn.: Appleton and Lange, 1994 (out of print).

Encyclopedia of Medical Associations. 7th ed. Bridget Travers, ed. Detroit, Mich.: Gail Research, Inc., 1997–98.

Encyclopedia of Medicine. American Medical Association, Charles B. Clayman, M.D., medical ed. New York: Random House, 1989.

Health Devices Sourcebook. Plymouth Meeting, Pa.: Emergency Care Research Institute, 2003.

Hospital Phone Book. Keith Cavedo, ed., Douglas Publishers, Inc., 2002.

BIBLIOGRAPHY

International Classification of Diseases (ICD-9-CM), Practice Management Information Corporation, 2000.

Isler's Pocket Dictionary: A Guide to Disorders & Diagnostic Tests, Procedures & Terms. 3rd ed. Charlotte Isler. Oradell, NJ: Medical Economics Co., 1990.

Joint Commission International Accreditation Standards for Hospitals. Joint Commission for Accreditation of Health Care Organizations. Oakbrook Terrace. Ill.: JCAHCO, 2002.

Law Every Nurse Should Know. Helen Creighton, R.N., J.D. Philadelphia, Pa.: W.B. Saunders & Co., 1986.

Legal Nurse Consulting Principles and Practice. American Association of Legal Nurse Consultants, Vickie Vaclavik, ed. Glenview, Il.: CRC Press, 2002.

Luckman and Sorenson's Medical Surgical Nursing: A Psychophysiologic Approach. 4th ed. Joyce M. Black and Esther Matassarin-Jacobs, eds. Philadelphia, Pa.: W.B. Saunders, 1993.

Medical Abbreviations: 24,000 Conveniences at the Expense of Communications & Safety. 11th ed. Neil M. Davis. Huntingdon Valley, Pa.: Neil M. Davis Associates, 2003. Web: www.neilmdavis.com.

Medicine Made Easy, 2nd ed. Sue Dill Calloway, R.N., J.D., and Mikel Rothenberg, M.D. Eau Claire, Wis.: Professional Education Systems, Inc., 1996.

Merck Manual of Diagnosis and Therapy; Merck Manual: General Medicine (vol. 1); Merck Manual: Specialties (vol. 2). 17th ed. Rahway, N.Y.: Merck & Company, Inc., 1999.

Merck Manual of Medical Information. 2nd ed., Mark Beers, ed., Simon & Schuster, 2003.

Mosby's Diagnostic and Laboratory Test Reference. 5th ed. Kathleen Pagana and Timothy Pagana. St. Louis, Mo.: Mosby-Year Book, Inc., 2000.

Nurse's Drug Loosleaf, Blanchard & Loeb Publishers, LLC, 2003.

Nursing 2000 Drug Handbook. Springhouse, Pa.: Springhouse Corp., 2002.

BIBLIOGRAPHY

The Official ABMS Directory of Board Certified Medical Specialists. 35th ed., Elsevier Science, 2002.

Orthopedic and Sports Medicine for Nurses. Sharon A. Gates & Pekka A. Mooar. Baltimore, Md.: Williams & Wilkins Co., 1989.

Physician's Desk Reference. 57th ed. Oradell, N.J.: Medical Economics, 2003.

Physician's Desk Reference for Nonprescription Drugs and Dietary Supplements, 23rd ed., Oradell, N.J.: Medical Economics, 2003.

Sloane-Dorland Annotated Medical Legal Dictionary. St. Paul, Minn.: West Publishing, 1987 with 1992 supplement.

Standards of Privacy of Individually Identifiable Health Information. The Federal Register, Department of Health and Human Services, 45 C.F.R., pts. 160 & 164. Final Rule, August 14, 2002.

Stedman's Medical Dictionary. 27th ed. (illus). Baltimore, Md.: Lippincott Williams & Wilkins, 2000.

To Err is Human: Building a Safer Health System. L. Corrigan Kohn & M. Donaldson, eds., Washington D.C. Institute of Medicine, 1999.

INDEX

INDEX

246

INDEX

INDEX

INDEX